D1569444

Coastal Lives

Critical Green Engagements

Investigating the Green Economy and Its Alternatives

*Jim Igoe, Molly Doane, José Martínez-Reyes, Tracey Heatherington,
Melissa Checker, and Bram Büscher*
SERIES EDITORS

Maximilian Viatori and Héctor Bombiella

Coastal Lives

Nature, Capital, and the Struggle for
Artisanal Fisheries in Peru

THE UNIVERSITY OF
ARIZONA PRESS

TUCSON

The University of Arizona Press
www.uapress.arizona.edu

ISBN-13: 978-0-8165-3929-1 (cloth)

Cover design by Leigh McDonald
Cover photo by Maximilian Viatori

Publication of this book was made possible in part by funding from the Department of
World Languages and Cultures, Iowa State University, and by Iowa State University
Publication Endowment, ISU Foundation.

Library of Congress Cataloging-in-Publication Data are available at the Library of Congress.

Printed in the United States of America
♾ This paper meets the requirements of ANSI/NISO Z39.48-1992 (Permanence of Paper).

For Anneke, Elio, and Nico

M.V.

A los pescadores artesanales de la caleta de Chorrillos "José Silverio Olaya Balandra"

H.B.

Contents

Illustrations

Figures

Maps

Coastal Lives

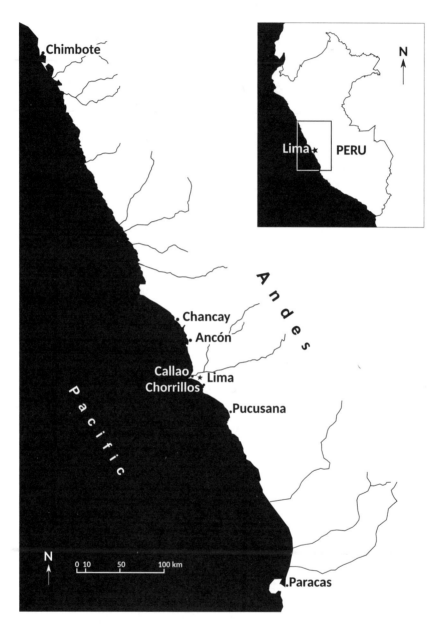

Map 1 Peru's coast. Cartography by Yibo Fan.

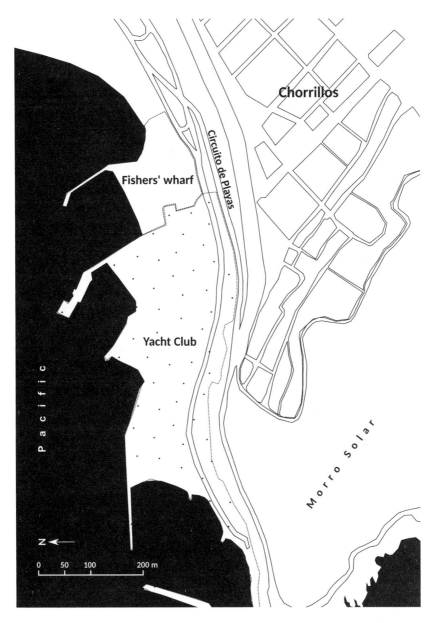

Map 2 The fishers' wharf and its surroundings in Chorrillos. Cartography by Yibo Fan.

Introduction

It was March 2016, and Peru's austral summer would soon come to an end, the sun and warmth replaced by the gray mist that characterizes the winters in Lima, Peru. The tide was up. There would be fish entering the bay with the rising water. Luis and Marcos decided to head out in the hopes that they would catch some fish for the evening market. They asked if we would like to come along. We agreed, and our small group made its way through the wharf in Chorrillos, a district of Lima. As we walked from the old union hall, with its roof mostly collapsed and ready for repair, we passed several men working in the small shipyard. They stood in the shade with their green nylon nets hung by the roof's beams, using new spools of line to repair the holes that *lobos* (*Otaria byronia*, South American sea lions) had torn in the nets. Once they were fixed, the men would head into the bay that night or the next morning. Past the shipyard were the vendors who sold beachwear and food for the tourists who came to use the adjoining beach. Beyond the vendors, there was an open-air corridor that led to a pier, where we clambered into a small rowboat.

We rowed out to Luis's and Marcos's larger *chalana* (skiff), a blue and white wooden boat that was about five meters long, which was attached to the moorage one hundred meters off the pier. In the middle of the boat was a small wooden box that housed the motor—a rusted contraption that tended to stall and required some coaxing from Luis to start. Between the motor and the bow was a rowing station with a plank of wood for a seat and two thick oars. Once

Luis had the engine running, we pulled the oars and slowly made our way under the pier, passing the beach full of tourists.

The buildings of Barranco and Miraflores, more affluent districts closer to Lima's center, were visible atop the sandy cliffs that separate the city from its narrow ribbon of coastline. To the south was the walled compound of the Club de Regatas Lima (Lima Yacht Club). Founded in 1875, the Yacht Club caters to Lima's wealthy elite, who play tennis, shop, or lounge in one of the many beach chairs. The socially and economically exclusive nature of the Yacht Club stands in stark contrast to the fishers' wharf, where approximately four hundred fishers and vendors make their living by supplying local residents and tourists with seafood. Chorrillos has been a productive fishing site for centuries, and in 1969, the federal government granted the local fishers' association (at the time a union) the right to administer the wharf, a right that is alienable. The wharf is part of Lima's Costa Verde, a stretch of the city's coastline that has been redeveloped to suit the needs of both local and international tourists. Recently, federal and municipal governments have pressured fishers to make the visibly poor wharf more amenable to tourism.

A pivotal moment in this process came in October 2015, when the administration of the Yacht Club announced that it was willing to help the fishers' association improve the space by holding an architectural contest for proposals to redevelop the wharf. The winning proposal included a computer-animated video, which depicted a completely sanitized dock with wood-slat buildings, a new concrete pier, people in swimsuits milling about, and a complete lack of fishers or market vendors. The Yacht Club invited a representative from the fishers' association to be one of the seven judges for the contest. While the fishers felt they should have been better represented on the panel, the artisanal fishers' association's leadership supported the plans because fishers felt this was their only opportunity to modernize the wharf. Moreover, many felt that private investment in the dock would mean increased revenue for the association, which would enable it to care for fishers and their families through the expanded provision of subsidized health insurance, scholarships, and holiday bonuses.

Ultimately, the plan for a new wharf stalled. The Yacht Club administration did not issue a public explanation. Among the fishers, there were rumors that the plan had been a tax break scheme for one of the club's members who owned a construction company that was in debt. By offering to do a public works project, supposedly his company's debt would be forgiven. Other fishers surmised

that the project had run aground because of the difficulties of obtaining necessary permissions from the multiple government agencies that held jurisdiction
over the wharf. In place of a renovated wharf, the Yacht Club built a new glass,
wood, and steel restaurant on the jetty that separates the Club's portion of the
coast from the fishing wharf. The restaurant is not open to the public—it is
accessible only by going through the Yacht Club's compound.

As we passed the new restaurant on our way out to fish, the waves rolled
higher, and the wind picked up. The southern end of the bay is sheltered by a
large hill, known as the Morro Solar—in Spanish "*morro*" means "hill" or "head-
land," while "*solar*" in this case refers to the solar observatory that shares the top
of the hill with a giant cross and a statue of the Virgin Mary, marking the end
of a pilgrimage that one can make up a winding path. Once we got closer to
the edge of the Morro Solar, we felt the full force of the Pacific Ocean, a steady
and cold wind coming from a horizon that appeared endless. There was also
a visible line in the ocean, which marked the calmer waters of the bay with a

Figure 1   Fishing boats in Chorrillos with Miraflores' skyline in the background. Photo
by Maximilian Viatori.

current streaming up from the south. It was at this point that the floats of Luis's and Marcos's net were visibly bobbing in the water.

Fishers in Chorrillos rely mostly on gillnets for their fishing. These nets are about fifty to one hundred meters long and a meter wide. They have floats along the top edge and lead weights along the bottom so that they suspend in the water in the shape of a tennis or volleyball net. Fishers position them in places where the fish are likely to enter the bay on changing tides, using nets with different sized gaps between the nylon strands to capture different fish species when they are in season. When the right-sized fish swim into the net, they can get their heads through the holes but cannot get back out because their gills become caught in the nylon.

As we approached the floats, Marcos cut the engine, and one of us got on the oars to steer the boat slowly along the net. The others donned large plastic bags to keep themselves dry and started to haul in the heavy net by hand. A blue plastic crate was on the floor of the boat for fish. The fishers pulled in the first few meters of the long net, heaping it onto the floor of the boat. There were no fish in it. They continued to pull in the net as we tried to keep the boat steady among the waves. Finally, the silvery, wiggling body of a fish appeared. Luis grabbed it, pulled it from the net, and tossed it into the plastic crate. The fish was a *caballa* (*Scomber japonicus*, chub mackerel), one of the more commonly caught fish in Chorrillos. Because they travel in schools, caballa are prime targets for gillnet fishing. As Luis and Marcos pulled in more of the net, there were more caballa in it. Soon, there were a dozen or more fish in the bottom of the boat.

Caballa do not have the sought-after white flesh of a *lenguado* (*Paralichthys adspersus*, fine flounder) but they do have firm gray flesh and are an inexpensive option for making a variety of popular dishes. They are one of several fish that constitute a mainstay for both fishers and consumers in Chorrillos but also suffer from high levels of contaminants. As with many coastal cities around the world, Lima's waters are heavily polluted by urban effluent. Approximately eight kilometers south of the bay is a sewage collection facility at La Chira beach, which spews out the mostly untreated sewage of roughly one-third of Lima's ever-growing population. The prevailing currents carry these contaminants up into the bay, where an eddy created by the jetties that have been built over the past century traps and circulates waste next to the fishers' wharf. Health officials in Lima have told the fishers that resident mollusks and fish are not always safe for human consumption. Fishers claim that they know which fish to target, focusing on species that only enter the bay to feed and spend much of their time in the open ocean. While this is the case for some species, caballa are near-coast fish that spend most of their lives in and around the waters of the bay. On many days, these fish offer the most abundant catches, and while consumers complain from time to time of becoming sick from eating fish in Chorrillos, demand for inexpensive fish has persisted among residents of the district.

We reached the end of the net, and the plastic tub was not even half full, so Marcos turned the motor on, and we moved farther north. Once they decided we were in a good position, Marcos and Luis fed the net into the water, and we repeated the process of rowing slowly along as the fishers pulled in the net. By the time we reached the end, the crate was almost full with caballa, a few small *lorna* (*Sciaena deliciosa*, drum), and one big *lisa* (*Mugil cephalus*, striped mullet). The fishers packed wet newspaper around the fish to keep them fresh and to ensure that they looked good to consumers in the market. Marcos estimated that the afternoon's catch would be worth about forty Peruvian soles, or about fourteen U.S. dollars, from which the fishers would have to pay for gas, repairs to their nets, and other expenses. Each would probably walk away with ten soles once the fish were sold, which would not go far in Lima's economy. As we motored back into the bay, both fishers complained about the poor quality of fishing in Chorrillos.

Fishers often comment on the changing nature of the ocean when they discuss poor catches. The productivity of Peru's fisheries is supported by the upwelling of cold water from the Atacama Trench to surface waters that are close to the country's central coast. During El Niños, this cold water is replaced by warm water, resulting in depleted catches of fish such as the Peruvian *ancho-veta* (*Engraulis ringens*, Peruvian anchoveta) that drives Peru's export fishmeal industry. Although climate scientists debate whether global warming has made El Niños more frequent, the phenomenon appears to be stronger as a result of climate change.[1] An El Niño event occurred from 2015 to 2016 that some scientists estimated was the strongest recorded El Niño. This was followed by localized coastal warming in 2017 that led to unusually warm temperatures in Lima and extensive coastal flooding. Fishers such as Marcos and Luis also attribute dwindling local catches to overfishing. The industrial fleet has spent decades overfishing anchoveta stocks, which many other fish depend on for food, and still come into the bay when they have not filled their holds to scoop up as many fish as they can.

Marcos expertly guided the boat back along the pier, where we jumped out and unloaded the container of fish. The brothers then took the boat back to the moorage, where it would bob and sway in the water until their next trip the following morning. Luis's adolescent son carried the fish back to the market. Every day during the summer, right before dusk, the fishers put moveable tables out in a small area next to the association's storage building and sold their fish. Restaurant owners from Chorrillos, residents, and tourists passed through, looking for fish for the night's meal or the next day. If all went well, Marcos's and Luis's fish would sell, and they would have money for their families' necessities, bills, or supplies for the next day of fishing. If the fish did not sell, they might put them in the cooler and try again the next day or take the leftover fish home for dinner. There were, Luis had told us several times before, many nights when they had little more than fish to bring home.

Fish, Class, and Politics

The lives of fishers such as Luis and Marcos reveal much about how natural environments and relationships of class and politics are not just entangled but also actively produce each other. In this book, we use the experiences of fishers in Chorrillos as an anchor for exploring the ways in which state officials, fishmeal producers, and developers have configured fish, labor, and coastal geographies in order to facilitate the ongoing production of wealth and for revealing the impact that such configurations have had on coastal ecologies and lives.

Those not familiar with Peru often associate the country with the Andes Mountains and well-known Inca cities and archaeological sites, foremost among them Machu Picchu, since these have been at the center of Peru's tourism promotion campaigns for decades.[2] Yet, Peru has one of the most productive fisheries in the world. The Humboldt Current is one of the world's great upwelling systems, which pushes cold water from the bowels of the southern Pacific Ocean to the surface of the waters that flow along the western coast of South America. In Chile and much of Peru, the current's waters come very close to shore, providing easy access to an incredibly abundant marine ecology. Fish from these waters helped to foster some of the earliest settlements in the continent along Peru's central coast and supported myriad fishing villages in the centuries after Spanish colonization of the Americas. During the first half of the twentieth century, fishers from the area around Lima participated in the country's first forays into fish exports, supplying *bonito* (*Sarda chiliensis*, eastern Pacific bonito) to canneries in Callao, Lima's main port.

Following World War II, Peru's fisheries changed dramatically as exports of fishmeal made from anchoveta assumed a rapidly expanding role in global markets and Peru's export portfolio. Peru's initial anchoveta boom, which lasted from 1956 to 1965, was followed by a series of crises precipitated by declines in fish stocks and subsequent reorganizations of capital and labor. This led to an increasingly monopolized fishmeal industry that has employed fewer and fewer people over the course of the past fifty years in an attempt to extract greater value from diminishing fish stocks through improved efficiencies. These reorganizations led to the development of novel languages of state fisheries policy and regulation, most significant among them the emergence of new classifications of fishing boats and fishers. Following the most dramatic reorganization of the fishmeal industry in the early 1970s, the state designated fishers who used small wooden boats to fish for food as *artesanal* (artisanal) in contrast to the industrial boats that chased anchoveta for fishmeal. From the 1970s on, the state worked with the fishmeal industry to lay off a significant number of workers, diverting them from the industrial fleet to the artisanal sector with the promise of state support for expanding the latter's capacity to supply food to Peruvian consumers. However, this support was limited because it was tied to state rents from a fishmeal sector that had either been in crisis or had found ways to pay little to the state, thus fishing Peruvian waters virtually for free. In the 1990s and early 2000s, the state further divided the artisanal sector into artesanales, who used small wooden boats that did not have mechanical winches to draw in their nets, and *menor escala* (small-scale) wooden industrial boats, most commonly referred to as *boliches* (purse seiners). The latter participated in the fishmeal trade until new regulations forced them out.

Over the course of the past three decades, the number of artisanal fishers has almost doubled as the industrial fleet has shed jobs. While the state has provided limited protections for these fishers—the most important being the establishment of a zone from the coast out to five nautical miles in which industrial boats cannot fish for anchoveta—such regulations rarely have been enforced. In contrast, the state has provided a group of eight corporations with a legal claim to the majority of the country's annual anchoveta catch, prohibiting the majority of small-scale industrial and artisanal fishers from engaging in the country's most profitable fishery. Thus, a critical component of securing value from Peru's marine natures for fishmeal corporations has been the ongoing enclosure of Peruvian fisheries for the fishmeal industry through projects of state space-making and the increased regulation of anchoveta catches in favor of large fishmeal corporations. This process has come at a cost to smaller anchoveta operations, which have been increasingly squeezed out of the fishery, and artisanal fishers, such as Luis and Marcos, whose catches of food fish for domestic markets have been impacted by industrial overfishing. Such enclosures are not ancillary results of industry reorganizations but are a central and ongoing component of securing value for the fishmeal industry, ensuring that it has ongoing access to sufficient anchoveta stocks.

The history and politics of Peru's fisheries development shows that the ocean is a historical-natural entity whose limitations are the products of the contingent ways in which capitalism has engaged ocean natures. We use *ocean natures* to highlight the myriad ways in which ocean life has been entangled with politics and capital and to show how shifts in ocean dynamics have imperiled particular systems of accumulation and governance. Cultural geographers studying "social nature" have demonstrated the dialectical interplay of nature and society in order to refute earlier conceptualizations of nature as an unchanging entity external to society (Harvey 1974; Smith 1984). Noel Castree (2001, 13–15) summarizes this approach when he asserts that "societies physically reconstitute nature" at the same time that "societies are 'in' nature (and vice versa)." In this vein, Jason Moore (2015, 2, 13) argues that capitalism is above all a system for "organizing nature," and it has survived not by "destroying nature" but by putting nature to work "for free, or at a very low cost." Capitalism cannot survive without producing and securing uncommodified "cheap natures" that enable the production of surplus value (Moore 2015, 15, 100–101). In other words, capital works through nature, identifying natures that can be commodified, while historical natures set limits on capital's ability to produce value (Moore 2015). Moore (2015, 95) stresses the importance of "extra-economic" practices that enable "unpaid work/energy to be mobilized, on a sustained but not sustainable basis, for capital accumulation," which he deems "accumulation by appropriation."

Fernando Coronil (1997) makes a similar point in his history of state politics and oil wealth in Venezuela. In countries with economies that depend on the commodification of natural resources, exports of these products represent "major sources of foreign exchange," the value of which is determined in global trade by the degree to which a country's "export sector possesses either cheap labor or a natural advantage" (Coronil 1997, 37, 65). In many instances, export industries rely on states to produce these advantages in the form of subsidies or increased restrictions on imports (Coronil 1997, 65). In Venezuela, the state claimed ownership of the country's mineral deposits in the name of the nation, enabling it to accrue significant rents from oil extraction. For Coronil, this example underscores the importance of "land"—here signifying the productive capabilities of nature—in a dialectic relationship with labor and capital for producing value. Furthermore, incorporating land into this equation makes it necessary to consider the central role that politics plays in value production rather than seeing it as secondary to the functions of the market (Lefebvre 1991).

Throughout this book, we consider the political practices through which state officials have asserted control of Peru's ocean natures in order to secure the conditions for ongoing accumulation. Dominant Western visions of the ocean have portrayed it as a wild void with a constantly changing shape that has resisted the cultural and territorial significations of land-based civilization. Stefan Helmreich (2009, 15) demonstrates that such images of a "wild and wondrous sea" continue to inform scientific research even at the microbial level. Framing the sea as an "unfamiliar universe of marine microbes," contemporary marine biologists contribute to its image as an "alien ocean" (Helmreich 2009, 15). In contrast to such images of the sea as a wild unknown, Phillip Steinberg (2001, 4–6) demonstrates that "each period of capitalism" has territorialized the world's oceans in specific ways. Steinberg and Kimberley Peters (2015, 255) argue that the ocean's unique materiality "both enables and disrupts . . . earthly striations." Oceans are in a constant state of reproduction as water moves both in rhythmic repetition, such as the "churning" of waves and predictable tides, and in "unstable cascades" that result from weather events and climatic shifts (Steinberg and Peters 2015, 250). As such, the ocean is best understood as a contingent volume composed of "heterogenous and independent" parts (Steinberg and Peters 2015, 255). Yet, schemes to govern the ocean reduce its three-dimensional nature to simplified "flat space" more amenable to mapping and areal regulations, such as "fishery certification zones" that "fail to capture the mobility of either the water or the fish" (Steinberg and Peters 2015, 253).

In Peru, such territorial simplifications have been critical for the enclosure of ocean natures because they have obscured local artisanal fishing rights and practice. Artisanal fishers, such as Luis and Marcos, engage with and are part of the complex assemblages that comprise the eastern Pacific's ocean natures. This engagement has enabled them to shift and adapt their practices as different fish species move, currents shift course, and climatic events change the ocean's temperature. In the process, they are part of a constant remaking of ocean natures, which have been critical for sustaining long-term artisanal fisheries. Industrial fish production and the regulatory enclosures that have accompanied it have made artisanal engagements largely invisible. Simultaneous with the anchoveta boom, the Peruvian state made concerted claims to "national" territorial waters out to two hundred nautical miles, a key element of which was the assertion that the state owned national waters and the fish in them and therefore had the exclusive power to regulate them as well as generate rent from their extraction. For most of the past seventy years, the state has used this power to provide access to abundant anchoveta stocks to the fishmeal industry for free.

This process has relied upon the production of a vision of Peru's portion of the Pacific Ocean that is oriented to the mass capture of a single species with regulations based on areal mapping of the ocean's surface and sonar sampling of anchoveta populations below the surface to estimate the total biomass of this species in a given year. This regulatory regime has been unable to account for the fluidity of ocean conditions or shifts in ecological assemblages, which is significant given that the eastern Pacific is subject to regular oscillations in water temperatures that affect fish populations and movements. The result has been a series of boom-bust cycles in industrial fishmeal production. Following each bust, state officials have sought to reestablish the profitability of the fish-meal industry by further enclosing ocean territory and fish stocks. Industrial fishmeal producers have argued against protections for small-scale and artisanal fishers (a significant portion of whom had previously worked in the industry) and have sought to exclude small producers from the anchoveta fishery. Such dispossessions have represented direct transfers of wealth from Peru's artisanal fishers to the fishmeal industry, while the former have repeatedly borne the negative effects of industrial reconfigurations in the form of reduced stocks, polluted waters, and competition among growing numbers of artisanal fishers for fewer fish.

Governing for Enclosure

In this book, we approach enclosure and dispossession not as end results but as processes that often unfold slowly over time. We do so in order to reveal the accumulated effects of gradual encroachments upon impoverished and politi-cally marginalized people's property, rights, and autonomy and to show the sub-tle ways in which new constraints and appropriations emerge and are worked out in day-to-day life. The declines in fish stocks that fishers such as Luis and Marcos have experienced are the result of both global climate changes and more than half a century during which the Peruvian state made anchoveta stocks available to an increasingly monopolized fishmeal industry. As the quantity and quality of existing fish stocks have diminished, industrial producers have sought to capture a growing portion of Peru's ocean natures to ensure their ongoing ability to generate income while advocating for increased restrictions on small producers. Such dynamics illustrate the degree to which particular configurations of capital have shaped the productivity of Peru's marine biomass, the limits of which have reinforced inequalities in class and wealth. Moreover, this illustrates the importance of politics for enabling and legitimating the appropriations, enclosures, and dispossessions that are necessary for securing unequal access to productive natures.

Geographer David Harvey (2003) argues that "accumulation by dispossession" is an ongoing strategy that capitalists employ to avert crises. Harvey takes as his inspiration work by Karl Marx and Rosa Luxemburg on the centrality of dispossession to capitalist accumulation (Harvey 2003, 137–147). Marx (1990, 874–875) theorized that "primitive accumulation"—the forcible enclosure and dispossession of common property—made later modes of capitalist accumulation possible and comprised the foundation of modern class inequalities. Luxemburg (1951, 509) asserted that such dispossessions were an ongoing aspect of capital accumulation which relied upon the existence of non-capitalist systems of production whose labor and natural resources could be forcibly appropriated via colonialism and imperialism. Harvey contends that dispossession is a repeated strategy for accumulation but argues that capitalism does not rely upon the separation of capitalist and non-capitalist systems of production. Rather, capitalist accumulation needs to continually acquire new assets through dispossession to avert crises (Harvey 2003, 139). In recent decades, Harvey argues that this has been accomplished through the privatization and financialization of once-public assets for the benefit of private corporations (Harvey 2003, 157–160).

Harvey's work provides critical insight into the political materiality of enclosure and dispossession and into the ways in which contemporary political economies facilitate unequal transfers of wealth. In her work on dispossession and the environment in Papua New Guinea, Paige West (2016, 2017) argues that attending to the symbolic representations that are used to justify material appropriations is equally important. West demonstrates that processes of accumulation and dispossession rest "on the discursive, semiotic, and visual production of both Papua New Guinea and Papua New Guineans as outside the natural order of things" (West 2016, 23). Such "discursive dispossession" has been a critical means through which Papua New Guineans have been denied sovereignty over natural resources and their conservation (West 2016). For example, top-down conservation programs have "wrest control of management of biological diversity" by casting "people from PNG as incapable, and living in a prior state, unable to manage anything" (West 2017). West (2017) argues that such instances reveal that dispossession "is increasingly intertwined with discursive and semiotic processes," which underscores the need to theorize the interplay between "representational rhetorics" and "material aspects" of dispossession.

In order to analyze the impacts of dispossession at various scales, we highlight the material, legal, and discursive components of ongoing enclosures of Peru's fish stocks, ocean territories, and coastal spaces as well as the ways in which such enclosures have enabled new modes of accumulation and dispossession. Throughout this book, we argue that cultural discourses about artisanal fishers as being uncivilized, unregulated, or existing outside of formal market relations have served to justify the state's enclosure of ocean natures for the industrial fishery. In the present conjuncture, government officials and industry representatives have framed the alterity of artisanal fishers in neoliberalized discourses of the responsible self, insisting that small-scale producers have not been sufficiently accountable to their communities or local ecologies to have earned the right to exploit Peru's ocean natures. In doing so, powerful actors have asserted that further enclosures are necessary for ensuring the health of the ocean and that artisanal fishers are to blame for their own dispossession.

Marine enclosures have taken a variety of forms in Peru. In the industrial anchoveta fishery, the government has instituted individual vessel quotas (IVQs), which award a portion of the year's maximum allowed catch to individual boats, based largely on the historical landings of particular fishmeal companies. This has resulted in the growing privatization and monopolization of the country's most lucrative fishery and has pushed out many small boats, which have now turned to pursuing other species and, in some cases, competing with artisanal fishers for nearshore stocks. Given the dispersed and widely variable nature of artisanal fishing, the government has not instituted a system of boat quotas for this fishery. Rather, it has created regulations to exclude most artisanal fishers from legally participating in the fishmeal trade and has instituted new regimes of licensing artisanal fishers and boat owners on the grounds that artisanal fishers exist outside the purview of the state and now must demonstrate that they are responsible producers to be able to participate officially in Peru's fisheries.

Our analysis of the lives of artisanal fishers explores how such enclosures have created new challenges for impoverished fishers to live what they consider dignified, culturally fulfilling lives.

Such pressures have affected not only the ways in which fishers engage with ocean ecologies but also their tenuous claim to the small wharf in Chorrillos. Part of the government's growing concern with making artisanal fishers and vendors visible to state regulatory and taxation practices has included the institution of new ways of organizing fishers' associations and more complex requirements for demonstrating that associations have earned the right to administer wharf spaces. In 1969, the state granted the local fishing union, a corporatist entity organized through what was then the Ministerio de Agricultura y Pesquería (Ministry of Agriculture and Fisheries), the right to the small wharf at the southern end of the Bay of Chorrillos. In the ensuing decades, the union used this right largely as a means of providing the necessary access that fishers and vendors needed to make a living as well as a resource for social support. The union charged small fees for tourists and vendors to use the area and, once a refrigeration unit was installed, charged fishers for ice. Furthermore, each year members of the union paid dues. The small revenue generated from these sources of income was used in part for the physical upkeep of the dock and in part to provide loans, scholarships, extra holiday food, and more to the families of the union's members. Recently, government officials have argued that unions are anachronistic forms of community organization and have forced fishing unions to reorganize as associations with fewer rights and no formal link to the Ministerio de la Producción (Produce, Ministry of Production), which oversees artisanal fishing. Furthermore, Produce, in conjunction with local municipal governments, has instituted a series of "best practices" for fishing, fish handling, and vending that require the local fishers' association to demonstrate that fishers and vendors are responsible users. These dictums have emerged at a time when the area around the wharf has become increasingly developed for tourism, and government officials and the neighboring Yacht Club members have viewed the physically dilapidated wharf as an eyesore. This has put fishers and vendors under greater official scrutiny and has placed increased pressure on them to improve the space and their practices, lest they lose control of the area.

While many aspects of this dynamic are unique to Chorrillos and coastal Peru, government demands that fishers and vendors improve themselves and their space are indicative of broader aspects of neoliberalized governance. Here we use *neoliberalism* to refer to the hegemonic ideology that markets and individuals' participation in them are the only viable solutions to governmental, social, and ecological problems. In Latin America, the complex ascendance of neoliberalized dictums of individualism and the supremacy of the market have altered notions of what it means to be a citizen and how the state functions (Hale 2002; Hetherington 2011; Krupa 2010; Ramírez 2011), have increased the role of financialization and debt in social life and governance (Biehl 2013; Han 2012), and have recast the grounds upon which different actors assert their rights to exist (Auyero 2012; Goodale and Postero 2013; Gago 2017). One of the central, defining ideologies of neoliberalized reforms in Latin America, and indeed throughout the world, has been the insistence that rights are not an inherent aspect of citizenship but privileges that individuals earn through responsible comportment.

In their analysis of contemporary neoliberalized regimes of the "actively responsible self," Peter Miller and Nikolas Rose (2008, 218) argue that individuals are expected to satisfy their "national obligations not through their relations of dependency and obligation to one another, but through seeking to fulfill themselves within a variety of micro-communal domains or 'communities.'" While such a move appears to enhance local, individual autonomy, it has ushered in new forms of seemingly a-political regulation—"audits, budgets, standards, risk management, targets" and other seemingly a-political mechanisms that seek to orient individual subjectivities to specific ends (Miller and Rose 2008, 218).[3] Reimagining society as comprised of a diversity of self-governing, autonomous entities makes it easier to abandon individuals or communities by repackaging class alterity as the failure to comport oneself in market-savvy ways (Povinelli 2011, 190). In her recent critique of neoliberalized governance, Wendy Brown (2015, 71) argues that such dynamics are made possible by the "combination of devolved authority and responsibilization of the subject." Individuals are "made responsible," regardless of their resources or lack thereof, for reconfiguring their practices to accomplish elite-specified outcomes (Brown 2015, 129).

For example, conservation projects increasingly have been oriented to creating environmentally responsible subjectivities through state interventions and certification schemes aimed at promoting certain practices by providing economic incentives for their implementation (Agrawal 2005; Luke 1999). In emphasizing economic growth as the only appropriate end of environmentally responsible behavior, recent projects of "neoliberal environmentality" (Fletcher 2010) have sidelined alternative ecologies, encouraged new forms of extraction (Adams 2015; Baletti 2014), and pressured small producers with few resources to demonstrate that they are responsible stewards (Martínez-Reyes 2016). One result of this has been that individuals who fail to demonstrate their ability to produce value according to neoliberalized metrics can be blamed for their own dispossession because they presumably failed to take responsibility for themselves or their environment. In this vein, Peruvian officials have presented new constraints on artisanal fishers' and vendors' autonomy and customary rights not as enclosures but as fundamental measures for creating a functioning "community" of self-responsible producers.

We argue that this insistence on building a responsible community ignores the existence of an already-existing, practiced "commons"—a web of social, cultural, and ecological relationships among people and nonhumans (Linebaugh 2008, 19)—and underscores how neoliberalized governance and the enclosures it furthers rely upon constant separations of people from historically rooted practices, humans from nonhumans, and fishers from the ecologies in which they are enmeshed.[4] In her seminal analysis of the history of the body in the development of capitalism, Silvia Federici (2004) shows how important separation is for appropriation. Specifically, she demonstrates that capitalism's separation of economic production from reproduction made women's work, which was necessary for reproducing the conditions that made wage labor possible, invisible in capitalist logics of work, thus enabling its appropriation for free. In his study of Irish fisheries, Patrick Bresnihan (2016, 126) refers to this process as "enclosure-through-separation." Bresnihan (2016, 7, 13) argues that the "generation of novel forms of inclusion and exclusion" involves the denial of certain "ways of knowing and relating."

In his analysis of the mediation of nature, Jim Igoe (2017, 6–10) argues that separation is a critical means through which nature continues to be produced and known. However, he demonstrates that nature is not imagined as something separate from humans. Rather, consumers are constantly being reconnected to selective representations of particular species, places, and conservation programs that have been separated from the messy realities in which they exist through processes of "dissociation, control, and commodification" (Igoe 2017, 7). These processes are central to an emerging "green capitalist policy zeitgeist" that portrays nature as having hidden value that can be unlocked through proper engagement with the market, thus creating an "idealized form of nature in which economy and ecology appear to harmonize" (Igoe 2017, 7–9; see also Büscher et al. 2014). Such idealized natures are possible because they "repress associated contradictions," thus providing people with images of nature they can consume without having to consider "their own entanglements in continuing histories and relationships of exploitation and harm" (Igoe 2017, 8–10). Elspeth Probyn (2016) makes a similar point when she argues that "green" seafood certifications simplify the sea by telling consumers that they can save imperiled oceans by buying fish that have been caught in the "right" way. Such simplifications of fishing and fisheries often overlook the "deep entanglement that fish, fishers, and ocean have forged over the millennia" in portraying fishers as engaged in an exploitative relationship with the sea while also absolving consumers of any role in the degradation of the world's marine habitats (Probyn 2016, 43).

In this book, we trace the ways in which emergent forms of green governance separate fishers and fish vendors from ocean natures and reconnect them to these natures in ways that enable new forms of enclosure and threats of dispossession by reducing fishing to a simplified set of economic relationships between fishers and coastal ecologies. Artisanal fishers in Chorrillos are engaged in myriad relationships with human and nonhuman entities in the coproduction of these ecologies. These myriad relationships are what make fishing possible, yet neoliberalized approaches to fishing regulation focus only on the latter— the narrow range of activities that comprise the economic production of fishers (Bresnihan 2016; Peterson 2014). This separation is a first step in asserting that fishers must establish their responsible adherence to best practices in order to gain access to resources or lose such access because they have failed to do so. The same is true of the wharf, which is not just an economic space, but also a place where myriad social, familial, historical, and cultural relationships among fishers and vendors reproduce a commons that makes economic production possible. As Peter Linebaugh (2008, 2014) and Bresnihan (2016) make clear, membership in a commons is a question of relationships and how people are actively engaged in practices that create, renew, and make a commons possible. In contrast, neoliberalized approaches to community frame membership as an alienable privilege that one earns through proper conduct (Miller and Rose 2008).

This tension between lived reality and the impositions of new forms of governance is one that has produced significant challenges for artisanal fishers and vendors. We argue that an in-depth consideration of these challenges is essential for understanding how attempts to forge "responsibilitized" (Brown 2015) subjectivities are inherently linked to and help to further enclosure and dispossession. We explore this struggle by examining artisanal fishers' and vendors' interactions with numerous government officials as well as their engagements with new regulations and governance practices. Fishers' and vendors' responses to the demands of neoliberalized governance have been complex and provide critical insight into the challenges that they have posed to existing practices that maintain ocean natures in Chorrillos and the subtle ways in which fishers and vendors have both resisted and incorporated neoliberalized understandings of responsibility in their attempts to rework and reimagine their relationships with each other. For example, in their discussions of new requirements, fishers often have accused the state of abandoning them to a host of localized government officials who constantly have harassed them but have provided little in the way of real support. Fishers have argued that these officials do not have full authority to regulate them, providing a rationale for not entirely complying with what they have viewed as externally imposed dictums of governance. At the same time, discussions among fishers and vendors about the future of the wharf have also revealed the degree to which neoliberalized discourses of responsibility and self-governance sometimes dovetail with traditional ideas about the moral responsibility of fishers to care for their families. Fishers and vendors oftentimes fall back on ideologies of responsibility to explain inequalities among themselves or between fishing ports.

In her analysis of land holding and agricultural production in rural Sulawesi, Tania Murray Li (2014, 8–9) argues that dispossession often unfolds in the "mundane" interactions of capitalist relations—driven by competition and profit—that rework social relationships and erode the basis of impoverished people's lives in "piecemeal" ways that are often "unexpected and unplanned." Li (2014) analyzes transformations in land ownership and inequality among highlanders in Sulawesi over the course of two decades to demonstrate how these people's engagement with cacao production changed kinship relations and ultimately led to dramatic inequalities in land ownership, leading many local people to become landless, while a small group of people prospered (until blights affected cacao production). Similarly, we argue that fishers' and vendors' daily struggles with and discussions about inequality and responsibility highlight the centrality of enclosure to capital accumulation and the role that politics plays in legitimating people's dispossession from rights and practiced commons by making such dispossession appear to be agentless, the result of poor management, or just the natural order of things. Furthermore, fishers' and vendors' experiences reveal the challenges of seeing and confronting these dispossessions amid quotidian interactions that rely upon and reinforce them.

Precarious Work

Understanding the day-to-day pressures that advance dispossession is not possible without a consideration of the economic precarity that artisanal fishers and vendors face on a daily basis. Artisanal fishers and vendors perform important labor in that they provide fish and prepared seafood for local markets and residents. Peruvians are among the highest per capita consumers of fish in the Americas, and artisanal fishers, such as those in Chorrillos, produce the majority of the fish that is consumed domestically. However, fishers and vendors receive little for the fish that they produce. Manual labor is devalued in Lima's urban economy both economically and socially. In her study of labor and forest conservation in Madagascar, Genese Marie Sodikoff (2012, 9) argues that the "devaluation of manual conservation labor" is not just a product of manual workers being paid less for their work. Rather, it is also "tied to the redeployment of a historical moral hierarchy that maintains the imbalance between unskilled, 'coastal' labor and elite others" (Sodikoff 2012, 9). The same is true of manual fishing labor in Lima, which is done by people with little social capital.

Artisanal fishers and vendors work in what economists, development specialists, and government officials often refer to as the "informal" economy. In this context, informality denotes work that is largely unregulated by the government, which means that workers have few protections such as basic insurance, guaranteed minimum wages, safe working conditions, or job security. Lima's economy is made possible by the cheap labor and services of the informal sector in which the majority of the city's workers are employed. Yet, government officials often decry informality as a hindrance to development and repeatedly engage in symbolic acts of clearing out informal vendors from popular spots in the city (Gandolfo 2013). City officials portray informal laborers as operating outside of the normal market economy, obscuring the reality that they are an integral part of Lima's economy. This represents a discursive means through which the labor of impoverished fishers is devalued as something that is a throwback to precapitalist forms of production while ignoring the central role that such labor plays in making contemporary forms of value production and accumulation possible. Roughly half of Lima's artisanal fishers make less than Peru's official minimum wage, which is one of the lowest in the region and does not represent a living wage in the increasingly expensive city. Furthermore, declines and fluctuations in fish stocks have added even greater precarity to the fishers' situation, given that they are not able to rely on consistent catches or market prices from one year to the next. Many artisanal fishers and vendors in Chorrillos have dealt with this precarity by trying to diversify their work and sources of income.

María Luz Cruz-Torres and Pamela McElwee (2012, 10) argue that "livelihood diversification is crucial in explaining how individuals and households negotiate improvements for their quality of life." For example, in her study of rural livelihoods in northwestern Mexico, Cruz-Torres (2004, 222) shows that as a result of "environmental degradation and economic impoverishment," people had to "combine resources generated through work in various economic activities available within, and beyond the limits of, their communities." The rural producers whom Cruz-Torres studied fished, engaged in small-scale agriculture, worked as rural wage-laborers, tended livestock, and entered the informal sector by selling goods. Engagement in these different kinds of work fell along "established gender patterns" that dictated "which tasks should be, or it is hoped, will be done by women and which will be done by men" (Cruz-Torres 2004, 223). Women were expected to tend to the labor of reproducing households by taking care of children, making food, and shopping for food while also working as vendors and as agricultural wage-laborers. While adding to their overall burden, work outside of the home meant women reduced their "economic dependence on men" and augmented women's "power and ability to make decisions within the household" (Cruz-Torres 2004, 243). This presented new challenges to household gender relations as some men resented women's increased economic power, since it upended men's traditional image of themselves as breadwinners.

Fishers and vendors in Chorrillos have engaged in similar strategies of diversification, taking advantage of the opportunities that they could find in Lima's urban economy for different sources of income. These strategies of diversification have fallen along gendered lines and have sometimes led to tensions between men and women over the value and importance of different kinds of work or the gendered identities associated with them. For working class artisanal fishers, manual labor is a critical aspect of their identities as adult men. Most fishers in Chorrillos engage in fishing as their primary form of work and main source of income. Fishing provides men with control over their day-to-day routine and recognition among their peers on the wharf that they are doing socially acceptable work. When fishing is poor, men seek other manual labor in the city, especially construction. However, such work is undesirable, and men usually only do it when absolutely necessary because working on a construction crew means surrendering their autonomy, working for a boss, and often making little more than what they earn by fishing. In the past, when fishing has been slow, some fishers also have turned to tourism, using their boats to give sightseers rides around the harbor. A few former fishers now focus on this as their primary source of income. While tourism is seasonal, it has been more predictable than fishing in many regards.

In Lima, working class women's identities traditionally have been linked to care of the household, performing unpaid and officially unrecognized labor necessary for the reproduction of fishing families. However, in all of the families we came to know in Chorrillos, women also worked in the informal sector as vendors, either on the dock as fish and food vendors or in other parts of the city. Some of the women we interviewed had worked as domestic servants, cleaning or caring for children for wealthier families, and some had occasionally picked up work cleaning offices or houses when times were really tough. Most preferred to avoid such work because the pay was low, abuse was regular, and they lacked the autonomy that they had as vendors. Working as vendors on the dock, women could set their schedules so that they could drop their children off at school before going to work or have their children with them when they were working. Indeed, in many of the food kiosks on the dock, children helped by running to get more ice, carrying drinks out to customers, and performing other tasks.

Such work has been necessary for survival in the city. Multiple pools of income generated by men's and women's labor has made coastal life and the small dignities that have accompanied it possible. However, women's growing economic power has also upset the notion of male fishers as traditional heads-of-household, and the centrality of food kiosks on the wharf, which are run by women, has challenged the notion that fishing is the engine of the dock's economy, not service and tourism. This, as we explore in greater detail in Chapter 5, has led to tensions among workers who use the dock for their economic activities. Women vendors and fish cleaners have argued that they are unjustly excluded from participation in the fishers' association, which makes decisions about how the wharf is used and administered. In response, some fishers have sought to assert their primacy in the administration and have advocated renovations to the space that would marginalize or remove food kiosks with the rationale that it would enable them to generate more rent and better care for their families. Through an analysis of fishers' and vendors' efforts to confront ongoing precarity and the tensions that have arisen out of these efforts, we show how dispossession and challenges to it are worked out in mundane, daily struggles over the value of different kinds of work and who does it.

Coastal Dialectics

We have chosen to examine fishing, class, and politics in Peru from a "coastal" perspective. Coasts are funny spaces within broader political and cultural geographies, which have tended to frame oceans as natures separate from land-based human civilization. The ever-changing, watery character of the ocean has long been perceived as a counter to human civilization, typified by the construction of territorially fixed settlements (Steinberg 2001). Within such geographies, coasts exist as liminal zones, where one leaves land and culture and enters the wilds of the ocean or vice versa. This is particularly true in Lima, where dunes and sandy cliffs largely separate urban settlement from the Pacific. Imagining the coast as a dividing line between the culture of terra firma and the nature of the ocean actively contributes to ignorance about the way in which the two are bound up by cultural, ecological, territorial, and economic systems. In contrast, we think of the coast as a privileged space of relationality in which the myriad connections that constitute human and nonhuman ecologies, territories, and political economies become apparent. In other words, by thinking through the "coastal," we seek to maintain the complexity of cultural, economic, and ecological worlds in view, which is critical for examining the politics that enable and challenge the configuration of particular ecologies and geographies of accumulation and dispossession.

A central argument of this book is that dominant ways of understanding nature, culture, responsibility, and entrepreneurialism obscure the coproduction of nature, class, and politics in particular historical moments. The belief that the ocean is the ultimate wild hides the degree to which ocean natures have been made to work for the accumulation of capital in fishing industries in Peru and around the world. The image of ocean natures as entities that are fundamentally different from urban culture masks the degree to which coastal degradation in the form of untreated sewage and pollution have provided Lima and other cities with a free sink for dumping waste. Discourses of self-responsibility and entrepreneurialism make class disappear as an analytical and organizational category by emphasizing the ideology that all individuals have a responsibility to take care of themselves and sustain communities regardless of the resources they have (or lack) to carry out such work. All of these discourses combine in different ways at different moments to make the enclosures that are necessary for ongoing and unequal transfers of value appear as though they are natural—the products of changing ocean conditions and of pollution for which no one

Figure 2 The fishers' wharf in Chorrillos. Photo by Maximilian Viatori.

is really responsible or the need to renew areas that have not been cared for by their users.

The only means for countering these erasures is to emphasize and make visible the historically specific ways in which nature, capital, and politics are configured. Doing so is not only critical for thinking about fishers' place within broader systems of inequality but also for thinking about environmental politics in new ways by considering how the degradation of coastal lives is an ecological issue that is simultaneously about class and politics. Crises in fish production are not just about surpassing the natural or sustainable catch limit for particular fish species but also about crises in the inability of capital to secure the necessary means for producing surplus value, which has led to more rapid reorganizations of capital, greater inequalities, and increased dispossessions in more aggressive pursuits of the cheap labor and ever-dwindling supplies of natures that have not yet been commodified and that are necessary for generating profit (Moore 2015). Treating these issues as separate, as being "just" about the environment, class, or politics, threatens to reinforce the unbundling of nature-capital-politics that makes the production of eco-spatial, class, gender, and other inequalities possible (Moore 2015).[5]

This book draws on the experiences of artisanal fishers as an analytical foundation for theorizing the coproduction of ocean life (both human and nonhuman), the accumulation of capital, and the articulation of class politics at particular conjunctures in local and global histories. Our analysis is based on ongoing archival and ethnographic research since 2012. During the summers of 2011 and 2012, Max conducted research in British Columbia on salmon conservation debates and the politics of salmon aquaculture (Viatori 2016a). Anchoveta meal from Peru and Chile has been an important component of aquaculture feed regimes around the world, and Max became interested in investigating the impacts that fishmeal production was having on fishers in Peru, given his long-term research interests in the region (Viatori 2016b). At the same time, Héctor entered the doctoral program in sustainable agriculture at Iowa State University with Max as his co-major professor. Both had worked previously in South America: Max had conducted ten years of research on neoliberalism and indigeneity in Ecuador (Viatori 2010, 2016c), and Héctor had worked on rights movements in Colombia for his MA in political science.

Given a shared background in South American politics and a growing interest in global commodity chains and food production, Max proposed exploratory research in Peru on artisanal fish production. Between 2012 and 2017, we made six trips together to Lima, which lasted from one week to two months. Additionally, Héctor traveled to Lima twice on his own when Max's academic commitments did not allow him to go. During each of these trips, Max employed Héctor as a research assistant. Héctor also used these trips to do research for his doctoral thesis on place-based activism and food production among artisanal fishers in Chorrillos. Over the course of working on this project, we developed and refined a collaborative approach to conducting ethnographic research with artisanal fishers. Before each trip, we discussed what we hoped to learn and who we wanted to interview. During the trips, we conducted many of the interviews together, conversing with different fishers or officials about their work and lives and their approaches to Peruvian fisheries. Afterward, we often talked about the interviewees' responses and noted different things that stood out. Given our different disciplinary backgrounds, this process helped us to identify various strands and patterns in the interviews and to identify areas of interest for future interviews. Upon returning from Peru, we often continued these discussions, thinking about and reflecting on what we had learned and how this would shape what we did on our next trip. In the instances in which Héctor traveled to Peru and conducted interviews for the project on his own, our interactive approach was all the more critical for ensuring continuity in the research. Our process differed from traditional approaches to ethnographic research in which a lone anthropologist studies cultural dynamics through individual participation in them. Recently, some anthropologists have highlighted the benefits of team approaches to ethnography, which can help researchers to keep different aspects of complex dynamics in view and better understand them (Brosius and Campbell 2010). This was certainly the case for this project, which demanded that we trace the complex ecological, political, and social relationships that comprised oceanic and coastal assemblages.

We chose to study these relationships in Lima and the surrounding area because they represent an important and historically significant concentration of artisanal fishers in Peru. According to a 2012 national government census of artisanal fishers, there are 2,107 artisanal fishers active in Lima Province—which bears the same name as the capital city and includes the thirty urban districts that comprise the Metro Lima area as well as thirteen surrounding rural districts—and an additional 1,241 working in Callao Province, which is coterminous with the city of Callao. This represents 7.5 percent of all Peru's artisanal fishers. Moreover, we decided to work in Lima because the anchoveta fishery is most active along Peru's central coast, and the Lima-Callao area was where the first export fisheries developed in the country, thus providing a deeper historical view of how industrial production has reordered coastal ecologies and the impacts this has had on artisanal fisheries and labor. Throughout our research, we spent a significant amount of our time in Chorrillos, which we chose to visit in 2012, because it is the primary artisanal fishing port in the Lima-Callao area. Artisanal fishers are also active in Callao. However, the port is dominated by container shipping and anchoveta meal production, which has marginalized artisanal fishers in the port's activities.

Our goal in studying fishing in Chorrillos was to be as involved as possible in the daily lives of fishers and vendors in order to understand what the challenges were of making a living from the ocean and to get firsthand knowledge of fishers' and vendors' struggles to maintain their access to the dock and to deal with increasingly degraded fisheries. At the outset of this project, we approached the president of what was the Sindicato de Pescadores Artesanales de Chorrillos José Olaya Balandra (Jose Olaya Balandra Union of Artisanal Fishers of the Bay of Chorrillos—it is now an association), which administered the dock.

Initially, much of our research involved unstructured, informal interviews with members of the association about their lives as fishers: what it was like to make a living through fishing, the difficulties they faced both on land and at sea, and how they felt about the current state of fishing in the bay and throughout Peru. These interviews helped us learn how fishers talked about environmental issues, class, and political power and how they used these understandings to orient their practices. Eventually, as we got to know individual fishers better, we participated more in the work and cultural life of the dock. We went out fishing to experience the physical difficulties of rowing a heavy wooden boat in the rolling waves of the outer bay and of pulling in a sunken net by hand. We also listened to discussions among association members about the future, which helped us understand how fishers talked about this issue among themselves.

The fishers' association provided us with critical insight into how fishers organized themselves and the dock economy as well as how the association's rotating leadership (new leaders were elected every two years) dealt with a number of government officials and navigated their relationship with the neighboring Yacht Club. Our research would not have been possible without the permission and support of the association. However, working through the association had a downside: It was comprised entirely of men. Life on the dock is largely structured by gender. Men fish, mend nets, and work on their boats. Women work as vendors, some selling fish or prepared foods to tourists, but most work in the food kiosks that line the wharf. Although there are aspects of this dynamic that are specific to Chorrillos, this division reflects broader national trends. According the 2012 census, approximately 97 percent of artisanal fishers are men. Because our first contact was through the association, our initial interviews and opportunities for participation were with men. Eventually, we got to know a number of the vendors, some of whom were the spouses of fishers we knew. Others we got to know through daily interactions, eating at their kiosks, or buying food from their stalls. Because vendors were not organized as an association, we relied on these individual relationships to get to know and interview women working on the dock. These interviews shed light on how women experienced dynamics of ecological degradation and the politics of the dock's future in ways that were sometimes overlapping but often different from men. We interpreted these differences not as peculiarities of life in Chorrillos—often the favored interpretation of government officials—but as indicative of how particular arrangements of nature, class, and politics interacted with gender inequalities.

All of our interviews, whether they were with fishers, vendors, or state officials, were open-ended conversations. In some cases, fishers and vendors were
reticent about their lives and the dock, not wanting to say too much to researchers whom they did not know well. Many, though, appeared to enjoy the process
and seemed to look forward to follow-up conversations because as fishers and
vendors often told us, they felt as though no one listed to them. Interviewees
saw the experience as an opportunity to set the record straight, to make it clear
what they thought the problems were with the bay, the dock, and Peru, and to
make the case that they had legitimate contributions to make to discussions
about the future of all three. As one older fisher said at the beginning of an
interview, he knew "stories that are not in books, which don't say how it was
[and] don't say the real [history of Chorrillos]." Similarly, another noted at the
outset of one of our interviews that there are "many people who are unaware
of all of this. I am telling you because I have family members who told me . . .
[I am telling you] so that you know it." This fisher went on to tell us about the
scarcity of fish, even in the high seas, which he and his relatives had witnessed
as fishers. Oftentimes, we entered the conversation with a particular set of questions in hand and with an idea of what we thought was important. Just as often,
fishers and vendors corrected this, shifting the discussion to what they knew
really mattered. In other words, rather than collecting data, the interviews were
a process whereby fishers and vendors engaged with us in thinking through and
theorizing the production of coastal lives.

Because the emphasis of our research was on understanding the politics
of coastal enclosures, we focused our attention on life and work on the wharf.
While we participated in cultural festivals and some aspects of life outside the
wharf, we did not spend significant time in researching fishers' or vendors' lives
outside of the dock. Part of this was a result of the spatial organization of life
and work in Chorrillos. The sandy cliffs that separate the ocean from the city
above provide no living space close to the water. Most of the people who work
on the dock live in a series of neighborhoods above central Chorrillos that were
settled through land invasions several decades ago. We did not have opportunities to investigate how other aspects of fishers' and vendors' lives oriented their
approaches to life and politics on the wharf, such as the participation of older
fishers in the land occupations that led to the creation of these neighborhoods.
Furthermore, we did not witness discussions between men and women about
the future of the wharf, their children's futures, and how best to achieve them.
This was also a product of the structure of our research trips. Rather than the

common ethnographic practice of spending a year or more living in an area, we made a series of repeated, shorter trips to Peru. In her study of dispossession in rural Sulawesi, Li (2014, 27) points out that the advantage of "revisiting as a method" is that it enables ethnographers "to track a set of processes as they took shape over time." Our shorter research trips meant that we did not have long periods of time to live with fishers. However, returning year after year allowed us to see the evolution of elite pressure to improve the space, attempts by the Yacht Club to push a renewal plan forward, and how discussions around these issues shifted and created moments of solidarity and tension among fishers and vendors.

While Chorrillos served as a place where we were able to see the depth of changes over a five-year period, we also conducted interviews with fishers as far south as Paracas and as far north as Ancón. We spoke with the leaders of local fishers' associations and individual fishers and vendors about their lives, the state of artisanal fisheries, and other topics they thought were important for understanding what was going on in Peru's central coast. These interactions provided us with a means of situating what we saw in Chorrillos within broader regional and historical dynamics and helped us to understand how people in different places articulated these differences. We also spent significant time interviewing and engaging with officials who were responsible for regulating industrial fishing in Peru, setting fisheries policy, and advocating for the fish-meal industry. Among these individuals were officers of the Coast Guard, high-level bureaucrats in Produce, members of government legal teams, and both government and nonprofit researchers. We rode along with Produce extension officers on their visits to different fishing wharves and spoke with them about the state of artisanal fishing. At the time of our research, there were few people in Peru who had an active interest in studying artisanal fishing. In a country where fisheries research and policy have been dominated by the considerations of the fishmeal industry, many officials and regulators treated our interest in artisanal fishing with curiosity, while others met us with open disdain, pointing out that artisanal fishers and those of the small-scale fleet were unregulated burdens on Peru's ecosystems. We also spoke with architects employed by the Costa Verde Authority—the government body charged with creating regulations for the development of Lima's coastline—about the development of the area around the fishing wharf in Chorrillos. As with fisheries policy, artisanal fishers were (and still are) largely invisible in plans to develop the Costa Verde. What these interviews revealed were the complex ways in which government officials justified and legitimated this absence by drawing on notions of responsibility, entrepreneurialism, and progress that overlooked the history of how coastal ecologies had been developed along Peru's central coast.

The individual stories that emerged from and were recorded in our interviews provided rich detail about the day-to-day struggles over enclosure and the subtle justifications for it. However, without consideration of the broader political and historical contexts in which individuals made particular assertions or chose to highlight specific aspects of their lives or concerns, focusing on individual experiences can obscure the bigger story of how accumulation and elite politics have reorganized nonhuman and human natures, class, and space. In order to analyze this process, we drew on a range of historical data.

Colonial and early republican censes of Lima's coastal populations as well as travel accounts that included descriptions of fishers and communities provide a view of the changing relationship of fishers to Lima's urban spaces and the forms of colonial and republican governance that accompanied them. Scientific and technical reports conducted by foreigners during the first half of the twentieth century and those conducted by the Instituto del Mar del Perú (IMARPE, Marine Institute of Peru) from the 1960s onward provide further insight into how government officials and private entrepreneurs envisioned possibilities for the development of Peru's fisheries and the types of changes that would need to occur in the organization of local fleets and fishers in order to realize these possibilities. A critical aspect of these discussions was often the identification of fishers as civilizational, ethnic, or class Others who required elite improvements to make them into more effective market producers or better urban citizens. For example, an analysis of media coverage of urban development and the cholera outbreak that swept through Lima in 1991 shows how elite Limeños increasingly viewed the Costa Verde's beaches as waste spaces in need of renewal while the fishers and vendors who used those spaces were blamed for spreading the epidemic, further marking them as socially backwards. Such instances, when compared across time, reveal how languages of governance shifted with changes in the organization of space, capital, and labor and how the alterity of fishers was repackaged to meet new demands for extracting value from coastal natures or labor. Such data is vital for providing a longer view of the changing situation of fishers in Lima and Peru.

Historical data was also our primary means of inserting nature into an account of fisheries politics, revealing how ocean natures have been an integral component of historical change. Moore (2015, 17, 30) argues that "the history of capitalism is one of successive *historical natures*, which are both producers *and* products of capitalist development" and emphasizes the importance of recognizing that capitalism works "through, rather than upon nature." In other words, capitalism organizes nature in historically specific ways, which includes unique ways of seeing and understanding nature through cultural production and science (Foster 2000). In turn, particular organizations of nature work through capitalism, setting limits on the ongoing accumulation of capital and precipitating eventual crises. Moore (2015, 28, 30) notes, "If humans are a part of nature, historical change—including the present as history—must be understood through dialectical movements of humans making environments, and environments making humans," because such an approach "allows for an understanding of modernity's historically specific natures as webs of liberation and limitation for the accumulation of capital."

Government records of catch rates, landings, and fisheries regulations demonstrate how historical natures emerged at different points in the development of Peru's fisheries and how capitalism both worked through and was limited by these historical natures. Analyzing industry reports and discussions of fisheries collapses and regulations, the development of new fisheries in trade journals such as *Pesca*, and scientific research on Peru's fisheries, demonstrates how particular constellations of nature and capital gave rise to and depended on specific epistemologies for identifying new natures for commodification or establishing ways to extract greater value from already-commodified ocean natures. Taken together, the historical components of our research demonstrate how state officials and industrialists organized ocean natures at different points in Peruvian fisheries history to produce value and how these organizations led to crises in fish, labor, and accumulation, which called for new systems of organization that required new encroachments and appropriations in attempts to ensure the profitability of industrial fisheries.

The Chapters in Brief

In this introduction, we have outlined a critical approach for uncovering the dialectical interplay among nature, capital, and politics in Peruvian fisheries and presented key themes for organizing the book, such as the centrality of enclosure for enabling new constellations of fish, space, and class. While these themes run throughout the book, each of the chapters approaches them from a different perspective in order to explore and emphasize particular aspects of these combinations or to trace the history of their changes.

No consideration of Peruvian fisheries is possible without first understanding how the development of the fishmeal industry in the 1950s and 1960s radically transformed the country's marine life-worlds. In Chapter 1, we draw on a range of archival data to show how the industrialized and globalized production of fishmeal led to significant reorganizations of Peru's marine ecologies and the impacts that such reorganizations have had on artisanal fishers. The initial fishmeal boom of the 1950s and 1960s occurred because the industry identified uncommodified natures in the form of massive Peruvian anchoveta schools that were easily accessible and could be exploited with little initial investment in new technology. Changes in the state jurisdiction of ocean territories and pro-industry labor policies also aided in securing these natures. While this particular configuration of nature, capital, and politics generated considerable profits for over a decade, overfishing and declining stocks led to crisis in the early 1970s, precipitating a reconfiguration of the industry that involved partial nationalization, layoffs, and attempts to increase the efficiency of the production process to squeeze greater value out of diminished stocks. This is a process that has shaped subsequent decades as the industry moved from one crisis to another, each of which was followed by reorganizations that increasingly monopolized the fishmeal industry, shed greater numbers of jobs, and relied on the state to capture a growing portion of Peru's fish for industrial production. Smaller fishmeal boats and artisanal fishers bore the brunt of these reorganizations as greater numbers of those left unemployed by the industry moved to food fish production at the same time that smaller boats were shut out of the country's most lucrative fisheries. In this chapter, we argue that contemporary ecological crises in Peru's fisheries are not the result of a lack of proper management, as proponents of a "tragedy of the commons" approach would have it. Rather, the state of Peru's fisheries is the result of previous management schemes and forms of enclosure intended to organize ocean natures in a way that made the production of surplus value possible for the fishmeal industry. A consideration of this dynamic is important for analyzing the ways in which capitalism, power, and knowledge combine to concentrate wealth and harm in different spaces.

In Chapter 2, we explore the importance of discursive dispossession for advancing and justifying material dispossessions through an examination of the history of elite discourses of alterity that have been attributed to Lima's coastal populations for centuries. Through a history of fishing and urban development in Chorrillos from the colonial era to the present, we show how fishers have endured a *longue durée* of racial, ethnic, and class Othering. During the colonial era, administrators, priests, and political elites identified the city's fishers and the areas where they lived as existing on the margins of urban civilization and Christianity and in need of intervention. While Indigenous fishers initially had their rights to local fishing territories protected, following the Bourbon Reforms—which curtailed local autonomy and sought to impose greater Spanish control of the colonies—local fishing rights became invisible within colonial and later republican law. Contemporary elite discourses of modernization that frame artisanal fishers as "traditional" producers who are inefficient and work outside the market economy obscure these fishers' long histories of engagement with different phases of colonial and liberal governance as well as their equally long history of participation in local, regional, and national markets. We argue that the erasure of these histories represents a significant attempt to not only obscure the irregularity and ad hoc nature of governing artisanal fisheries—which has been carried out by a host of state and non-state actors with often-conflicting priorities—but also justify contemporary encroachments as matters of course or necessary aspects of progress.

In the following chapters, we explore these dynamics from an ethnographic perspective, showing how the day-to-day work of fishers relies upon and in turn produces economic practices and politics that link human and nonhuman natures in specific ways and how neoliberalized governance threatens fishers' ability to maintain these links.

In Chapter 3, we situate Chorrillos within regional dynamics of coastal development. In comparison to two other artisanal fishing ports in Lima Province, Ancón and Pucusana, fishers in Chorrillos have fared poorly in recent decades, landing fewer fish and accumulating less capital than their counterparts. Through an analysis of the development of Lima's fisheries, we show that socioeconomic disparities among Lima's ports are the products of their different histories of engagement with the industrialization of Peruvian fisheries and coastal urbanization. This uneven development has had a profound impact on the resources available to fishers to assert their autonomy and defend their access to particular places. Yet, as we demonstrate through several recent instances of local place-based activism and green marketing schemes, government officials, entrepreneurs, and fishers regularly make comparisons between ports in Lima Province, attributing geographical disparities to fishers' willingness or apparent unwillingness to take initiative and improve their situations. In doing so, we argue that artisanal fishers and officials acknowledge coastal inequalities while contributing to their production by attributing these inequalities to differences in physical geography and individual comportment. This appraisal of coastal geographies subtly reinforces the notion that extending and expanding markets will solve ecological issues, and those who are not responsible will eventually go out of business and will be forced to move on to other kinds of work.

In Chapter 4, we expand our analysis of neoliberalized discourses of responsibility by exploring their impacts on the daily functioning of the wharf in Chorrillos. Through a series of ethnographic encounters between government officials and artisanal fishers—a new census of artisanal fishers, a government review of the local fishers' association, and the implementation of new licensing requirements—we show how contemporary governance projects reduce complex ecological and social relationships to a narrow range of individualized economic practices that can be made visible to state regulators. While dictums of individual responsibility have not undercut the relationships that make up a multispecies commons in Chorrillos, we argue that they have challenged them and have contributed to tensions among fishers and fish vendors about the future of the wharf and their places in it. In the second half of this chapter, we explore this dynamic by tracing discussions within the fishers' association and among fishers and vendors about what was wrong with the dock and who was responsible for it. The growing importance of the tourism economy and government pressure to renovate the wharf have led to ongoing discussions about which parts of the dock are failing and which need to be refurbished. In these discussions, fishers have identified the fish market and food kiosks as problem areas that should be replaced with private restaurants, thus laying the ideological groundwork for the potential displacement of vendors. Similarly, the government's restructuring of the old fishing union into a local association has exacerbated divisions among fishers, tourist boat operators, and individuals who had run afoul of the union, creating new challenges to the fishers' association's right to administer the wharf. These instances reveal the importance of seemingly mundane negotiations about work, responsibility, and the future for understanding how enclosure is contested, stalled, or slowly advanced.

In Chapter 5, we provide a more in-depth view of discussions among fishers and vendors about the future of the dock and their places in it as well as the future of fishing as a way of life. This chapter highlights the voices of young artisanal fishers who have chosen to pursue fishing because it affords them greater dignity than work in the city, of older artisanal fishers who feel the state has abandoned them and they have lost all hope of progress, and of women fish vendors who, despite economic hardships, prefer to work on the dock where they have autonomy over their daily routine. We present and analyze discussions among fishers and vendors about fishing, the state of the wharf in Chorrillos, and the future. One of the themes that emerges from these discussions is dignity and fishers' and vendors' beliefs that working on the dock has afforded them greater dignity than wage work in construction or domestic service in Lima's economy. However, many also felt that this dignity has been undermined by the increasingly precarious ecological and economic status of the local fishery. For example, fishers complained that they were fighting with hungry lobos and greedy boliches for fish and pointed to this competition as evidence that the state no longer afforded artisanal fishers the necessary protections that they needed to survive. Such feelings of abandonment led fishers and vendors to conclude that they could rely only upon themselves and their individual hard work to get ahead.

Such commentaries represent important avenues for thinking about how fishers and vendors experienced their situations and came to understand their political subjectivities. Fishers' and vendors' resentment about structural inequalities and the importance of dignity existed in tension with their beliefs that some individuals had fared better than others because they made smarter financial decisions or worked harder to get ahead. The tension between these attributions of structure and agency suggests how important struggles over accounting for harm and dispossession unfold in the interstices of everyday life and how depoliticized understandings of individual responsibility wend their way into daily considerations of inequality and its causes.

In the book's conclusion, we explore the significance of the experiences of artisanal fishers for thinking about and making sense of nature, class, and politics during contemporary climate change. Prominent frameworks for understanding global warming highlight human activity as a force of geological change while simultaneously reinforcing a distinction between an a-historical human species and an external physical nature. In contrast, our analysis of the lives of artisanal fishers demonstrates the intertwining of nature, class, and politics. The critical implication of this is that ecological crises are also and always socioeconomic crises, and any just means of dealing with global warming must, in addition to addressing climatological changes, highlight the ways in which people of different classes assume the unequal burdens of environmental destruction.

A Note on Names and Measurements

Throughout the book, we have given our research participants pseudonyms to protect their anonymity and also because we were less concerned with their individual opinions and more with how their comments reflected their positions as fishers, vendors, officials, or entrepreneurs. We have used the real names of public figures, such as the presidents of Peru or the mayors of Lima. We have followed Peruvian regulatory practice by referring to maritime distance in nautical miles and land-based distances, weights, and volumes using the metric system.

CHAPTER 1

Ocean Natures

D uring our first trip to Lima, we scheduled a meeting at one of the city's universities with a fisheries expert who conducted research on fish production and served as a regular consultant to government agencies and fishing companies. After a long taxi ride through congested traffic, we arrived at the campus and made our way to the correct building, where a secretary showed us to a conference room. There was a long table with a green felt top and wood paneling on the walls which displayed fading portraits of former program heads, many of whom were involved in the development of agricultural and fisheries policy in Peru. We sat in the room by ourselves, talking about what we had learned so far and what we wanted to do in the coming days. Eventually, our interviewee showed up, apologized for making us wait, and then sat across the table from us. He slowly folded his hands and asked what aspects of Peruvian fisheries interested us. We replied that we wanted to know about the ecological impacts that industrial overfishing was having on local waters and fish species. We also added that we were interested in the effect that industrial fishing was having on artisanal fishers. He responded to this with a long and vociferous diatribe about the environmentally sound nature of the Peruvian fishmeal industry. He told us that industrial boats were not able to overfish because fisheries law required them to have satellite tracking devices on each boat so that state officials could ensure they did not stray into protected waters. He also told us that each boat had a closely monitored quota of fish that it could land during each season. In contrast, he argued that artisanal fishers used horse-drawn nets and other arcane methods to pull however many fish they could out of coastal waters, destroying local ecosystems in the process. The answer to this, he asserted, was the imposition of greater restrictions on artisanal fishing to ensure the sustainability of Peru's fish stocks, foremost among them anchoveta.

Industry consultants and government officials regularly expressed this opinion during our research, both in interviews with us and in public discussions about the future of Peru's fisheries. This was especially true in debates about how to sustain industrial-level captures of anchoveta, which are processed into fishmeal, Peru's most important non-mineral export. Economists and fisheries biologists concerned with the long-term sustainability of Peru's anchoveta fishery have argued that the current state of the country's fish stocks is due to poor management and a history of open access. Following orthodox economic thought, they have stressed that fisheries are distinct from other natural resources in that fish are not owned by anyone—they are a common resource. The problem with this is that in an open-access or regulated open-access fishery, as new boats enter the fishery, the value of rent dissipates, forcing individual boats to land more fish to generate a profit, which results in a downward spiral in which an overly large fleet is chasing too few fish. The solution, many fisheries policy experts claim, is to design more effective management protocols with clearer rules, better accountability for both fishers and government regulators, and fine-tuned incentives to ensure that "stakeholders" behave in ways that ensure a healthy fishery.[1]

We argue that by framing fisheries declines as prototypical examples of a "tragedy of the commons," these explanations obscure the central role that politics have played in unequally distributing access and benefits among different sectors of Peruvian fishers. The biologist Garrett Hardin (1968) popularized the notion of the "tragedy of the commons" in a *Science* article. He argued that unregulated and naturally finite resources are doomed to overexploitation as the human population continues to grow because society is comprised of individuals pursuing their own best individual interests without concern for the common good. Hardin (1968, 1246) argued that the "belief that everyone born has an equal right to the commons is to lock the world into a tragic course of action." In the place of common access to resources, he advocated for enclosures and private property rights based on "mutually agreed upon" forms of "mutual coercion," arguing that "injustice is preferable to total ruin" (Hardin 1968, 1247–48). This approach has become accepted wisdom in neoliberal economics and natural resource management and has often been deployed as an argument for the necessity of individualized private property. In the case of fisheries, this has taken the form of privatizing ocean natures and fish stocks through the appropriation of IVQs, which have created a share that can be bought or sold to a small number of boats (Crean and Symes 1995; Longo et al. 2015; Mansfield 2004; McCormack 2017). In most cases where individual vessel quotas have been instituted, a large portion of once-active fishing boats have been forced out of the trade.[2]

In his sweeping ecological history of the Pacific world, Gregory T. Cushman (2013, 337) argues that the collapse of Peru's anchoveta fishery in the early 1970s cannot be explained as a "tragedy of the commons" given that it "was among the most carefully supervised and rigorously regulated the world had ever seen." During the late 1960s, "environmental scientists attained unprecedented authority over Peru's marine fisheries" (Cushman 2013, 328). It was an "overinflated faith" in technocrats' abilities to maximize the fishery's sustainable yields through science and regulation that contributed to anchoveta's crash (Cushman 2013, 328). The anchoveta fishery was (and continues to be) rooted in an unsustainable mode of global production whereby fish were extracted from a marine environment prone to dramatic changes and exported as livestock meal to industrialized countries so that consumers in those countries could eat ever-growing quantities of chicken and pork (Cushman 2013). While government officials and entrepreneurs presented Peru's "Blue Revolution" (Bailey 1985) as a vehicle for transforming the lives of its citizens through national development, Cushman asserts that it contributed little to alleviating hunger or poverty in the country. Rather, it represented a massive transfer of Peru's marine resources to consumers in wealthy countries, leaving rates of malnutrition in Peru largely unchanged.

Similarly, Peru's anchoveta fishery has been made possible by, and continues to rely upon, ongoing dispossessions through which an increasingly monopolized fishmeal industry has gained control of a significant portion of anchoveta stocks by pushing smaller producers out of the fishery. In the first portion of this chapter, we conduct a historical analysis of the material and political development of Peru's anchoveta fishmeal industry in order to demonstrate how state- and industry-backed regulatory regimes contributed to repeated crises in anchoveta production rather than ensuring the sustainability of stocks.

State regulatory regimes relied upon the production of a simplified, official vision of the ocean and its nature that enabled the accumulation of rent from the mass capture of a single species, the anchoveta. Moreover, state regulations have followed broader trends in global fisheries management by reducing fishing to a set of economic relationships (Bresnihan 2016; Peterson 2014). Such an approach has occluded the role that pro-industry state policy and fishmeal processing have played in the creation of existing limits to the ocean's productivity while also marginalizing alternative approaches to fisheries management. The result, we argue, has been that industrial regulatory regimes have been unable to account for fluctuations in fish stocks and environmental oscillations that characterize the eastern Pacific's ocean natures. This has produced a series of boom-bust cycles and regular crises in the fishmeal industry. State officials and industry owners have sought to move past these crises through repeated enclosures and dispossessions, which have excluded small-scale and artisanal fishers from the country's most lucrative fishery and concentrated the harms of industry reorganizations in impoverished artisanal fishing communities.

In the second half of this chapter, we examine the most recent instance of enclosure and dispossession when industry leaders successfully rebuked the Ollanta Humala Tasso (2011–16) government's expansion of the anchoveta fishery to allow small-scale and artisanal boats to capture the fish for human consumption. The heads of the largest fishmeal companies in Peru and their public spokespeople argued for greater enclosure of the anchoveta fishery as absolutely necessary for conserving the fish's populations, asserting that the privatization of anchoveta stocks was the only way to ensure that industrial extraction of the species could continue. They based this in part on the portrayal of artisanal fishers as producers who, existing outside the modern capitalist system, were on the margins of ecologically necessary government regulation and who sought to capture as much fish as they could for the purpose of immediate economic gain. Such discourses obscure the reality that artisanal fishers play a role in more-than-human relationships that maintain nearshore fisheries and also fish for a variety of economic, social, and cultural reasons, as we demonstrate in Chapters 4 and 5. Such exclusions reveal the degree to which class politics have shaped ocean natures and access to them and, in turn, how the limitations of such natures have reinforced inequalities in politics and capital accumulation. They also highlight why industry-backed regulatory regimes have not resulted in a more sustainable industrial fishery but only led to more enclosures and dispossessions.

Anchoveta

Mature anchoveta are usually no more than a few inches long, but what these fish lack in size, they make up for in sheer biomass. Great schools of the fish concentrate along Peru's coast, where upwelling of cold water from the Humboldt Current provides the ideal conditions for the fish. These are not the fish that one commonly finds in grocery stores, packed in salt or oil and tinned. Peruvian anchoveta are worth far more as fishmeal, which is used throughout the world in farmed fish and livestock feeds. During the second half of twentieth century, anchoveta made Peru the largest exporter of fish in the world and contributed to the dramatic reorganization of the country's ocean nature and coastal labor.

The impetus for Peru's fishmeal industry came from the country's bird guano producers. During the nineteenth century, Peru experienced a boom in the mining of bird guano deposits, which were exported to industrializing countries (Gootenberg 1993). At the turn of the twentieth century, Peruvian officials concerned with the conservation of the country's guano birds created the Compañía Administradora del Guano (CAG, Guano Administration Company) to oversee their protection and ensure the sustainability of the industry, which came to rely on deposits from living birds, whose primary source of food was anchoveta and other small pelagic fish. Following a crisis in guano production at the end of the 1930s, Cushman (2013, 290) notes that "CAG technocrats gave birth to the original plan to replace Peru's guano birds with a fishmeal industry," arguing that the country could increase production "from the sea by directly exploiting a lower level of the Humboldt Current food chain." To promote this venture, the government of Manuel Prado Ugarteche (1939–45) gave CAG the exclusive right to fish anchoveta and a loan to build a fishmeal plant. However, the "wartime interruption of regular shipping, rapid inflation, and problems arising from capital" meant that the plan never materialized and CAG "never produced a gram of fishmeal" (Cushman 2013, 291).

It was private entrepreneurs who quickly came to dominate the industry and eventually wrest control of Peruvian anchoveta from guano producers. During World War II, Peru experienced a boom in bonito production, supplying the tuna relative to the American market in quantities that had not yet been seen in the Peruvian fishery. The boom ended shortly after the war when the American tuna fishery rebounded and the U.S. government prohibited the labeling of canned bonito as tuna. As bonito exports declined in the late 1940s, some

Figure 3 Unloading bonito on the dock in Ancón. Photo by Maximilian Viatori.

producers used "bonito scraps to produce a low-protein fishmeal" (Roemer 1970, 82). When the plants did not get enough bonito, they looked for other fish to make up their extra capacity, turning to anchoveta (Roemer 1970). This development marked a dramatic shift in Peru's fisheries, which rapidly switched from catching food for human consumption to capturing anchoveta for fishmeal. It was not long before the country was exporting anchoveta meal in great quantities.

Several factors contributed to the competitive advantage of Peru's fishmeal sector in global markets.[3] First, the country had a surplus of cheap coastal labor as shortages of arable land in the highlands drove growing numbers of peasants to coastal cities in search of work. To keep labor costs low, the Sociedad Nacional de Pesquería (SNP, National Fisheries Society), an organization founded in 1950 to represent the rapidly expanding industrial sector, lobbied the government to exclude fishers from existing labor protections by classifying them not as wage or piece workers but as "task workers," a move that enabled boat owners to avoid paying social security (Caravedo Molinari 1977, 113). Second,

Peru's southern and central coast provided these boat owners with easy access to anchoveta populations. In this region, the Humboldt Current tracks right along the continental shelf, keeping anchoveta schools remarkably close to shore. This feature of Peru's geography meant that fishers could target anchoveta with existing nearshore boat technologies. Third, successive Peruvian governments adopted pro-export policies that benefited the fishmeal sector at the expense of guano producers and domestic agriculture (Cushman 2013, 290–99). Furthermore, Peruvian governments took part in a push to extend state maritime sovereignty in the eastern Pacific. In 1952, delegates from Chile, Ecuador, and Peru drafted what came to be known as the Santiago Declaration, which asserted their countries' rights to "possess exclusive sovereignty and jurisdiction over the sea along the coasts of their respective countries to a minimum distance of 200 nautical miles from these coasts" in order to protect maritime resources that could be quickly depleted by foreign fleets for the future development of national industries.[4]

In 1950, Peru's fishmeal exports totaled 167 million Peruvian soles. By 1964, that number had risen to over 1.2 billion soles as Peru became the largest exporter of fish in the world. Booming fishmeal exports provided the Peruvian state with significant foreign revenue, contributing to a positive trade balance that allowed the government to pay for expanding imports. However, by the mid-1960s, international demand failed to keep pace with the growing supply of fishmeal, and prices declined, leaving many fishing and processing operations heavily indebted and some bankrupt. Anchoveta stocks also showed signs of overfishing. The newly created IMARPE partnered with a special Food and Agriculture Organization of the United Nations (FAO) mission in 1965 to analyze anchoveta stocks and recommended the country's first closed season, which the government implemented the same year to protect stocks by limiting the number of days that they could be fished.

Throughout the remainder of the 1960s, biologists from IMARPE received expert help from foreign fisheries biologists to refine "methods for estimating the maximum sustainable yield each season" (Cushman 2013, 324). For many in the fishmeal industry, this was a worrying development as it signaled the unwelcome possibility of state interference in industry matters. However, industry leaders accepted the closures in part because of the work that IMARPE officials did to convince them that it was necessary for the long-term health of the fishery and in part out of fear that if they did not, then the government would threaten to nationalize the industry in order to protect it (Smetherman and Smetherman 1973, 345). Despite having some of the most "rigorous technical procedures for managing a marine fishery," Peru was not able to avert a collapse in anchoveta stocks, because while IMARPE limited the number of days that anchoveta could be pursued, the fleet was so large and efficient it could still easily overfish existing populations (Cushman 2013, 324). As the situation continued to worsen, both ecologically and economically, state officials did indeed exert greater oversight of fishmeal production, albeit ultimately in favor of the industry.

Fishing for the State

In 1968, members of the Peruvian military led by General Juan Velasco Alvarado overthrew the government of President Fernando Belaúnde Terry (1963–68) in a bloodless coup. As Liisa North (1983, 246) puts it, historically, the military had "substituted for the party the oligarchy was incapable of generating." However, Velasco's military government broke from this tradition. Velasco was a member of the provincial, popular classes and a number of the officers in his government came from humble origins (McClintock 1983, 280). This group of "progressive" officers sought to transform Peru by ending its dependence on the United States, making foreign investors more responsive to domestic economic needs, and developing a "third path to development that was neither 'capitalist nor communist' through such innovative measures as worker-managed enterprises" (McClintock 1983, 280; McClintock and Lowenthal 1983, xi; Aguirre and Drinot 2017).

Velasco set out to more closely regulate anchoveta stocks in order to extract greater rent for the state, which he planned to redistribute to the food fishery to promote domestic production and consumption. Despite possessing one of the most abundant fisheries in the world, throughout the mid-twentieth century, Peru imported table fish along with a growing array of costly foodstuffs. Between 1969 and 1971, the Velasco government passed a series of laws that restructured the fisheries industry.[5] These laws reinforced the state's legal jurisdiction over and ownership of all resources in the Pacific Ocean from shore to two hundred nautical miles, created the country's first stand-alone Ministerio de Pesquería (Ministry of Fisheries, separating it from agriculture), and established publicly held companies to oversee fishmeal production and promote domestic fish consumption.[6] These efforts achieved long-term success in encouraging

Peruvians to eat more fish, contributing to a doubling in average fish consumption in the decades that followed (Cushman 2013, 326). However, state attempts to restructure the industry to diversify ownership and increase worker benefits were limited and short term in their success. In his analysis of Peru's fishing industry during the 1970s, Baltazar Caravedo Molinari (1977, 118) argues that the government's policies actually helped to speed up the demise of small and mid-sized producers and helped to consolidate the fishmeal industry into a few large producers. As with so many of the military government's economic policies (McClintock 1983), reforms in the fishing industry benefited those who were already in a strong economic and political position. This was a process that only intensified with the ecological and economic crises of the 1970s.

Anchoveta catches continued to decline, and a significant El Niño in 1972–73, combined with overfishing, led to disappearing stocks. In 1973, the government instituted a moratorium on anchoveta fishing for most of the country. When the fishmeal industry looked to be on the verge of collapse, the Velasco government nationalized the four largest companies to create the Empresa Nacional Pesquera Pesca Perú SA (National Fishery Company Pesca Perú, or as it came to be known, Pesca Perú), which possessed the exclusive right to fish and process anchoveta in Peruvian waters. Caravedo Molinari (1977, 118) argues that nationalization did not conflict with the interests of large industry holders because it occurred at a moment of total crisis and provided industry owners with an opportunity to "restructure their capital." Government officials furthered this process by halving the number of registered boats and laying off roughly the same percentage of the industry's workers in an attempt to make the industry more efficient.[7]

Widescale unemployment presented the government with a significant problem. Many fishers and workers in the fishmeal plants had migrated to places such as Chimbote to find work in the fishing industry; therefore, they could not be easily relocated nor could they find opportunities for work in other sectors due to a lack of opportunities (Paulik 1981). The government attempted to mitigate this issue by increasing participation and profit sharing in Pesca Perú for those fishers and workers still employed in fishmeal production and by encouraging those who had been laid off to shift into the food fish sector. This led to a flood of surplus labor into the artisanal fishing sector, almost doubling its numbers. While the artisanal sector was tasked with absorbing the surplus labor from the industry, the government was not able to provide the necessary infrastructure, distribution networks, or credit to make food fishing a viable means of providing stable employment to a growing number of fishers. Government officials intended to promote artisanal table fish production by diverting profits from the fishmeal industry to provide food fishers with credit. However, the funding necessary to promote such schemes withered with the crisis in anchoveta production. Furthermore, artisanal fishing suffered in many ports where fishmeal processing took place. The waters around Chimbote, Callao, Supe, and other anchoveta ports became "eutrophied dead zones," forcing artisanal fishers to "travel far away to locate fish," conditions which ultimately forced many to "abandon the trade entirely" (Cushman 2013, 313; Wintersteen 2014).

Nonetheless, preventing the anchoveta industry from collapse and ensuring its future profitability remained the focus of government fisheries policy and regulation. The state largely achieved this by absorbing the industry's debts and then returning assets to private hands once the crisis abated. While industry representatives were (and remain) generally averse to state interference, nationalization in the early 1970s provided fishmeal entrepreneurs with an opportunity to avoid bankruptcy. Moreover, nationalization was short lived. In 1975, military officers in southern Peru led by General Francisco Morales Bermúdez Cerruti (who was, at the time, also the prime minister and the minister of war) overthrew Velasco. As president, Morales Bermúdez (1975–80) instituted orthodox economic policies to address the worsening economy. In 1976, workers in the fishmeal industry carried out a series of strikes. In response, Morales Bermúdez declared a state of emergency and initiated massive lay-offs to break labor organizing and eliminate worker participation and compensation schemes in Pesca Perú. In an even more significant move, the government reprivatized the anchoveta fleet and began selling off its food fish operations and processing plants. This initial wave of privatization, a process that culminated in the 1990s, enabled a significant reorganization of capital in Peruvian fishing.

The Nation's Industry

During the 1980s, anchoveta stocks failed to rebound to their pre-1973 levels, and the fishing industry suffered declining profits and increased indebtedness as the global economy entered a recession. To address this situation, government officials encouraged private boats to exploit previously overlooked species, particularly *sardina* (*Sardinops sagax*, Pacific sardine), catches of which increased between 1976 and 1980. However, "redirecting effort did not resolve overfishing, but simply extended it to new fisheries"—in 1980, IMARPE had to close sardine fishing for one year to protect the stocks, which were already being overfished (Aguilar Ibarra et al. 2000, 512). Overfishing combined with a strong El Niño in 1982–83 led to further stock declines, with closures in the anchoveta fishery in 1983 and 1984. Anchoveta and sardine seasons were closed again through parts of 1987 and 1988. In 1967, Peru's fishmeal exports exceeded two million metric tons. By 1987, that number had dropped by more than half as the fishing industry struggled to generate value as a result of rising costs, weakened markets, and diminished fish stocks, making the sector an unattractive option for capital investment. In order to deal with this ongoing crisis, the state largely absorbed the fishmeal industry's debts while shifting the burden of employing fishers to the artisanal sector. This is a process that intensified with the advent of neoliberalized reforms in Peru's fisheries in the decade that followed.

Upon entering office in 1990, President Alberto Fujimori (1990–2000) promised to restart the country's faltering economy through increased foreign investment and government support for the poor. In 1992, Fujimori instituted a self-coup, dissolving Congress and declaring a state of emergency so that he could issue laws by decree and restructure Peru's economy and politics, including a revamping of the fishing sector. Fujimori pushed for the complete privatization of the fishmeal industry by dissolving Pesca Perú's control of a significant share of the country's fishmeal processing capacity as a means of encouraging new investment. The process had begun before Fujimori's government with the 1976 reprivatization of the anchoveta fleet and the government's sale of a considerable portion of Pesca Perú's assets during Belaúnde's (1980–85) second term. In the late 1980s, Congress began to lay the legal groundwork for the regionalization of government industry, decentralizing control of property and management. However, Fujimori's privatization of the fishmeal industry represented part of a major shift in the state's control of marine resources and a new set of regulations regarding who could fish what and where. This shift enabled a greater concentration of wealth and influence in the fishing industry while increasingly squeezing out smaller producers.

When government officials announced the privatization of Pesca Perú in 1992, the first thing they did was cut half of the approximately 3,500 jobs in the company in an attempt to make it more attractive to interested buyers. Between 1993 and 1998, Pesca Perú also sold off its twenty remaining plants to investors, relinquishing the government's control of fishmeal processing. Minister of Fisheries Jaime Sobero Taira justified the privatization by arguing that Pesca Perú was inefficient and should have been producing "more fishmeal for a lower price and using less primary material" and by asserting that the participation of the private sector in Peru's fisheries was "indispensable and necessary" to promote "efficiency and productivity" (El Comercio 1992a, 1992b). In its 1992 analysis of Peru's fishing industry, FAO (1992, x) noted that the privatization of Pesca Perú raised serious questions given "its size, economic importance, production volume, and the key role that it plays in the national economy and development strategies." The report cautioned that a partial or full privatization would mean that the government would "also be transferring the associated exclusive right to join a highly profitable activity which exploits a common property national renewable natural resource" and thus foregoing a significant source of potential revenue that could be used for the public good.

That was exactly what happened. In a 2002 report for the Comisión Investigadora de Delitos Económicos y Financieros 1990–2001 (Investigative Commission for Economic and Financial Crimes), a congressional subcommittee argued that the privatization of Pesca Perú had cost the government dearly. In their forty-seven-page report, five Congress members asserted that the government had recouped just 15 percent of the total estimated value of Pesca Perú and, among other irregularities, suggested that the state may have hidden the significant cost of processing the privatization of Pesca Perú in its finance reports (Congreso de la República del Perú 2002, 45–6). In short, the privatization of Pesca Perú represented a significant transfer of capital and market share from the state to private fishing companies in order to make the latter more profitable.

This privatization was one component of the Fujimori government's reorganization of the fishing sector. In 1992, the administration also issued a new fisheries law and several executive decrees that redefined the state's role in regulating fishing and introduced a new schema for classifying fishing activities. In late December 1992, Fujimori's "emergency government" passed the new Ley General de Pesca (General Fisheries Law), Decree no. 25977, with the only approval coming from the president's ministers since Congress had been dissolved. The law declared that the "hydro-biological resources contained in the jurisdictional waters of Peru are the patrimony of the nation" and that it was the responsibility of the state to "regulate the integrated management and rational exploitation of these resources" (Article 2).

While subtle, the notion that Peru's marine resources belonged to the nation was an important one with considerable legal ramifications. The fisheries journal

Pesca published an extended analysis of the law by lawyer Edwin Masseur Stoll. In his commentary, Masseur Stoll (1993, 4) remarked, "It is without doubt that the current declaration is more appropriate than those contained in previous provisions and represents a step forward in respect to the position that predominated in the country for more than twenty years, according to which they [marine resources] were the patrimony of the state. As a result, state monopolies and the granting of 'concessions' for the development of fishing activity disappear." This was a clear reversal of the legal basis for Velasco's nationalization of the fishing industry, namely that the state owned Peru's marine resources and therefore had the right to control and exploit them for its and its citizens' benefit.

What is intriguing about the language that Fujimori's administration employed in the law is the rhetorical separation of the nation from the state so that "national" could stand in for the interests of private businesses when opposed to state control. Article 3 of the bill stipulates that the state's responsibility was to promote "private investment by adopting measures that contribute to the encouragement of the study, conservation, extraction, cultivation, processing and commercialization of fishing resources." As Masseur Stoll (1993, 4) commented, the law favored "private initiative," which "acting freely in a business-like manner and subject only to the laws designed to preserve the biomass and its diversity, will guarantee the sustainable development of fishing." This is a shift that paralleled the neoliberalization of fisheries policy in other parts of the world whereby the state assumed the role of creating the necessary conditions for the accumulation of capital and the development of the industry but increasingly promoted self-regulation as the best means for adapting to changing ecological and economic contexts (Bavington 2010). During the Fujimori years, this meant that the fishmeal industry was allowed to expand regardless of prior collapses in anchoveta production and their impacts on other fisheries.

The Fujimori government sought to ameliorate the negative impacts of this expansion with new protections for artisanal fishers. The General Fisheries Law mirrored Fujimori's broad project of facilitating private capital in combination with populist measures to encourage support among the country's poor by creating the first legislation to define artisanal fishers as a specific legal category while offering government support for the sector. Article 4 of the law stipulated that "the state will lend the necessary support for the development of artisanal fishing activity and the training and capacitation of artisanal fishers," defined in Article 20 as those individuals fishing with small boats or using predominantly manual labor in their catch techniques. Article 27 of the law also created the Fondo Nacional de Desarrollo Pesquero (FONDEPES, National Fund for Fisheries Development) to provide credit to artisanal fishers; FONDEPES announced in 1993 that it was funding the construction of two hundred new boats for artisanal fishers.[8] Furthermore, Fujimori's Supreme Decree no. 017-92-PE reserved the zone from zero to five nautical miles for artisanal fishing and prohibited the use of purse seine nets in this zone as a means of both protecting these important ecological zones and supporting food fishing.

These measures provided critical legal bases in the decades that followed for establishing and advocating for artisanal fishers' rights. However, they did not signal unconditional government support for artisanal fishers but rather emerged in concert with neoliberalized forms of governance that established these rights as conditions to be earned by responsible, individual entrepreneurs. If one examines the language of the General Fisheries Law carefully, the primary support it offers to artisanal fishers is in the form of training and capacitation, which in the ensuing years was focused largely on licensing to establish that artisanal fishers were responsible producers for emerging markets. While the five-nautical-mile limit offered crucial grounds for protecting artisanal fisheries from industrial depredation, the decree that created it and ensuing legislation provided little in the way of funding or resources for enforcing this limit. As such, the industry did not oppose the institution of the five-nautical-mile restriction at this point.

By 1994, anchoveta catches rebounded to their 1971 levels, and the fishmeal industry was again thriving. The FAO encouraged Fujimori to make cuts in Peru's fleet and institute more stringent catch limits, which the government largely ignored. Indeed, there was a surge of boats built during the 1990s with an influx of new capital. While the General Fisheries Law required that owners decommission old boats before new ones could be commissioned, in practice this rarely happened. Moreover, many new boats were commissioned to fish for food but not for anchoveta that would be converted into meal. Yet, the owners of both decommissioned boats and those authorized to fish only for food experienced little trouble in using such boats for the anchoveta fishery, leading to a doubling in the mid-1990s of the number of boats providing fish to the processing plants.

Additionally, the institution of the five-nautical-mile protection ignored the fact that artisanal fishers not only fished nearshore waters—many of which had become increasingly polluted in urban areas and zones around fishmeal processing plants—but also often ventured farther out to capture food fish. One of the staples of the central coast artisanal fisheries, bonito, is often caught at distances of forty nautical miles or more from shore. These practices remained invisible in state oceanic geographies, oriented as they were to industrial anchoveta production. Finally, the Fujimori government's definition of artisanal fishers was very broad in that it only specified that artisanal fishers relied primarily on manual forms of labor (as opposed, for example, to winch-operated nets) and did not use purse seine nets. It was not until after Fujimori left office that the government established a size limit for artisanal boats with Supreme Decree no. 012-2001-PE, which stipulated that they could not have a hold capacity greater than 32.6 cubic metric tons and could be no longer than fifteen meters in length. This included quite large boats that approached the size of boliches. Government support tended to privilege the latter.

005

Landings of anchoveta peaked in the mid-1990s and then dropped following the 1997–98 El Niño but largely stabilized in the ensuing decade and a half. In the face of continuing global demand and rising fishmeal prices, the industry sought to extract greater value from anchoveta catches through improved technological efficiencies, the consolidation of smaller companies into large conglomerates, and the shedding of jobs. The ongoing monopolization of the anchoveta catch by a smaller and technologically advanced industrial fleet accompanied growth in Peru's small-scale industrial fleet, given that older industrial boats had not been decommissioned during the Fujimori government. In particular, the fleet of wooden boliches expanded rapidly in the 1990s and early 2000s. In 1998, the Fujimori government passed Law 26920, which allowed boats over 32.6 cubic meters of hold capacity to harvest anchoveta for fishmeal. This move provided economic relief for the small-scale industrial sector but did so at the cost of significantly expanding the anchoveta fleet (Aranda 2009, 149). Furthermore, because boliches were not subject to the same regulations as the large-scale industrial boats, such as the requirement to carry satellite-tracking devices, they could easily fish within the five-nautical-mile zone undetected.

By 2000, Peru's fleet was estimated to be up to five times larger than needed to catch the average annual limit of anchoveta (Paredes and Gutierrez 2008). This dramatic over-capacitation presented a risk to the profitability of Peru's fishing industry and threatened to put even more fishers out of work. One means by which government bureaucrats, boat owners, and fishers dealt with this was to seek out new fisheries to meet the capacity of the small-scale industrial fleet and satisfy growing international demand for food fish. IMARPE conducted pilot programs on previously unexploited or underexploited species of fish. The greatest success of these efforts was the development of the *pota* (*Dosidicus gigas*, jumbo flying squid) fishery, the only fishery to have experienced significant growth in the first decades of the new millennium.

The government also protected the largest fishmeal companies' access to anchoveta stocks by more stringently regulating the fishery and the participation of smaller boats in it. During Alan García Pérez's (2006–11) second term as president, the government instituted a system of IVQs in 2008. Quotas were awarded to boats "based on the best years of landings since 2004" (Aranda 2009, 149), a system that provided legal reinforcement for the monopolization of the catch by the largest fishmeal companies. Eight companies dominated Peru's fishmeal sector, accounting for over 60 percent of the anchoveta landed each year.[9] Unsurprisingly, the legislation was backed by the SNP, the industry association that represents the interests of the "big eight" fishmeal companies. However, the Asociación Nacional de Armadores Pesqueros de la Ley 26920 (Association of Ship Owners of Law 26920), which represents the owners of small-scale industrial boats, vehemently opposed the quota system since it effectively excluded them from the legal fishery. The new system encouraged fishmeal producers to consolidate their quotas in a smaller number of vessels, thus improving efficiencies, and put greater effort into landing high-quality anchoveta for prime and super prime fishmeal in order to add value (Evans and Tveteras 2011, 17). In the years that followed the institution of the IVQ, the average grade of Peruvian meal increased along with the average price for anchoveta. However, this development encouraged small-scale and artisanal fishers to illegally harvest anchoveta for fishmeal within the five-nautical-mile limit and sell it to black-market refineries, potentially threatening the export value of prime Peruvian fishmeal (Evans and Tveteras 2011, 17). Furthermore, the IVQ system did not include any measures for mandatory or voluntary boat decommissions, effectively maintaining the capacity of Peru's small-scale fleet (Aranda 2009).

This is an issue that the Humala government addressed in 2012 when it issued Supreme Decree no. 005-2012-PRODUCE, referred to in Peruvian fisheries circles as 005. The decree aimed to protect Peru's anchoveta stocks, improve the quality of fishmeal exports, and encourage the employment of small-scale and artisanal fishers by developing a domestic market for anchoveta as a food fish. The decree changed the way that Peru's marine waters were divvied up among different categories of fishers and how those categories were demarcated. Under the new law, the boat limit for artisanal fishers was reduced to 10 cubic meters of capacity, the wooden boliches of the small-scale industrial fleet were between 10 and 32.5 cubic meters of hold capacity, and large-scale industrial boats were over 32.5 cubic meters. Artisanal fishers retained the exclusive right to fish the first five nautical miles from the coast for anchoveta but could only do so for direct human consumption. In turn, the boliches could fish no closer than five nautical miles for anchoveta, and only 10 percent of their catches were licensed for fishmeal—the rest had to go to canning. Finally, large industrial boats could fish no closer than ten nautical miles for anchoveta that would be processed into fishmeal. The most significant impact of the legislation was to regulate the boliches, many of which had been categorized as artisanal. These boliches were harvesting anchoveta for sale to mostly unlicensed processing plants, which not only impacted local artisanal fisheries but also the industry, which was concerned that low-grade fishmeal would damage its global reputation. In conjunction with this new regulation, the government announced it would conduct the first national census of artisanal fishers. The census represented an attempt to mollify industry leaders by showing that the state was acting to more closely monitor artisanal fishers and was not just placing new restrictions on the anchoveta industry.

Industry leaders fiercely resisted the decree. Some fish processing companies owned boliches and were able to skirt the IVQs on their larger boats by buying fish from boliches. The decree effectively closed this loophole. However, the amount of fishmeal produced in this manner was relatively small, so this alone does not explain the stiff resistance that the industry mounted against the new law. Rather, it appears to have emerged out of industry concern that the state was taking on too great a role in regulating anchoveta stocks. While the government required both boliches and artisanal boats to fish almost exclusively for human consumption, industry leaders saw the legislation as a threat to their official monopoly of anchoveta stocks at a time of diminished abundance. While stocks were mostly stable in the first decade of the new millennium, there were still dramatic oscillations in the decade that followed due to overfishing and fluctuating climatic conditions. In 2012, the government dramatically cut the overall quota for anchoveta by 68 percent during the summer fishing season because of concerns that warmer water near the coast and overfishing had led to a more than 40 percent reduction in stocks. The dramatic cut was meant to allow more anchoveta to spawn. The government increased the quota in 2013 but cut it again the following years as developing El Niño conditions negatively impacted anchoveta reproduction. The reduction in supply led to a spike in the price of prime fishmeal, which increased by 50 percent in 2014. If they maintained access to and control of anchoveta catches, large fishmeal companies would ensure their profitability given the increasing value of anchoveta meal in the global market. In a time of fluctuating stocks, it was the industry that wanted the power to define the boundaries of ocean production. Industry leaders felt that Humala's government directly threatened their ability to do so.

Humala campaigned as a center-left candidate promising to exert more control over Peru's extractive industries, particularly mining, for the good of the state and its poor citizens. While he quickly adopted an extractivist approach to economic growth upon entering office, his appointments for the minister of Produce were career technocrats—the first time in Peru's history that the post did not go to someone from the fishmeal industry. The first minister, José Urquizo Maggia, was a member of the Peruvian Congress. After serving for one year, Urquizo was asked to serve as minister of defense. In his place, Humala appointed Gladys Triveño Chan Jan in May 2012. Triveño was a lawyer who had worked in the finance sector but had no direct experience working in the fish industry. Piero Ghezzi Solís, an economist who took over from Triveño in 2014, argued at the outset of his appointment that the industry was not paying the government enough for the right to fish because the fees had remained the same for over a decade.

The fact that these appointees were outsiders was something upon which fishmeal industry representatives pounced, arguing that 005 was drafted by a minister who did not know the realities of the fishing industry and therefore had advocated for regulations that did not make sense. The SNP led this charge, using its considerable influence to encourage a campaign against 005 in the country's media sources. The capital city's newspapers ran numerous articles decrying the problems with the law and the woeful impact it would have on the country's fisheries. In an interview published in *Gestión*, Lima's business newspaper of note, the SNP's lawyer, Aurelio Lloret de Mola, argued that the minister was "misinforming" the president on the subject of fisheries policies (Gestión 2013). Industrial boats were not putting artisanal boats out of business, and the fishmeal industry was not depleting the ocean's biomass, he asserted.

The problem, Lloret de Mola claimed, was with the boliches that were illegally fishing the five-to-ten-nautical-mile zone for anchoveta that were then processed for poor quality meal. Supreme decree 005 "was legalizing this piracy," the lawyer argued (Gestión 2013). Similarly, an article in *El Comercio* reported that the SNP had hired a consultant to study the effect of 005 on the anchoveta fishery, and the study found that the decree had increased the trade in illegal fishmeal and reduced the direct human consumption of anchoveta (Ortiz 2014). The report's authors concluded that "none of the objectives that brought forth the regulation have been fulfilled" (Ortiz 2014).

These are points that Guillermo, a former Produce official and editor of a publication that tracks and offers commentary on Peru's fishing industry, laid out in greater detail in two interviews we conducted with him in 2012 and 2013. In both conversations, he made it clear that the government had made a mistake by appointing individuals to ministerial and vice-ministerial positions who did not have backgrounds in the fishing industry. Guillermo argued that "for the first time in history the president said no to the industry" with the drafting and implementation of 005. The decree was a political and not a business decision, Guillermo contended. However, that was not what he saw as the main problem with the regulation. The issue was that the personnel in Produce did not know how to implement it. "When you get a group of people together who are inexperienced in the topic [of fishing], this is what you get," Guillermo lamented. "How can you manage a sector you don't know? I am intelligent, I will learn, but the country does not have the luxury of having a minister that takes three, four months to learn, and with only three months of learning, you will not get people who have the experience of [those with] twenty to thirty years in the business. What we are experiencing is the result of this." Guillermo went on to assert that because the minister was not from the industry, the team that drafted and implemented 005 was assembled according to criteria of personal connection and trust, rather than expertise. "Where are you going to go with a team like this?" he quipped. "Nowhere."

In addition to these complaints, Guillermo also argued that the regulation was problematic because it separated the large-scale industrial fleet from the small-scale and artisanal fleets. He claimed that the government negotiated almost exclusively with the SNP over fisheries regulations because the small-scale and artisanal fleets were "atomized" among "eight hundred unions and associations." However, the reality was that one could not, Guillermo believed, draw a clear line between industrial and artisanal fishers. Small-scale boats fished anchoveta for processing plants, and artisanal fishers provided bonito and squid to the frozen fish industry. Despite this, there were "vast differences" in how the government treated and regulated each sector, which Guillermo felt were biased in favor of artisanal fishers. The solution, he believed, was to subject all boats and fishers to the same set of regulations, regardless of size or what they fished.

When we asked him if the 2012 national census of artisanal fishers was an effective step in this direction, he was quick to criticize it, noting that it had moved slowly and that the government had yet to make much of the data publicly available. Moreover, the census was only half of the equation. Guillermo insisted that in order to regulate artisanal fishers, the government needed to know not just how many artisanal fishers there were but also "how much biomass is available, how much there is [that is] likely to be extracted" by these fishers. Otherwise, Guillermo explained, the government could not establish if artisanal boats were overfishing. "The truth of the matter," he argued, was that artisanal fishers did not want this to happen; they fought being formally regulated because "people prefer to remain informal because they don't pay taxes." Guillermo noted that the industrial sector paid something to the government, something back to the nation for using its fish. In contrast, he said, "It seems unjust to me that among the thirty million inhabitants [of Peru], a small group [of artisanal fishers] enjoys the benefits of raw material from the seas, they profit from it, and they pay absolutely nothing to the owner of this resource, which is the constitutionally recognized nation. I'm telling you [they pay] absolutely nothing . . . the informal artisanal [sector] is compensating the nation absolutely nothing for any of the kilos of fish it extracts." Furthermore, he stressed that artisanal fishers were not "compensating the country for the environmental impact they cause."

The argument that small-scale and artisanal fishers should be subject to the same regulations as the industrial anchoveta fishery was something that we heard from government officials and industry advocates throughout our research. They asserted that small-scale and artisanal fishers were doing the most ecological damage to Peru's marine resources and that the only way to address this was to subject them to the same laws and regulations. However, this argument ignored two important realities. First, artisanal fisheries have been more or less sustainable for centuries. The areas where artisanal fisheries have suffered most have been in those ports and bays where industrial fish processing and fishing has impacted negatively nearshore fisheries through pollution and overfishing. Second, there is tremendous diversity among small-scale and arti-sanal fishers in Peru in regards to what they fish, when they fish it, and where they fish, as we discuss in the next chapter. This is one of the reasons why a truly national-level organization of artisanal fishers does not exist—the needs and realities of fisheries vary considerably from one area to the next. Similarly, the state lacks the resources to patrol and enforce every small-scale or artisanal fisher active in every fishery. State officials have chosen instead to institute a set of new enclosures based on licensing fishers and boat owners who have undergone training to demonstrate that they are "responsible" users of common resources, as we show in Chapter 4.

In contrast to Guillermo's comments, Raúl, one of the team of lawyers who drafted 005, told us that the law benefited everyone in Peruvian fisheries, from the fishmeal industry to artisanal fishers. Although it was aimed specifically at the anchoveta fishery, he asserted that it helped to protect the whole fish food chain because anchoveta were a primary food source for the fish that were caught for human consumption. In contrast to Guillermo, Raúl identified the ministry's lack of connections with the fishmeal industry as a plus. "It is important to note that the people who have entered the administration have not had links with any sector," he said. "The second thing is that they have come with experience as regulators." For Raúl, this meant that the team who was responsible for developing fisheries regulations did so from a more objective stance, considering what needed to happen to ensure a sustainable fishery and establishing a system of regulations and incentives that would accomplish this. Decree 005 required regional governments to provide the ministry with an updated registry of all boats, signaling a break with the old practice of turning a blind eye to unregistered or decommissioned boats. Raúl claimed that the regu-lation allowed the ministry to "know where they are, who they are, and the pres-sure they are putting on the resource." Raúl argued that "to have a regimen of quotas without a regimen of supervision is a hand wave and nothing more" and something to which 005 put an end, especially for small-scale industrial boats. Moreover, the fact that the small-scale fleet was required to switch from fishing anchoveta for fishmeal to human consumption in the five-to-ten-nautical-mile zone should have pacified the industry, which was concerned about low-grade meal from the boliches making it into the market.

That was not the case. The fishmeal industry fervently rejected the ten-nautical-mile limit for its large boats. José Antonio, an expert in sustainable fisheries research, told us that "the fight between the ministry and the Society

[SNP] has been strong, aggressive, [and] personal." In a 2012 interview we conducted with him, José Antonio remarked, "The industry has an interest in promoting the view that they do not like 005 . . . It is a forced view that says everything will be the same or worse. And I ask, 'Why?' Because, in the first place, it is an egotistical view from the industry, which has fought against 005 because of the ten-mile limit." The reason, he believed, was that the state was attempting to exert greater control over the sector, and as a result, the fishmeal industry was not "able to do what they feel like as they did before." In retaliation, the industry and its media allies generated public discourse surrounding 005 emphasizing that an inept state was attacking the industry. The problem with this, as José Antonio saw it, was that it obscured broader issues, such as the overall health of Peru's fish stocks or the impacts of climate change on the fishery, by reducing the discussion of the decree to a state versus industry polemic. José Antonio argued that this sidestepped the fact that regulation had improved in the last decade. "Before you took all that you could," he said, but now there was better biological baseline data to establish quotas and limits. The generation of such data was critical to making any fisheries regulations work. Furthermore, José Antonio claimed that the industry's vociferous public attack on 005 effectively stalled government efforts to implement new regulations.

Indeed, shortly after the issuing of 005, the industry pressured the government to temporarily change the five- and ten-nautical-mile limits in Peru's southern coast to three and seven nautical miles, respectively, because anchoveta schools in that region tended to stay closer to shore than in the central coast. In the organization's newsletter, SNP representatives argued that 005 was unconstitutional because it created an "exclusive zone" in which only small-scale and artisanal boats could fish, a measure that they asserted would hurt and ultimately "bankrupt" the fishmeal industry (SNP 2012). In November 2013, Peru's Supreme Court declared 005 unconstitutional, arguing that reserving the capture of anchoveta in the five-to-ten-nautical-mile zone for small-scale industrial boats was in direct violation of Article 9 of the General Law of Fisheries, which stipulates that any new regulations have to be based on clear scientific data and socioeconomic factors and that Produce had not provided a sufficient base of scientific data to support the adoption of the new regulation.

In response, Produce officials argued that the decree was meant to protect the sustainability of Peru's anchoveta biomass and overall marine biodiversity since the greatest fish species diversity exists within the first ten nautical miles from shore. Immediately following the Supreme Court ruling, Produce issued a second decree (DS 011-2013) with supporting scientific research that reasserted the ten-nautical-mile limit. The following year, Lima's Fourth Superior Civil Court ruled that the decree was unconstitutional. Produce appealed the ruling, and the SNP pushed for the Supreme Court to confirm the unconstitutionality of the decree. In the meantime, Produce issued yet another modified decree, attempting to stay ahead of the legal challenges to 011. Supreme Decree 001-2015 reasserted the limits to industrial anchoveta capture, reserving the first ten nautical miles from shore for artisanal and small-scale fishing for the species for direct human consumption, except in the southern portion of the country, where the limits were reduced to 3.5 and five nautical miles. In short, while the SNP sought amenable judges who would block Produce's anchoveta regulations in court, Produce continued to issue new decrees as a means of attempting to reign in the industry. This fight eventually came to a halt with the election of a new government in 2016, which favored the fishmeal industry.

The new president, Pedro Pablo Kuczynski Godard (2016–18), worked for the World Bank and the IMF, directed Peru's Central Reserve Bank, and held various ministerial positions in different Peruvian governments beginning in the late 1980s.[10] In contrast to the left-leaning Humala, whose administration tried to regulate fisheries in a way that provided rational legal access for all sectors, Kuczynski's government reinforced the supremacy of the fishmeal industry in regulating Peruvian fisheries. According to several former and current Produce employees with whom we spoke in 2017, under the Kuczynski government, Produce had "returned to normal," by which they meant that it was run by the fishmeal industry. Kuczynski appointed Bruno Giuffra Monteverde, an economist and corporate consultant, as the head of Produce. Upon taking office, Giuffra announced a campaign to simplify and restructure Produce's bureaucracy in order to remove unnecessary roadblocks for the development of Peruvian fisheries. He also declared that he would move to have DS 011 repealed, arguing that greater restrictions needed to be placed on small-scale industrial boats and that setting aside the five-to-ten-nautical-mile zone for them was a "farce" that had only contributed to a black market for fishmeal (Gestión 2017).

In November 2016, Produce issued a ministerial resolution (RM 433-2016-Produce) signaling the development of a new set of regulations for the capture of anchoveta for human consumption "with the objective of strengthening the framework of juridical and economic stability that encourages private investment in fisheries." In January 2017, the Supreme Court declared 011 to be unconstitutional, opening the door for a new set of anchoveta regulations. In place of

005 and 011, Giuffra's office proposed a reduced set of boundaries for fishing for anchoveta for direct human consumption, allowing all sectors to fish closer to shore while removing special protections for small-scale industrial boats. The new regulations stipulated that artisanal boats and small-scale industrial boats were allowed to fish for anchoveta for direct human consumption from three nautical miles and out, except in Tumbes, in the north, where they could not fish closer than five nautical miles for anchoveta. Large industrial boats were not allowed to fish closer than five nautical miles. In other words, throughout most of the country, artisanal and small-scale fishers only had exclusive rights to fish anchoveta from three to five nautical miles. The ministerial resolution that outlined the new regulations also included the caveat that Produce could, "with the recommendation of IMARPE," suspend artisanal and small-scale fisheries for anchoveta if necessary for the "conservation of the resource."

Conclusion

Anchoveta emerged in the mid-twentieth century as a driving force in Peru's export economy as a result of shifts in fisheries technology, policy, and markets, which made it possible for producers to identify the small fish as an uncommodified nature that could be exploited profitably. Employing discourses of national good, state officials enclosed the productive waters of the Humboldt Current—rich with anchoveta and other sea life—for the fishmeal industry, sidelining the interests of domestic agriculture, guano exporters, and food fishers. This first wave of commodification and appropriation produced a boom in anchoveta landings and fishmeal exports, driven by the fishing industry's access to free nature and cheap labor.

Since the late 1960s, crises in Peru's marine production arose because this initial system of organizing nature and labor no longer enabled the fishmeal industry to appropriate value from Peru's ocean natures, forcing government officials and industry leaders to find new ways of securing cheap nature and labor. In the late 1960s and 1970s, Peru's military governments sought to strengthen the state's legal ownership of the ocean as part of its efforts to extract greater rent from the fishmeal industry and redistribute it to the country's artisanal fishers in an effort to boost food fish production and reduce expensive food imports. These efforts occurred as anchoveta stocks neared collapse. Rather than redistribute fishmeal profits, the state momentarily took ownership of the industry, nationalizing its debt and laying off half of its workers, before returning a more efficient and increasingly monopolized fishmeal sector to private hands. Neoliberal restructuring in the 1990s deepened this process as the government gifted its remaining fishing assets to private industry and instituted regulations that supported the ongoing appropriation of fish value by an increasingly small number of companies. New regulations have further concentrated access to Peru's fish stocks in the hands of a few companies while industry representatives have presented vehement (and largely successful) opposition to protections for small-scale fishers in an effort to maintain the industry's unlimited access to cheap ocean natures.

These subsequent reorganizations of Peru's ocean natures led to equally dramatic recompositions of the country's fisheries and fleets. Prior to the anchoveta boom, Peru's fisheries were dominated by artisanal fishers pursuing table fish. The boom in fishmeal production reoriented the fishery and fishing policy to the production of meal, diverting resources and government attention away from the country's food fisheries. However, small-scale food fisheries did not disappear. The reverse occurred as successive reorganizations and downsizing in the fishmeal sector produced surplus labor, which the government directed to the artisanal sector in attempts to avoid employment crises. While the artisanal sector has become the largest portion of the fishery in terms of employment, state attempts to direct revenue and subsidies to artisanal fishers have come to little given the state's ongoing need to ensure the fishmeal industry's access to cheap nature. Moreover, given the prioritization of the fishmeal sector, artisanal fishers became the economically, politically, and socially marked category in discussions about Peruvian fisheries policy. State officials and industry representatives repeatedly have highlighted the presumably informal black market and ecologically unsound nature of artisanal fishing, contrasting it to the supposedly efficient, well-regulated, and environmentally sustainable large-scale industrial fleet. This highlighting of the supposed dysfunction of artisanal fishers has served to gloss over the role that industry restructuring has played in creating and expanding the category of artisanal fishers as well as the fact that limits on Peru's fisheries are the result of the ways in which the country's ocean natures have been made to work for the fishmeal industry for over half a century.

CHAPTER 2

Coastal Others

"Who built the city up each time? In which of Lima's houses,
The city glittering of gold, lived those who built it?"
—Bertold Brecht (1947, 109)

The statue of San Pedro (Saint Peter) swayed as the fishers carried him on their shoulders across the wharf. He sat in a miniature boat surrounded by flowers, and his head and body were adorned in regalia made of velvet with gold embroidery. Led by the local priest, the fishers slowly made their way to the water. It was June 29, 2013, the saint's feast day, and the wharf vibrated with people pushing to see their patron saint, crossing themselves in reverence, or snapping cellphone pictures of the procession. The fishers took the statue to the edge of the dock where a boat was waiting to carry San Pedro, seated in the bow, into the bay. The priest climbed into the wooden boat along with a fisher dressed as the independence hero and namesake of the local association, José Silverio Olaya Balandra. The leaders of the association and officials from the municipal government boarded the boat. Fishers offered rides to the faithful and charged more to follow San Pedro once he was on the water. The procession had begun. The cavalcade of brightly colored boats first went to the neighboring Yacht Club, where San Pedro was greeted at the jetty by a shower of flower petals and songs. Afterward, the boats made a loop through the harbor before returning to the wharf, where fishers threw out flowers as offerings to San Pedro in return for a good year of fishing.[1]

The local fishers' association has been responsible for the San Pedro procession since its initial founding in 1927, although fishers were involved in the process long before that. For the other 364 days of the year, when it is not featured in a procession, the statue of San Pedro sits in the fishers' association's office on the dock in Chorrillos, largely hidden from public view. In this regard, the Feast of San Pedro and the fishers' role in it are suggestive of their broader position in the social geography and cultural politics of the capital city. Throughout Lima's history, artisanal fishers have conducted socially necessary labor in the city's economy, supplying residents and domestic markets with fish. Moreover, as the Feast of San Pedro demonstrates, fishers also have contributed in significant ways to Lima's cultural life. However, artisanal fishers and vendors have been marginalized within urban cultural, political, and spatial hierarchies. Lima's elites consistently have viewed the coast as a marginal area that is distant, both geographically and culturally, from the city's centers of power and have framed artisanal fishers as problematic Others who are out of place in the city. Such discourses of alterity, we argue, represent critical means through which encroachments on artisanal fishers' and vendors' autonomy have been advanced and through which threats of dispossession have been justified in Lima's rapidly changing urban landscape.

The almost ten million people who live in Lima's metropolitan area comprise approximately one-third of the national population. During the colonial era, Lima was the most important Spanish port on the western side of the continent and served as the nucleus for the exportation of mineral wealth from Andean mines. Lima now serves as a hub for the flow of global capital, much of it focused on exporting still-rich mineral resources. However, urban renewal oriented toward making the city more attractive for tourists and wealthy residents has transformed Lima's core into a site for investment (Gandolfo 2009). For decades, the city also has received waves of migrants from Peru's rural areas, individuals and families displaced by the financial crisis of the 1980s and the civil war between the government and the Maoist Sendero Luminoso (Shining Path) guerrilla. These interrelated processes have produced growing urban inequalities and tensions among Lima's wealthy residents and the impoverished majority, whose "informal" settlements ring the urban core and house roughly two-thirds of the city's total population (Dosh 2010; Matos Mar 1984).[2]

This situation is not unique to Lima. Throughout Latin America, contemporary waves of neoliberalized urbanization, which increasingly have privatized once-public spaces for the benefit of real estate investors, tourists, and the rich, have deepened enduring inequalities (Holston 2008; Fischer, McCann, and Auyero 2014; Leal Martínez 2016; Swanson 2010). Geographer David Harvey (2008, 32, 37) argues that the price of this has been increasingly fractured urban

Figure 4 The parks and thoroughfare of Lima's Costa Verde near the fishers' wharf in Chorrillos.

landscapes, where quality of life has become a commodity that only wealthy citizens are able to enjoy through individualized consumption. Urban renewal projects, which have privileged the city as a space for global tourism and real estate speculation, have challenged many people's right to participate in decisions about how urban space is produced—what Henri Lefebvre (2003, 194) deemed the "right to the city." In numerous instances, impoverished urban residents have been dispossessed of this right through forced evictions to make way for the construction of luxury hotels, condominiums, and stadiums (Bin 2017).

Artisanal fishers and vendors have faced a similar struggle to maintain their right to the wharf in Chorrillos in the face of recent coastal development. While the area was once the favored bathing spot of the city's elite, it became a neglected space during the mid-twentieth century where the booming city's sewage was dumped directly into the ocean, an issue that continues to plague some of the area's beaches. However, in recent decades, this "waste" space has been the focus of redevelopment to make the Costa Verde, which extends from just south of Callao to Chorrillos, a bypass route for the city's congested thoroughfares and an area that is more attractive to both foreign and domestic tourists. Government officials and members of the neighboring Yacht Club have singled out the dilapidated but functioning wharf as an eyesore, an unwanted reminder of the area's recent past and the poverty that rings the city. Drawing on neoliberalized discourses of self-responsibility and entrepreneurialism, elite actors have justified the need to intervene in the development of the wharf by claiming that fishers and fish vendors have failed to take the initiative to solve local economic, infrastructural, and environmental problems, a dynamic that we explore in greater detail in Chapter 4.

In this chapter, we demonstrate how these discourses draw from and build upon earlier elite narratives of Lima's coastal fishing populations as cultural, racial, and spatial Others. Local elites have portrayed artisanal fishers as traditional actors who have operated largely outside the market economy and modern state regulation. In contrast, we show that Lima's coastal fishers have participated in local, regional, and global markets since the colonial era. The notion that artisanal fishers' current problems are the product of their contemporary transition to a market economy is the latest instantiation of a *longue durée* of elite encroachments and interventions aimed at extracting greater value from fishers' land, labor, and catches. Examining the history of these interventions is critical for understating contemporary dispossessions for several reasons. First, elite discourses about the alterity of artisanal fishers promote dispossession through a discursive erasure of fishers' history of engagement with and participation in the city's social relationships, markets, and ecologies. Making these engagements visible is essential for contesting contemporary dispossessions and for showing how artisanal fishers' and vendors' current situation has resulted from the accumulation of earlier dispossessions. Second, analyzing the history of elite interventions in artisanal fishers' and vendors' lives demonstrates that contemporary ideologies of individual responsibility and market solutions, which are presented as an apolitical means for evaluating urban citizenship, in fact rest upon and in many ways continue to promote elite cultural, racial, and class assumptions about the inappropriateness of artisanal fishers and vendors in Lima's urban, cosmopolitan society. Finally, an examination of these dynamics underscores the importance of analyzing symbolic politics for understanding how dispossession unfolds. Paige West (2016, 23) argues that material dispossession rests upon "discursive dispossession"—representations of people as incapable because they "exist outside the natural order of things." By tracing the history of such discursive dispossessions, we demonstrate how elite Limeños have repeatedly

sought to deny artisanal fishers and vendors autonomy over their livelihoods
and the right to participate in decisions about how urban coastal spaces should
be used and developed.

Peripheral Spaces

At the time of Spanish conquest, fishing villages dotted Peru's coastline. In and
around what would become Lima, Indigenous peoples settled near coves and
beaches in present-day La Chira, Chorrillos, Lurín, Bellavista, Callao, Ancón,
and Chancay. In her pioneering historical work on coastal Peru, Maria Rostworowski (1981, 118) notes that Chorrillos was known as the "place of fishermen." During the first century of conquest, Spanish colonization and disease
decimated these coastal populations. Chorrillos was no exception, having been
"totally destroyed" (Elmore 1904, 112). In the latter half of the seventeenth
century, Spanish Lieutenant Francisco Carrasco reestablished the community
as San Pedro de los Chorrillos (Saint Peter of the Springs), granting land to
fishers from nearby Huacho and Surco. In the centuries that followed, Chorrillos became the "most important center of fishing" in Lima and the largest
Indigenous settlement on Lima's coastline (Saénz 2005, 130).

During the colonial era, and indeed in the centuries that followed, the coast
"was a peripheral space of the city" where communities of Indigenous fishers
were relatively isolated from Lima's urban nucleus (Sáenz 2005, 123–25). Colonial administrators saw too many risks in building urban settlements on the
coast, given the threat of pirates and military attack, plus the potential for natural disasters, such as the tsunami that wiped out Callao in 1746 (Walker 2008).
The Spaniards built Lima on the Rímac River approximately twelve kilometers
from Callao, which served as the city's gateway to the sea. In keeping with European ideals of city planning (Rama 1996), the Spaniards built Lima on a grid,
which served not only to instill geographic but also social order to the city and
project imperial power into its space. As sociologist Aldo Panfichi (1995) notes,
the farther one lived from the center, the lower one's social status. Indigenous
people and Black slaves generally were forced to live outside the perimeter of
the city's walls. With this objective in mind, colonial administrators created the
Arrabal de San Lázaro in 1563 and the Pueblo de los Indios del Cercado in 1571.
The former was constructed across the Rímac River from Lima for the growing
number of Black slaves with leprosy. The Spaniards intended the latter as a

means for concentrating in one place Indigenous peoples, who provided services to Lima's well-to-do residents, to facilitate their physical control and ideological domination (Panfichi 1995). While such centers were meant to maintain the separation of different categories of people within colonial administration, they in fact served as sites for the production of ethnic and racial heterogeneity among Indigenous peoples, Afrodescendants, migrants from Japan and the Philippines, and poor Spaniards, whose "mixed" progeny challenged colonial hierarchies and produced new forms of urban culture, albeit ones that continued to be denigrated by the Spaniards (Panfichi 1995).

Because of their geographical location far from Lima's walls, the area's fishing settlements escaped the gaze of colonial officials, affording fishers a degree of local autonomy not shared by Indigenous peoples living in Lima's walled centers or around rural centers of power such as churches and estates.[3] Colonial authorities encouraged Indigenous fishers to continue with their work, which provided Lima's and Callao's residents with food. Fishers were excused "from the agricultural labor draft" because of their occupation, which meant that they "could live out their lives without much Spanish meddling" (Charney 2001, 24). Historian Alberto Flores Galindo (1981) argues that as a result of their relative isolation, fishing settlements remained resolutely Indigenous into the republican era. In a survey of census data from the eighteenth century, Flores Galindo notes that while 26 percent of Peru's total coastal population (including Lima) was Indigenous, the percentage of Indigenous peoples in most fishing settlements was well over 90 percent with few Spanish priests and no secular authorities. The ability to maintain cultural and political separation from the Spaniards may have drawn Indigenous peoples from the valleys around Lima, where expanding sugarcane production, among other crops, placed greater demands on Indigenous labor and land (Flores Galindo 1981). In this context, fishing may have been a form of "silent protest against agrarian dispossession" (Flores Galindo 1981, 161).

Fishers did take advantage of their legal status as Indians to organize as *gremios* (guilds) and used the colonial legal system not only to defend their fishing grounds from other groups but in some cases to also petition for land to which they were entitled by colonial law (Charney 2001, 57; Rostworowski 1981, 85). This was particularly the case in the eighteenth century once coastal Indigenous populations rebounded and the growing populations of urban centers increased demand for fish. For example, two fishing guilds in Callao excluded other *castas* (castes) from their "fishing area and boasted of having been given rights to fish from the bridge that connected Lima to San Lázaro, to the mouth of the sea by several viceregal provisions" (Charney 2001, 57). Fishing guilds also used the colonial legal system to file complaints against each other over encroachment on communal fishing territories. For example, in 1784, fishers from Bellavista complained that fishers from Lurín and Chorrillos were fishing in their waters (Rostworowski 1981, 85). In such cases, members of local fishing guilds argued that they had a historical right to specific fishing grounds, asserting that they had fished them since "time immemorial" (Rostworowski 1981, 85).

The peripheral and semi-autonomous nature of Lima's fishing communities took on a different meaning toward the end of the eighteenth century with the advent of the Bourbon Reforms in colonial Latin America. Among other things, these reforms sought to strengthen the Crown's power and presence in colonial life and weaken the role of Creoles (individuals of Spanish descent born in the Americas) in administration. For Indigenous peoples, the reforms meant greater tax burdens and meant both Spanish and Creole attempts to more closely govern Indigenous peoples and extract greater value from their labor.[4] Colonial administrators began to view Lima's coastal zones as areas in need of better control, evangelization, and civilization—a process that brought Lima's Indigenous fishers further under the control of the colonial state (Sáenz 2005, 143). Colonial administrators who visited fishing communities were aghast at what they saw as the idolatry, lasciviousness, and wildness of fishers, who would "not tolerate subjecting themselves to Spaniards" (Flores Galindo 1981, 164).

Spanish officials also emphasized fishers' apparent laziness and—amid growing demand for fish and increased litigation among fishers—asserted that fishing should be open so that others could participate in the trade. In 1566, the Visitador Gregorio González de Cuenca ordered that the sea be declared common to all, a measure that caused considerable protest from Indigenous fishers, who argued that beach areas and fishing grounds were restricted to those who lived closest to them (Rostworowski 1981, 84). In the face of these protests, the visitador revoked his decree. However, in the late eighteenth century, Spanish authorities repeatedly decreed fishing to be free to all. For instance, in 1789, a Crown attorney concluded that, because fishing was a "public object," it should be open "not only to the Indians, but also other castes," thus creating a means of subsistence for the indolent (Flores Galindo 1981, 163). Such declarations do not appear to have had an immediate impact on Indigenous peoples' access to fishing grounds, as local traditions of access continued to dominate day-to-day use. However, they were significant in that they initiated a process of making

Indigenous fishing rights invisible to the law, thus laying the groundwork for later state claims that the sea was a national common. This is an idea that took on greater significance in the mid-twentieth century with the rapid industrialization of Peruvian fishing, as we showed in Chapter 1.

Seeing Alterity

In the nineteenth century, Lima's elites began to encroach more and more on the autonomy of Indigenous fishers. As fishers became further integrated into the city, elite Limeños and foreign travelers framed them as racial and cultural Others who existed on the margins not only of the metropolis but of the burgeoning Peruvian nation as well. Following independence from Spain, Creole elites adopted rhetorical components of liberal citizenship in a manner that kept colonial racial hierarchies largely intact (Thurner 1997; Walker 1999). With the advent of scientific racism in the late nineteenth century, urban elites increasingly noted the cultural, ethnic, and linguistically marked nature of Indigenous and Afrodescendent peoples in order to exclude them from full membership in Peruvian society. Given the locally constrained nature of Limeño elites' reach, these discussions did not always have immediate impacts on much of Peru's Indigenous population. However, Creole concerns about the appropriateness of Indigenous peoples did have growing significance for Lima's fishers in what was becoming an increasingly urban coastline.

At the turn of the nineteenth century, and especially in the decades after independence, wealthy Limeño and expatriate families built summer houses in Chorrillos, contributing to the "progressive displacement" (Sáenz 2005, 132) of Indigenous fishers. Despite this creeping displacement, Chorrillos remained an important fishing center during the nineteenth century. Indeed, travelers and government officials described the area as a "community of fishers" (de Arona 1894, 52). In his *Estadística Histórica* of Lima, José María Córdova y Urrutia (1839, 123) noted that, in the town of Chorrillos, there were numerous *ranchos* (huts) made of balsa and a few "decent and comfortable houses" constructed by wealthy families. Córdova y Urrutia (1839, 19) did not include these "decent" families in his census of Chorrillos, which he noted was comprised of 1,051 Indigenous peoples (581 men and 470 women) and twenty castas (in this case referring to individuals of "mixed" descent). In Chorrillos, fishing was "practiced at every hour," and on both sides of the bathing area, there were fleets of canoes and small boats (Córdova y Urrutia 1839, 103). The few not employed as fishers made their livings from the growing resort economy, working as *bañadores* (assistants who helped the rich get into the sea to bathe) or running small food stalls.

By the mid-nineteenth century, Chorrillos had become the most important seaside resort for Lima's wealthy and "the local indigenous community had found a new source of income by providing services to visitors," such as renting small homes to tourists on holiday (Higgins 2005, 202). Chorrillos reached its apex as a "flourishing holiday resort" in the 1860s and 1870s during Peru's guano boom, and it was during these decades that wealthy Limeños built grand homes along the district's coast, which featured an "elegant seafront promenade" (Higgins 2005, 202). However, during the War of the Pacific (1879–83), Chilean troops sacked and burned much of Chorrillos. Following the war, the baths and jetty were rebuilt along with the exclusive Yacht Club, which had been founded in 1875. The expansive Casino de Chorrillos (Chorrillos Casino), built in 1896, drew socialites from around Lima for its parties and dances. In 1906, an electric tram replaced the old railway connecting Chorrillos with Lima, thus improving Limeños' access to the area. Although neighboring Barranco displaced Chorrillos in the early twentieth century as the most fashionable resort district in Lima (Higgins 2005, 202), Chorrillos continued to be an important destination, especially for growing numbers of middle-class urbanites.

In his description of Chorrillos, Juan de Arona (1894, 109), a correspondent for the Real Academia Española, described the community as comprised of "wise, grave, respectful Indians," echoing both Peruvian and European ideologies of Indigenous peoples as a servile class. Furthermore, external commentators increasingly referred to the fishers in Chorrillos as *cholos* and *cholas*, terms used in this context as derogatory means of indicating Indigenous people who are supposedly out of place in an urban context. The notion that Chorrillos' Indigenous fishers existed on the cultural, spatial, and even temporal margins of the city was most clearly indicated in elite commentary on Indigenous women. Within Peruvian discourses of national identity and character, Indigenous women were (and continue to be) often framed as the most staunchly traditional and therefore non-modern Others (de la Cadena 2000).

In his 1866 guide to the city, the Limeño statistician, lawyer, and journalist Manuel Atanasio Fuentes sought to demonstrate to domestic and international audiences that Lima was a modern city by emphasizing the predominance of upper class social "types" in Peruvian urban society while also highlighting the diminishing presence of Blacks and Indigenous peoples (Poole 1997, 151–157).

Fuentes made the case that Indigenous people lacked "potential as modern citizens," given their docility and apparent rootedness in the nation's past. Of the few Indigenous "types" presented in the volume, Fuentes chose the *pescadora* (fisher woman) of Chorrillos. Alongside a drawing of a woman on a donkey with a basket of fish at her side, Fuentes wrote (1866, 156):

> The chief occupation of the *Chorrillanos* (Indians of Chorrillos) is fishing. The women carry the fish to Lima for sale, either at the market or in the streets. Before the railway was made from Lima to Chorrillos, the *pescadora* (fisher's wife) acted as carrier and messenger to all the families of Lima. Some time elapsed before the *Chorrillanas* (women of Chorrillos) dared to venture on the railway. They were unable to conceive how carriages without horses could whirl along so fast, *unless the devil had a hand in it*. Even at the present day, the *pescadora* prefers the jog-trot of her mule, although the quiet animal takes three hours to go from Chorrillos to Lima.

Fuentes's description of the Chorrillana clearly marks her temporal Otherness by emphasizing her seeming inability to comprehend modern technology and its benefits, compounded by the irrationality of her insistence on continuing to use a mule, despite the longer trip. Moreover, in emphasizing—and exaggerating—the distance between Chorrillos and Lima, Fuentes conveys the social distance he imagines between the residents of the two places. Carlos Prince (1890, 2), a French expatriate living in Lima, later reproduced the drawing and description in his *Lima Antigua*, the first volume of which consisted of anecdotes and sketches of different social types who were "gradually falling out of sight" in the city's social landscape.

Some elites and government officials hoped that migrants from Europe would replace these "premodern" types and thus would help modernize (and whiten) Peru's national labor pool. As was the case in a number of other South American countries, during the latter half of the nineteenth century, a number of Europeans, in particular Italians and Spaniards, migrated to Peru. In 1872, the Peruvian government created the Sociedad de Inmigración Europea (European Immigration Society), which encouraged European immigration by providing economic assistance to help migrants make the trip. The government's intention was to attract immigrants to Peru to work on growing coastal haciendas. However, upon arrival, most rejected contract labor, pressing instead for land that had been promised to them for individual cultivation. The result was that many ended up in Lima, forming small businesses and specializing in economic activities, among them fishing. Sicilians and Genoans who had worked as boat builders and fishers in their home country found their way to the ports of Callao and Chorrillos, where they lived and worked side by side with Indigenous fishers. Government officials and travelers noted the increased number of Italians in Lima's ports who extracted "a great quantity of fish of all sorts" (Maurtua 1906, 308). The 1905 census data for Callao indicated that there were 338 fishers, among them sixty-six women and forty-one foreigners, mostly recent Italian immigrants. The full impact of these immigrants on Lima's fisheries is not clear in existing historical records. However, rather than Europeanizing fishing communities or displacing Indigenous fishers, they appear to have been integrated into existing social and cultural dynamics.

State, Industry, and Labor

During the twentieth century, Indigenous peoples did not fall out of sight in Lima; instead, the reverse happened. Growing numbers of Peruvians, especially Indigenous families from rural areas, moved to the city in search of work. Chorrillos' seafront remained oriented to fishing and elite recreation. However, the district's urban center became a zone for working-class residents and light manufacturing, while its periphery boomed as a result of land invasions by impoverished Peruvians seeking housing. This shift occurred against a backdrop of broader changes in governance and the relationship among governing elites, the state, and subaltern populations. In response to the challenges of emerging leftist and populist parties, elites in Lima increasingly argued for a central state to organize and "protect" the working class from subversive agents with roots in the provinces.[5] Historian Paulo Drinot (2011, 13) argues that these elite narratives of state intervention were deeply racialized because they assumed that industrial "labor was commensurable with progress and indigeneity was commensurable with backwardness" and therefore it followed that "labor was incommensurable with indigeneity." In more blunt terms, the "allure of labor in Peru coexisted with, indeed was conditional upon, the repulsion of indigeneity" (Drinot 2011, 14).

Through the creation of new labor laws, ministries for overseeing labor conditions and social welfare, labor unions and associations, and governments in the 1920s and 1930s sought to protect existing laborers and foster the process of redeeming Indigenous peoples through their participation in organized labor. However, Peru's industrial sector remained quite small and the country did not embark on a process of state-led import substitution, unlike the countries of South America's southern cone. Drinot argues that, despite the shortcomings of Peruvian industrialization and state interventions, elite projects and policies aimed at regulating labor represented significant instances of emergent forms of governance. Not only did attempts to police labor promote an elite gaze on "troubling" aspects of Peruvian society (race and gender foremost among them) but they also established the state as the mediating entity of social welfare.

This was true in Lima's fisheries, which became objects of state concern and new regulations. The state began requiring (in law, if not always in practice) that fishers register with the local port authority to obtain a license to fish their local waters. In 1927, fishers in Chorrillos registered themselves as a mutual aid association through the Ministerio de Marina y Aviación (Marine and Aviation Ministry), which was responsible for the regulation of fishing in Peru (in 1935, it became part of the newly created Ministry of Agriculture). The idea behind such associations was that they would create a clearer and more direct line of organization between local fishing communities and a centralized Peruvian state, thus enabling more efficient regulation and projects of cultural and economic improvement. Associations such as the one in Chorrillos cared for local ports, aided members in need, and served important religious functions, such as coordinating the annual festivities for the Feast of San Pedro. However, state officials remained concerned that fishers in the city and throughout the country were locked in presumably "premodern" forms of identity, social organizing, and economic production that hindered attempts to modernize the country's fisheries. Despite possessing one of the world's most productive fisheries, Peru imported fish for domestic consumption.

With such concerns in mind, in 1941, CAG—the Peruvian corporation commissioned by the state to oversee the conservation of guano-producing sea birds and by extension the marine fisheries that nourished them—commissioned the U.S. Fish and Wildlife Service to produce a report on the state of Peruvian fisheries and make recommendations for their development. In their analysis of the social organization of Peruvian fishers, the foreign consultants commented at length on Peruvian fishers' boats, technologies, and social organization. They cataloged the different kinds of boats that fishers employed, noting that many persisted in the use of canoes and *caballitos de totora* (small boats made of reed that were capable of landing only small quantities of fish at any one time). Furthermore, mechanization was absent—fishers relied on manual labor to catch, land, and process fish for domestic markets. The consultants drew implicit parallels between the presumably premodern technologies used by fishers and their social organization. They noted that the majority of fishers in Peru were "Indians or racial mixtures in which Indian blood predominates" (Fielder, Jarvis, and Lobell 1943, 63). They also commented that while fishers in Chorrillos and Callao were organized into associations, these associations did not function as cooperatives because they did not "acquire communal supplies or gear for the members or pool fish to sell jointly" (Fielder, Jarvis, and Lobell 1943, 64). Each member was responsible for buying his gear and selling his fish in a manner that did not take advantage of efficiencies of scale. Through improved organization and the creation of cooperatives, the consultants argued that Peru's fishers could increase their productivity and produce more fish for the growing domestic market.

Such commentaries and recommendations were indicative of state discourses about artisanal fishers throughout much of the mid- to late twentieth century. Government officials repeatedly highlighted the seemingly anachronistic nature of fishers as evidenced by their racial-ethnic-class character and their manual fishing methods while providing little-to-no state support for artisanal fishers. This dynamic contributed to the ongoing devaluation of artisanal fishing labor and obscured the central role that such labor played in the development of Peru's export-led fisheries in the mid-twentieth century. By the 1940s, there were over two hundred fishers registered in Chorrillos, which when combined with those in nearby Callao, accounted for almost one-third of the total number of registered fishers nationwide. These fishers drove Peru's first export boom in fish during World War II, which relied on an abundance of cheap labor provided by Lima's fishers to catch bonito for canning and sale to the United States (Maldonado Félix and Puertas Porras 2011). The same is true of the initial anchoveta boom in the 1950s and early 1960s, which relied largely on fishers' cheap manual labor to provide Peruvian fishmeal producers with an economic advantage in the global fishmeal trade.

The discursive marginalization of artisanal labor not only denied the role of fishers in the development of Peru's fishing industries but also enabled state officials and industrial producers to expel artisanal labor and enclose artisanal fisheries to weather crises in industrial production. The boom in anchoveta production was made possible by an abundance of undervalued coastal labor. However, ongoing crises in the late 1960s and 1970s led to a reliance on improved technology to increase efficiency and reduce costs. In order to deal with over-capacitation in the anchoveta fleet, the government cut the number of registered boats in half and weakened labor organizing by laying off workers. One result was the increased monopolization of production by a few firms when the industry was later denationalized. Another was a dramatic increase in the number of artisanal fishers in Peru. Balthazar Caravedo Molinari (1977, 117) notes that, as a result of economic crises and subsequent reorganizations in the fishmeal industry, "the number of workers involved in fishing for food rose from 13,275 in 1967, to 24,654 in 1972."

As with many other ports in Peru's central coast, Chorrillos grew as a result of these dynamics. In contrast to Callao, which supported a growing fleet of industrial boats, Chorrillos remained an important port for supplying fresh fish to Lima's population. In 1943, there were 69 boats (including canoes) and 232 registered fishers in Chorrillos. By 1970, those numbers had grown to 144 boats and 420 fishers. In 1969, the fishers' association in Chorrillos became a union and was registered the following year through the newly created Ministry of Fisheries. This transformation provided fishers with the ability to administer the thirty-meter iron dock that existed at the time and the surrounding beach. The government gave the union responsibility of administering the dock with the condition that the union administered it in a suitable manner, providing the necessary services for its functioning by collecting regular dues from members as well as daily or annual fees from other dock users.

This shift was part of a broader corporatist approach advocated by General Juan Velasco's left-wing military government (1968–75) to make the poor equipped to function as producers for the national good. Government attempts to organize artisanal fishers and other small-scale producers and laborers paralleled agrarian reforms in the highlands, which sought to better integrate Indigenous farmers into regional and national economies through the creation of peasant associations. Peru continued to rely on extensive food imports. Velasco sought to increase domestic food production to 40 percent of consumption as a means of stabilizing food costs and reducing foreign dependency. Ultimately, the interests of the export industry took precedence over domestic production, as we demonstrated in Chapter 1. However, the government's interest in small producers represented an important point of contact between powerful actors and artisanal fishers, one that not only provided a window into the latter's relationship with the state but that also shaped that relationship in significant ways in the decades that followed.

In the late 1960s, IMARPE conducted a pilot study of Chorrillos, which it published as a special report in 1970 with the goal of assessing the degree to which artisanal fishers could become more efficient food producers for domestic markets and what kinds of inputs they would need to do so. The report's authors, Alba Bustamante and Marco Borda (1970), noted that fishers in Chorrillos landed approximately 1,700 metric tons of fish each year, which they caught in a zone that extended from the bay to fifteen nautical miles out to sea. At the time, the fish landed in Chorrillos represented just over two percent of the national total of fish caught for human consumption. Bustamante and Borda argued that, despite the high quality of fish, production in Chorrillos had stayed the same for the past decade in large part because of poor infrastructure, a lack of capital and basic services, and limitations of the marine environment. The best fishing in Chorrillos was during the summer when a variety of fish moved into the area. However, the abundance of beach-goers congested access to the dock thus interfering with the unloading of fish and leading to unnecessary spoilage. Furthermore, there was a lack of local economic capital that prevented fishers from investing in larger or more technologically advanced boats, and the absence of a strong cooperative meant that fishers were subject to fish buyers who kept prices low in order to maximize their profits. Finally, while the quantity of different fish in the bay was high, the fish rarely reached average size because of "sporadic incursions by *bolicheras* that destroy [fish in the bay] without any distinction" and the permanent presence of local fishers (Bustamante and Borda 1970, 10). The limited fishing season also meant that a considerable number of fishers migrated to the nearby ports of Pucusana and Ancón when fishing in Chorrillos was slow.

The report's authors also suggested that a lack of desire among fishers hampered the development of a more productive fishery, noting that in their opinion the boats and fishing methods had changed little in the prior twenty or thirty years. Chorrillos' fishers were stuck in the "artisanal stage" and seemed to lack an interest in building boats or adopting new technology in order to catch more fish and earn a better living (Bustamante and Borda 1970, 31). The one bright spot was that fishers who used larger boats were generating enough money potentially to form a "new group of small industrial fishers" (Bustamante and Borda 1970, 31). These comments reveal how the construction of artisanal fishers' alterity shifted in the mid-twentieth century. While earlier accounts, such as the 1943 USFWS study, highlighted the racial makeup of fishers along Peru's central coast, similar language was absent from IMARPE's 1970 report on Chorrillos. In part, this reflected changes that urbanization produced in local demographics, as an increased number of migrants from other areas of Lima and Peru began working in Chorrillos. Additionally, lower class Limeños felt growing pressure to disavow any connections to indigeneity. Current-day fishers and vendors in Chorrillos highlight their identity as *criollos* (Creoles), *mestizos* (people of "mixed" European and Indigenous descent) whose families migrated from the highlands, or the descendants of Italian migrants. However, the lack of racial discourse in the report also highlights the Velasco government's goal to convert poor Peruvians into peasants and workers, emphasizing their position in the country's economy and their role in production over racial or ethnic identities while reinforcing their marginal status in the country's political economies. Instead of highlighting the racial alterity of fishers, Bustamante and Borda emphasized what they believed was the temporal alterity of Chorrillos' workers, who continued to be stuck in an earlier phase of technological and economic development. This narrative erased artisanal fishers' contributions to the development of the industrial fishery. Furthermore, such depictions remade artisanal fishers into objects of development in need of outside improvements and expertise to transition to modernity. While economic development for artisanal fishers was put on hold in the decades that followed, their marginalization as modernity's Others persisted.

Waste Space

Through much of the mid-twentieth century, government officials marked artisanal fishers in Lima as racial-ethnic Others in need of state redemptory projects to convert them into modern producers for growing urban markets. In the 1980s and early 1990s, elite discourses about artisanal fishers shifted, emphasizing their alterity through dictums of informality, illegality, and cultural inappropriateness. As was the case for much of Latin America, the 1980s became popularly known as the "lost decade" for Peru. The global economic recession in the early 1980s hit Peru's economy, which was dependent on raw material exports, hard. By the end of the decade, the country was heavily indebted and strapped with runaway inflation. The country also suffered through a civil war between Maoist guerillas and the army, which left an estimated seventy thousand people dead. As a result of the country's economic crisis and the war, growing numbers of rural people looking for work and fleeing violence migrated to Lima, whose population grew by two million people between 1980 and 1995. Lima's new residents added to the city's periphery with land invasions and joined the growing portion of the city's workers employed as *informales* (informals). In her discussion of the cultural discourses of illegality and deviation in Lima, Daniella Gandolfo (2014) notes that the city's elites came to use the idea of "informal" to convey "class outrage and disgust" at the "open defiance of the law" and "hodge-podge aesthetics" that they came to associate with the city's street vendors.

Such outrage and disgust at the ad hoc, messy, and quasi-legal nature of fishing and fish vending in the city was most cogently expressed during a cholera outbreak in 1991. The outbreak was the first cholera epidemic in Peru since the nineteenth century and it killed over three thousand people. Initially, the epidemic was blamed on a ship that had docked in Chancay and several other ports near Lima and that had several crew members who were sick and whose excrement was presumably dumped overboard. Whether this was the source or not was never verified. In any case, Peruvian health officials theorized that the quick spread of the disease along the coast (and then later to other parts of the country) was due to the consumption of raw fish and shellfish from contaminated near-coast waters in places such as Callao and Chorrillos. The health crisis highlighted growing problems of urban pollution along Lima's coastline and the poor state of the city's water treatment infrastructure. However, government officials placed much of the blame not on the state's inability to provide clean water for its booming urban populations but rather on the hygiene of poor fishers, vendors, and residents.[6]

Like many coastal cities, Lima dumped its untreated sewage into the Pacific Ocean at three main sites and several smaller drains along its coastline. The largest of these sewage collectors was located in La Chira, a small beach in southern Lima, approximately eight kilometers south of Chorrillos. The facility in La Chira was constructed in 1963 when there were two million residents in all of Lima and the southern cone of the city was not densely populated. By the time of the cholera outbreak in 1991, Lima had a population of 6.5 million. La Chira continued to collect and dump wastewater into the ocean, and the same was true of Lima's two other main collection plants in San Miguel, near Miraflores, and La Taboada, just north of Callao. Because the predominant currents run south to north along most of Peru's coast, the wastewater from these plants, but especially La Chira, is pushed along Lima's coast. The result at the time was a high level of harmful bacteria in the city's nearshore waters and widespread contamination of much of the marine life that inhabited these shallow waters.

In the face of the outbreak, Peru's Health Minister Carlos Vidal Layseca prioritized public health messages for curbing the disease's spread that emphasized the importance of personal hygiene, such as washing hands, and avoiding the consumption of uncooked fish in the form of the popular seafood dish *ceviche* (*cebiche*), made by mixing raw fish, lime juice, red onions, garlic, and hot pepper. This declaration sparked what some called the "Ceviche War" between Vidal, President Fujimori, and the fish industry. The health minister's warnings that the consumption of raw fish and shellfish spread cholera contributed to a sudden drop in fish sales in Peru and an embargo on imports of Peruvian fish products by other countries in the region. Artisanal fishers lost an estimated five hundred thousand dollars of revenue in the first months of the epidemic. Twenty-five years later, when we asked fishers about the cholera outbreak, they spoke about it as one of the most trying times in their lives. They continued to go out and catch fish, but no one would buy it, so they had no money. They noted that they and their families continued to eat fish from the bay because that was almost all they had during those months and they believed it was not a risk for cholera. During the outbreak, *El Comercio* (1991), Lima's conservative newspaper of note, published a brief interview with a fisher from Chorrillos. The article noted that, because no one would buy fish from the vendors in Chorrillos, many fishers had turned to giving tourists rides as a means to try and earn some money. The fisher who was interviewed said that "the work is not easy because there is a lot of competition, some have boats with motors, I only have my arms, which thankfully are still strong."

In response to the crisis, Fujimori chose not to develop an official campaign against cholera for fear that such measures would further impact his country's agricultural and piscatorial exports and instead publicly assured Peruvians that it was safe to eat ceviche. In a controversial move, Fujimori and his wife as well as Enrique Rossi Link and Félix Canal Torres, the ministers of agriculture and fisheries, visited a number of ports and ate ceviche on television to reassure consumers. Vidal lambasted Fujimori's actions noting that "there is one ceviche for the rich, and another ceviche for the poor" (Brooke 1991). Fujimori's ceviche, Vidal asserted, was made with fish from the open ocean as opposed to the nearshore fish that was used to make cheap ceviche. Vidal resigned his post on March 18 under pressure from the Fujimori administration as the number of cases began to wane. His successor took a lower-profile approach to the epidemic and dropped public proclamations that fish was unsafe to eat.

Official focus on the suitability of fish for consumption, as well as the government's focus on personal hygiene as a means for combating cholera, sidestepped broader structural issues that enabled the epidemic and did so in a way that shifted blame for the disease's spread to social undesirables. In his analysis of the epidemic, Marcos Cueto (2001) points out that infrastructural problems played a key role in the spread of cholera. The outbreak was made possible by considerable deficiencies in Peru's water and sewage systems. Seventy-five percent of the cholera patients admitted to Lima's hospitals claimed they had not "eaten fish or ceviche in the first month of the epidemic" (Cueto 2001, 116). However, in Callao alone, an estimated "forty percent of the population drank water contaminated with fecal residues" (Cueto 2001, 103). The health ministry's focus on personal hygiene for combating cholera ignored the fact that many Peruvians did not have access to clean water with which they could effectively wash their hands and sanitize food preparation surfaces. Moreover, this emphasis on personal hygiene suggested that individuals were responsible for becoming ill with the disease, which became a social indication of the filth of victims and the spaces they inhabited. Cueto (2001, 124) notes that "filth was ascribed to 'others' and to somewhere outside the home," most often to "street peddlers, the beaches, the fruit eaten away from home, the piles of refuse and the flies." The connection between cholera and filth became so strong that "being sick with cholera" became "proof not just of being poor, but also of being socially undesirable" (Cueto 2001, 125).

Media coverage of the epidemic reflected and perpetuated this idea that filth and a general breakdown in personal hygiene among the poor were responsible for cholera's spread. For example, an article in *Caretas* (1991, 55), a popular news magazine, proclaimed, "In Lima, the dirtiest capital in Latin America, the cholera epidemic found the most favorable environment for its spread. The street filth, abetted by whomever confused the city with a kitchen (or a latrine) seemed to disappear at the beginning of the epidemic, but, in reality, it has not left." It was the uneducated, poor masses who did not know how to comport themselves properly in the city who were responsible for producing the filth that made the epidemic possible. While many reports focused on street vendors as the emblems of this problem, it was Lima's beachfront that emerged as the most undesirable of the city's spaces. An article in *El Comercio* (1991b) noted that the "anti-hygienic state of our beaches, the proliferation of trash and the health risks related to the lack of potable water" made going to the city's beaches a danger to one's health. And yet, as another article noted, poor people still used drainage canals along the beaches to bathe and wash clothes, seemingly ignoring the "grave contamination of the sand and marine waters" (El Comercio

Figure 5 A red flag warns swimmers that the waters of one of the Costa Verde's beaches are not safe for swimming. Photo by Maximilian Viatori.

1991c). Many news reports noted that the beaches surrounding the dock in Chorrillos—the Pescadores and Agua Dulce beaches—were some of the most contaminated areas in the Costa Verde. The docks and jetties that were con-structed in the bay during the second half of the twentieth century created an eddy effect at the southern end of the bay where the dock was located. The water in this area moved slowly and warmed more frequently, making it an ideal site for the reproduction of bacteria. As one report noted, cholera bacteria were not found in these waters, but given the area's "high contamination by black water," monitors found elevated levels of other bacteria, water-borne pathogens, and other "nasty things" (El Comercio 1991d).

The cholera epidemic brought to the fore the reality that Lima's coastline had become a site of contamination, a zone that had been sacrificed slowly to the needs of the city's growing population and industry. For decades, Lima's elites had abandoned the area as their preferred recreational site in favor first of the beaches north of the city in Ancón and later south near Pucusana and Asia. The contamination of Lima's coastal waters, impoverished people's continued use of them, and the beaches as sites of recreation and commerce, co-constituted the zone as a site of filth and its users as social undesirables. Such discourses directed attention away from the structural factors and enduring inequalities that had concentrated waste and contamination in an area used primarily by working- and lower-class people, instead emphasizing the irrational individual "choices" of these people to continue to use contaminated coastal spaces to fish and swim.[7] This way of framing poverty and environmental contamination has become a fundamental aspect of justifying a range of elite interventions into the lives of coastal fishers aimed at the renewal of neglected coastal spaces and the apparent need to ensure that fishers and vendors adhere to best practices for handling and selling fish and caring for the spaces that they use.

Greener Shores

For Lima's wealthy residents, the cholera outbreak was one of several signs (among them the sprawling shanty-towns, faltering government services, and guerilla bombings) that their city had deteriorated to the point of collapse. In her ethnography of urban renewal in Lima, Daniella Gandolfo (2009, 34) argues that this sentiment helped to drive the "most aggressive effort since the urban population explosion of the 1930s and 1940s to redefine Limeños' relationship to their city and its history through ideas of cleanliness, order and beauty to which, it is assumed everyone should aspire." Upon assuming office in 1996, Lima's Mayor Alberto Andrade Carmona made efforts to recuperate the historic center by relocating street vendors to wholesale markets, instituting cleaning programs to combat unhygienic conditions, and renovating historic buildings.[8]

Lima's coastline underwent a similar renewal as a space for tourism, park-based recreation, and real estate speculation in the form of luxury apartment and condominium construction. From the late 1990s on, the upper coastal shelf from Miraflores to Chorrillos became packed with luxury condominiums and apartments as well as one of the city's most exclusive shopping centers, Larcomar, which overlooks the Pacific Ocean from Miraflores. District municipal governments in Miraflores, Barranco, and Chorrillos developed portions of the lower coastal shelf for tourism and recreation in an attempt to rid the seaside of its reputation as an open sewer for the city. This renewal of the Costa Verde began as the lifelong project of architect Ernesto Aramburú Menchaca, who often noted that Lima was built with its back to the sea and who led efforts to construct beaches along the Costa Verde in the 1960s and 1970s with an expressway that would connect the city's residents to the sea. In the early 1980s, he successfully lobbied for the creation of an authority to oversee the zone's ongoing development and coordinate efforts among the six district municipalities—Chorrillos, Barranco, Miraflores, San Isidro, Madgalena del Mar, and San Miguel—that shared the Costa Verde. In 1995, a federal regulatory norm created the Autoridad del Proyecto Costa Verde (APCV, Costa Verde Project Authority), a decentralized body responsible for conducting feasibility and environmental impact studies of the zone and for creating regulatory norms for the Costa Verde's coordinated development. The president of the APCV is appointed by the mayor of Lima, and its governing board is comprised of the mayors of the six district governments that share the Costa Verde, plus a representative from the government of Metro Lima and an at-large appointee, both of whom are also appointed by the mayor of Lima.

Shortly after its creation, the APCV issued a fifteen-year plan for the Costa Verde's development, the objective of which was to develop the "touristic-recreational-cultural potential" of the zone to facilitate its "integration" with the rest of the metropolis (APCV 1995, 6). The APCV's plan emphasized the "social role" of the zone for the "city/capital" and its role as "cultural patrimony" with the object of promoting a better standard of living and relationships among the residents of the metropolitan community (1995, 36). The APCV emphasized the "physical" development of the area through the improvement of beaches for recreation and the expansion of the zone's expressway. The APCV's plans did not incorporate fishing as a component of the zone's redeveloped future. The architectural drawings in the plan did not include fishers, even those for the Pescadores Beach in Chorrillos, but rather provided images of enhanced tourism and recreational facilities with a few sailboats in the bay, an expanded Yacht Club, and improved mooring for pleasure boats. Looking at the plans, one would not even know that the bay supported a productive fishery because fishers were literally written out of the Costa Verde's future.

In the more than two decades since the APCV released its comprehensive plan, development of the zone has unfolded at a steady pace, albeit not always in the way that the APCV's architects have planned. The APCV has no enforcement authority; so while district governments are supposed to submit plans for development of their sections of the coast to the APCV for approval, this has not always happened in practice. New hotels and luxury condominiums have been built closer to the edge of the Costa Verde's unstable sand cliffs than the

APCV regulations recommend. However, despite the challenges of the APCV's governing structure, development of the Costa Verde, especially its southern half, has remade the area into a beautified space for tourism and real estate speculation.

Despite their exclusion from the APCV's plans, fishers are still active in the Costa Verde, and the beaches next to the fishing wharf in Chorrillos are as busy as ever during the summer tourist season. However, as a result of the push for tourism-oriented development and recent expansions of the neighboring Yacht Club, the wharf in Chorrillos increasingly has come to stand out as a singular space of poverty and crumbling infrastructure along the Costa Verde. This has led to increased government scrutiny of the wharf and the fishers' apparent mismanagement of it, as we demonstrate in Chapter 4. Officials have justified increasing their regulatory gaze by highlighting the alterity of artisanal fishers not as racial or class Others but rather as individuals who have failed to be responsible for their own proper conduct and their "community." In doing so, elite actors have blamed fishers and vendors for the impoverished condition of the local wharf. At the same time, the decentralized nature of coastal development has meant that fishers and vendors have had access to few municipal government resources to maintain or rebuild the dock to bring it in line with the aesthetics of coastal renewal, as we show in Chapter 4. Government officials have emphasized that fishers and vendors need to draw on their own resources, which they get from charging use fees for the wharf, to come up with their own solutions for renovating and improving the space or to face losing control of it. In this manner, officials have framed the potential dispossession of local fishers not as a product of persistent urban inequalities or a lack of government support but instead as a result of fishers' inability to comport themselves appropriately according to neoliberalized dictums of responsibility and market-driven initiative.

Conclusion

Contemporary elite concerns with making artisanal fishers and vendors responsible entrepreneurs continue a long history of encroachments and enclosures. Colonial administrators, religious clerics, and government officials identified fishers and vendors in Chorrillos as Others in need of intervention. In each instance, powerful actors emphasized the presumably ad hoc, irrational, or messy nature of coastal fishing and the individuals engaged in it. Such postulations of alterity erased fishers' ongoing engagements with and role in various political economies, providing ready-made justifications for "finally" incorporating them into civilized society, the city, the nation, or the market, and thus dispossessing them of resources and autonomy. Recently, dominant discourses of urban renewal have promoted neoliberalized notions of citizens as individuals who earn their right to portions of the city by demonstrating that they are entrepreneurial agents who comport themselves in accordance with elite-specified outcomes such as coastal beautification. Such ideologies deny the importance of places such as the wharf in Chorrillos as spaces for cultural, and not just economic, reproduction. The coastline in Chorrillos has functioned for centuries as a place of refuge, a space where Indigenous peoples and new migrants could live with some economic, political, and cultural dignity. As such, threats of dispossession not only jeopardize fishers' access to productive resources but also endanger the right of the less powerful to the city in Lima's changing urban landscape.

This dynamic illustrates the importance of discourses of racial, class, and cultural alterity for understanding how powerful actors have promoted and justified various acts of dispossession. Such dispossessions have not just been material, such as elites' attempts to claim the value generated by the labor of impoverished artisanal fishers or the space they have used to make their livelihoods, which is now potentially more valuable as a tourist destination. Rather, elite claims that artisanal fishers and vendors do not fit and are not appropriate within Lima's changing urban landscape have also furthered a denial of fishers' and vendors' autonomy and right to participate equally in decisions about how coastal development should proceed and to what (and whose) ends. Furthermore, tracing artisanal fishers' and vendors' long history of struggle with elite governance reveals that dispossessions are never the result of seemingly apolitical considerations of the market but instead rest on and are advanced by historically rooted racial, class, and cultural discourses of alterity.

CHAPTER 3

Comparative Geographies
of Responsibility

From the 1950s to the present, an increasingly monopolized fishmeal industry has established its claim to Peru's most lucrative ocean natures at the expense of small-scale and artisanal fishers. Following a series of ecological and economic crises in the 1970s and 1980s, the industry reorganized to maintain its ability to generate profit despite diminished anchoveta stocks. The artisanal food fishing sector bore the unequal burden of these reorganizations, absorbing waves of workers who were laid off by downsizing in the fishmeal industry and dealing with the impacts of industrial overfishing. At the same time, industry leaders have opposed protections for artisanal fisheries that threatened their monopoly over anchoveta stocks. In Chorrillos and the greater Lima metropolitan area, these enclosures paralleled artisanal fishers' experiences with urban renewal and infrastructural development. Growing pollution and sewage discharges contaminated urban fisheries in Lima and marked them as waste spaces in need of renovation. In Chorrillos, renewal projects to make Lima's Costa Verde more attractive to tourists have threatened to dispossess impoverished fishers of their access to the historical use areas that they need to sustain their livelihoods. In this chapter, we explore the ways in which these reorganizations of coastal ecologies have produced geographical inequalities among Lima's artisanal fishing ports and we argue that neoliberalized comparisons of responsibility obscure the role of capitalist "world-ecologies" (Moore 2015) in producing coastal disparities by attributing them to differences in local behavior.

Considerable disparities exist among the four main ports where artisanal fishers in Lima and Callao Provinces are active. Beginning in the north and moving south, these ports are Ancón, Callao, Chorrillos, and Pucusana. According to IMARPE and Produce statistics, in the first decades of the new millennium, approximately two hundred fishers in Chorrillos landed about one thousand metric tons of fish per year. In Ancón, five hundred fishers regularly brought in five thousand metric tons of fish per year, while four hundred fifty fishers in Pucusana accounted for between eight thousand and fourteen thousand metric tons each year. Like Chorrillos, Ancón and Pucusana are relatively small ports that are used by artisanal fishers pursuing food fish. In contrast, Callao, which is located just west of Lima's city center, is the busiest shipping port in the country. Each day, approximately three thousand containers move through the port in addition to thousands of barrels of oil, tons of grain, and fishmeal in bulk carriers. Among the containers and the warehouses, there are also fishers who use the port to unload their catches. There are one thousand two hundred registered artisanal fishers and divers in Callao. While about one-third of them use small boats to fish nearshore waters, most operate or work on larger artisanal boats (many of which approach the size of boliches) to pursue anchoveta and *jurel* (*Trachurus murphyi*, jack mackerel)—these fish account for seventy percent of the reported one hundred thousand to one hundred fifty thousand metric tons of fish landed by artisanal fishers in the port.

These differences are the products of uneven development along Lima's extended coastline, which has created significant disparities among artisanal fishers both in the political and economic challenges they face and in the resources they have to deal with them. In groundbreaking works on the centrality of geography to capitalism, David Harvey (1982) and Neil Smith (1984) show that uneven development is integral to capitalism because it creates spatial inequalities, which capital can then exploit to produce geographical advantages by, for example, moving to find cheaper labor or cheaper nature to exploit.[1] Through combined processes of connection and differentiation, capital production and accumulation produce historically specific natures, spaces, places, and identities that are linked in unequal exchanges (Smith 1984). Smith emphasizes that this is never a finished process but one characterized by ongoing tensions as capital seeks new inequalities that can create novel advantages while also confronting political resistance at different scales.

Neoliberalized modes of production and accumulation have reconfigured urban, rural, and natural spaces around the world and have contributed to increased differentiation and growing disparities (Escobar 2008; Lowe et al. 1993; Heynen et al. 2007). Environmental anthropologists have demonstrated that in many parts of the Global South, the neoliberalized production of nature has contributed to uneven development by promoting rural spaces as sites either for expanded corporate production of raw materials and agricultural commodities or for conservation and its related forms of global tourism (Doane 2012). Both have been advanced through emergent forms of dispossession, which have enclosed and privatized communally held resources and made it more difficult for local people to maintain their livelihoods (Grandia 2012). This has been compounded by the ongoing devaluation of local labor in places such as rural Mexico, Madagascar, and Tanzania, which have become attractive sites for global capital investment and conservation tourism in part because of a surplus of cheap, increasingly landless labor (Martínez-Reyes 2016; Sodikoff 2012; Walley 2004). Furthermore, neoliberalized modes of uneven development have led to the growing concentration of global waste and contamination in previously colonized, industrialized, or underdeveloped spaces (Millar 2018; Stoler 2013). For example, Heather Anne Swanson (2015, 101) shows that shifting the ecological destruction of intensive salmon farming to production sites in coastal Chile enabled the development of "eco-friendly fisheries management" in Japan. Such disparities highlight the importance of unequal geographical connections in the production of value around the world.

Through a historical analysis of investment in and the development of Lima's fisheries, we argue that disparities among Lima's ports are the products of the divergent ways in which each port was integrated into or bypassed by the industrialization of Peruvian fisheries from the mid-twentieth century on and by the development of different coastal zones for export industries, tourism, or housing. This uneven development has had a profound impact on the resources available to fishers to assert their autonomy and defend their access to particular places, which we demonstrate through an analysis of fishing activism in the port of Ancón, where a proposed megaport project threatened the artisanal fishery. By joining together with wealthy condominium owners, the local fishers' association was able to halt port construction plans by arguing that the bay of Ancón was a unique space in the geography of Peru's central coast—one that combined important archaeological history with the protection of a special coastal ecosystem that supported artisanal fishing and local tourism. Given that Ancón is located outside of the city, it escaped the waves of industrialization and urbanization that contaminated Chorrillos' and Callao's bays, which made

Ancón an ideal site for wealthy urbanites looking for pristine beaches outside the city center. Ultimately, the government rejected the port project in Ancón.

Politics and cultural discourses about place are equally important for promoting uneven development because they provide narrative justification for why certain places need revitalization or redevelopment or why capital investment should be blocked from others. Analyzing place and memory in Argentina, Gastón Gordillo (2004, 3) argues that "places are produced in tension with other geographies." One critical means through which this occurs is comparison. In his book on environmental politics in Hong Kong, Timothy Choy (2011, 11) shows that ecologies, species, and landscapes come "to matter epistemically and politically" through their comparison on multiple scales with other ecologies and landscapes. We argue that everyday comparisons of fishing ports are critical means through which fishers and government officials acknowledge coastal inequalities while contributing to their production by attributing these inequalities to differences in individual responsibility. As we demonstrate in the second half of this chapter, government officials and fishers regularly make comparisons between ports in Lima and Callao provinces, attributing geographical disparities to fishers' willingness or apparent unwillingness to take initiative and improve their situations. Such comparisons recognize inequalities among fishing ports but obscure the role that uneven development has played in shaping these disparities and producing the "unique" aspects of specific port economies.[2]

Taken as a whole, this chapter demonstrates the importance of a geographically minded analysis for understanding how and why particular configurations of nature, capital, and politics have produced spatial inequalities. Paying attention to local differences is critical for understanding why fishers in different places have varying resources for sustaining themselves, accessing new markets, and defending their rights to the coast and the sea from encroachment. However, such local analyses only make sense when considered in the broader context of how coastal spaces have been organized within regional and global political ecologies. Rather than overlook or devalue local variation, situating individual artisanal fishing ports within broader regional geographies shows that differences among ports are not, as many fishers and officials claim, about local idiosyncrasies or variations in physical geography. Geographical inequalities are the products of the interplay between nature, capital, and politics and the uneven development that results from their configuration within historically specific systems of production and accumulation. We argue that such an analysis is critical for understanding how contemporary dynamics of encroachment and dispossession have unfolded in particular places and why fishers have been more or less successful at contesting them in different ports. Yet, neoliberalized geographies of comparison undermine such understandings by framing artisanal fishers as entrepreneurs competing with other entrepreneurs and reducing complex geographical inequalities to dubious comparisons of local responsibility.

Producing Difference among Lima's Ports

The development of export-based, industrialized fisheries in the mid-twentieth century dramatically altered the economies, labor relations, and ecologies of fish production in central Peru and initiated the geographical differentiation that exists among the region's fishing ports, as we demonstrated in Chapter 1. Understanding the history of this differentiation and the role that regional and global political economies have played in producing it is key for explaining why artisanal fishers in Ancón and Pucusana have done better in recent decades than those in Chorrillos. This is particularly critical given that many fishers and officials reinforce existing disparities by reducing them to considerations of entrepreneurial responsibility.

Prior to the anchoveta boom of the 1950s and 1960s, bonito processing and exports in the 1930s and 1940s made Callao the center of Peru's burgeoning fish export trade. Fishers from the port benefited from the fact that Callao was already Peru's primary shipping port and that fish processing plants were built in close proximity to the wharf, making it a multipurpose site for landing, processing, and shipping fish. At the time of the bonito boom, the greatest concentration of Peru's registered artisanal fishers was in Chorrillos and Callao. However, given Callao's supremacy as a processing and shipping hub, fishers based in Chorrillos unloaded their catches in Callao. The wharf in Chorrillos remained a hub for landing and processing smaller quantities of nearshore fish. The bonito boom began a process of differentiation among Lima's fishers. Those who were able to enter the export fishery had the potential to accumulate more capital and buy larger boats, and the port in Callao amassed greater capital and infrastructure to take advantage of export markets while other ports remained relatively localized in their production.

The explosion in fishmeal production in the 1950s deepened these differences. Callao was one of the early centers of fishmeal production. In the 1950s, there were thirty-six plants in Callao, a number of which had been built to process frozen fish but then were refitted to take advantage of the more lucrative fishmeal trade. In the 1950s and 1960s, there were large and easily accessible schools of anchoveta off the coast from Callao north to Supe, making it possible for fishers to capture anchoveta with existing technologies. It was a combination of capital, infrastructure, access to markets, and fish ecology that made Callao the most important fishing port along Lima's coastline. By the end of the 1960s, fishers in Callao were landing over one million metric tons of anchoveta a year. This made Callao second only to Chimbote, the northern city that had sprung up to exploit the massive anchoveta schools off the coast there, in annual tonnage of fish landed.

Pucusana, Chorrillos, and Ancón remained relatively small ports. However, during the second half of the twentieth century, important differences emerged among these ports as a result of the uneven ways in which economic and ecological changes impacted them. During the 1950s and 1960s, there were small but economically viable anchoveta schools off Pucusana's coast. In 1948, Blue Pacific Fishing SA (formerly Pesquera Naplo SA) opened a plant in Pucusana to process frozen fish, but like many fish processing factories along Peru's central coast, switched to fishmeal production in 1957. Throughout the boom period of Peruvian anchoveta fishing, landings in Pucusana grew steadily. In 1957, Pucusana's fishers landed 18,970 metric tons of anchoveta (Tilic 1963). By 1970, that number had grown to over 100,000 metric tons (Vasquez et al 1970). Only a minority of Pucusana's fishers engaged in the anchoveta fishery. However, it was significant for the development of the port in the decades that followed because it contributed to differentiation among fishers in Pucusana. A small number were able to purchase and operate larger boats that could go farther out and capture more fish, and the existence of processing and shipping infrastructure provided access to markets in Lima and beyond that could handle greater quantities of fish. The majority of Pucusana's fishers continued to use smaller boats to pursue a range of table fish. In 1970, they landed over 3,100 metric tons, which went to local and regional markets for sale as fresh or frozen fish (Vasquez et al. 1970). In the decades that followed, as anchoveta stocks went from boom to bust to a tepid recuperation, the food fishery became more and more economically important in Pucusana. However, the anchoveta fishery laid the groundwork for the increased production of table fish in the decades that followed because it gave a portion of fishers the ability to fish farther out and for greater quantities. At the same time, fishmeal operations were small enough—in comparison to ports such as Callao and Chancay—that Pucusana did not suffer the widescale ecological devastation that occurred in those ports' waters, thus maintaining relatively intact nearshore fisheries.

As happened in many Peruvian ports, during the 1970s and 1980s, anchoveta virtually disappeared off Pucusana's coast. The same happened in Chancay, just north of Ancón, which boomed during the 1950s and 1960s and then crashed in the 1970s when fishers could not find viable schools to exploit. These shortages were a result of overexploitation during the 1960s combined with the 1972–73 El Niño. Peru's fisheries have always been subject to significant changes as a result of the upwelling cycles that shape the temperature of the eastern Pacific and the availability or scarcity of different fish species. This variation wreaked havoc on Peru's industrial fish production, resulting in successive boom-bust cycles. IMARPE surveys reported that there were no landings of anchoveta in Pucusana during the high seasons from 1981 to 1991 (Ñiquen and Bouchon 1995). However, there was an uptick in landings of sardines, which had become more plentiful as anchoveta declined. During the early 1980s, the Peruvian government encouraged fishers to pursue sardines as a substitute for anchoveta. However, the former was quickly overexploited, and the numbers landed never approached those of anchoveta during the boom years. Indeed, in Pucusana, sardine landings were a fraction of what anchoveta captures had been. When anchoveta stocks rebounded in the early 1990s, landings in Pucusana went up again and in 1993, briefly returned to their pre-1973 levels. However, this was only a momentary blip. By 1999, IMARPE reports showed that anchoveta landings were down to 5,800 metric tons, and since 2003, Pucusana's fishers have reported no landings of the fish.

However, during this period, landings of food fish increased, growing to over 8,000 metric tons by 2003. José Antonio pointed out that while the El Niños in 1972-73 and 1981-82 negatively impacted the fishmeal trade, they pushed artisanal fishers to find new opportunities. During El Niño years, warmer waters generally depress near-coast fisheries, which depend on a range of fish species that prefer the normally cold waters of Peru's coast. When coastal fishing declined in the early 1970s and 1980s, José Antonio argued that artisanal fishers—an increasing number of whom had better boats and improved technology that had spread with the fishmeal trade—began searching farther and farther from shore for fisheries to exploit. "El Niño promoted the diversification of fishing in the high seas," he noted, adding that "fishers learned that they could fish farther out and that there were resources they could capture . . . [for a] better price." For example, José Antonio noted that prior to these years *perico*

(*Coryphaena hippurus*, dolphinfish or mahi-mahi), a relatively large pelagic fish, did not garner a very high price in domestic markets, but in the past decade, fishers have received good prices for it because there is export demand for it. Given that Pucusana is about seventy kilometers from central Lima, fishers are able to access the country's most important domestic and export markets for their fish at a time when global demand for frozen table fish has increased. They do this by selling their fish to buyers, who then truck the fish to Lima to sell in large quantities.[3]

The same has been true for Ancón. A small city located approximately forty-five kilometers north of Lima, people have been fishing in Ancón for millennia, and the area continues to support a vibrant fishery. During the mid-twentieth century, Ancón became the preferred beach resort for Lima's rich as the beaches around the city became more and more polluted and frequented by growing numbers of working-class Limeños. The bay in Ancón is now ringed by apartment high-rises in the midst of which is a small dock and wharf with seafood restaurants.

For much of the area's history, there have been fewer fishers in Ancón than in Pucusana or Chorrillos. According to an IMARPE survey that was done in 1996, Ancón had 208 fishers and 92 boats, Chorrillos had 285 fishers and 125 boats, and Pucusana had 325 fishers and 114 boats (Escudero Herrera 1997, 12). Similarly, landings were lower in Ancón than in Pucusana or Chorrillos. This changed in the early 2000s, when fishers in Ancón began to slowly surpass those in Chorrillos. At present, Anconeros outnumber fishers in Chorrillos and produce about five times more fish in an average year than Chorrillanos. This is a remarkable trend and one that emanates from a variety of factors. First, fishers in Ancón did not participate in the anchoveta economy so the local fishery was not distorted by the ecological destruction and socioeconomic differentiation that accompanied industrial fishing in other ports, such as Callao or Chancay. Ancón's status as a tourist enclave also saved the coast and bay from industrial development and helped to keep the littoral zone relatively intact, which meant that the port continued to support a vibrant nearshore fishery as other local ports, such as Chorrillos, declined. This provided the economic basis for the expansion of the fishery to include high seas fishing, which was driven not only by fishers' post-El Niño discoveries of new species that could be fished farther from the coast but also by growing export demand for such fish.

Mario, one of the former presidents of the artisanal fishers' association of Ancón, outlined the makeup of the fishery for us in one of the interviews we conducted with him. "There are three types of fishing," he said, "*pesca de altura* [high seas fishing], *pesca de ribera* [nearshore fishing], and *pesca de buceo* [diving]." Pesca de altura, which in Ancón is done with boats in the six to seven ton range, involves fishing in what Mario referred to as *aguas continentales* (continental waters) close to or outside the 200-nautical-mile limit that divides Peru's exclusive economic zone from international waters for large species such as *atún* (*Thunnus albaceres*, yellowfin tuna) or *pez espada* (*Xiphias gladius*, swordfish). Pesca de ribera involves fishing within five or so nautical miles from shore with small boats for *pescado blanco* (fish with white flesh), such as the prized lenguado or *corvina* (*Cilus gilberti*, corvina drum). Finally, pesca de buceo comprises diving in rocky areas along the coastline primarily for shellfish. In order to move growing quantities of fish that could not be absorbed by the limited local market, Ancón's fishers' association developed strong relationships with buyers who could link artisanal fishers with fish markets and processing facilities in Lima. Mario estimated that only 20 percent of what artisanal fishers caught in Ancón was eaten locally by tourists and residents; the remaining 80 percent was sold to intermediaries who then trucked the product to Lima for sale in the big fish markets.

In contrast to Pucusana and Ancón (and certainly Callao as well), fishing in Chorrillos has remained primarily small-scale and focused on coastal fishers. During our research, there were only a few larger boats that fished the high seas. These boats had been built over the course of several years on the beach in Chorrillos as the fishers who owned them gathered money from work and small loans from other fishers and vendors. Nearshore fishers repeatedly told us that there were not more big boats in Chorrillos because during the winter, the waters in Chorrillos were too rough and windy and would damage larger boats. However, artisanal fishers in several ports south of Lima, working out of unprotected bays with heavy winds, have developed high seas fisheries. More than differences in physical geography, the specific history of development and investment (or its lack) better explains why Chorrillos now lags behind other ports in the region in terms of the amount of fish that is landed. With direct access to a large urban population in Lima—different fish markets, a bevy of nearby seafood restaurants, and individual buyers from surrounding neighborhoods—fishers in Chorrillos developed few collective relationships with buyers interested in larger quantities of fish for markets outside the immediate locality. Fishing remained predominantly coastal and individualized. Most fishers in Chorrillos have arrangements with local restaurants and sell directly to them on a one-on-one basis. While such arrangements limit the amount of fish that individuals can land and sell at any one time, they ensure a steady stream of revenue for individual fishers. Those who do not have such arrangements set up tables and sell their fish on the wharf to tourists. Moreover, because of the location of the wharf, Chorrillos is not a good place for transporting fish in any quantity to regional markets. The wharf sits on a narrow strip of beach at the base of the cliffs of the Costa Verde. As development along this part of the coast has increased and more cars have used the expressway that runs between the cliffs and the wharf, traffic congestion has become increasingly worse. Furthermore, the parking lot in Chorrillos is quite small and dominated by tourists and food kiosks, making it difficult to increase the truck traffic that would be necessary to land and transport increased quantities of fish.

In Ancón and Pucusana, fishers did not have the same direct access to large urban markets, which led to the development of strong buying cooperatives, transportation links to urban markets, and investment in high seas fishing with greater potential for return. Recently, growing domestic and global demand for food fish has meant that fisheries in these ports have become linked to new markets, contributing not only to a boom-bust dynamic in some of these fisheries but also the production of disparities among artisanal ports in Peru's central coast. Data from an IMARPE survey published in 1997 provides an interesting snapshot of these three ports and the ways in which the differences among them were evolving at a time when Peruvian fisheries were on the rebound (Escudero Herrera 1997). Pucusana was the only port of the three where a portion (about 10 percent) of the boats operating were larger purse seiners, eight of which had motors of fifty horsepower or greater, suggesting the ongoing presence of bigger vessels equipped to catch large quantities of fish at long distances from the coast. However, there was a full range of boats in Pucusana, from purse seiners to small coastal boats, with roughly even numbers of boats in each category, indicating the degree to which the fishery had diversified so that fishers were exploiting everything from near-coast to high seas fisheries. In contrast, the range and size of the boats in Ancón and Chorrillos were smaller. In Ancón, the majority (58 percent) of the boats were chalanas of six to eight meters in length—good all-around boats that could land moderate quantities of fish from coastal waters to higher seas. However, in Chorrillos there were more *zapatos* (42 percent) than any other type of boat. Zapatos are small, flat-bottomed boats that are used to fish very close to shore for species such as *pejerrey* (*Odontesthes regia*, Pacific silversides) and usually have less than a ton of hold capacity. In Chorrillos, there were no boats over ten meters in length. Over the past twenty years, these differences have continued to evolve as fishers in Pucusana and Ancón have landed more and more fish while the fishery in Chorrillos has declined as nearshore fisheries have become more and more compromised.

Ancón

In Chorrillos, older fishers have encouraged their children to not go into fishing because it is an increasingly difficult way of making a good living. In contrast, Mario proudly told us that in Ancón there were young fishing families who were able to slowly buy their own boats and make a living from fishing because the quality of the fishery was still very good. However, the announcement in 2007 that the federal government was moving forward with approval for the construction of an industrial megaport in Ancón threatened the prosperity of the city's expanding fishery. There are no major ports between Callao and Chimbote, and the government has been keen to add several in this portion of the coastline as a means of expanding import-export hubs.[4] The proposal for the project recommended the construction of a 700-meter access pier with a 620-meter loading dock at the end, creating a large "T" in the southern half of Ancón's bay. The result would have been a new facility where four large container ships could have been unloaded simultaneously and where an estimated two thousand truckloads of cargo would have circulated daily. In order to service container ships, the proposal also recommended that the bay be dredged.

In 2008, the government awarded the concession for the megaport's construction to Santa Sofía Puertos SA (SSP), a Peruvian company that specializes in port investment and construction and that is part of the larger Peruvian-based Grupo Romero, which owns a number of finance, agribusiness, and infrastructure companies. Upon receiving the concession, SSP representatives stated that they would begin at once with an ecological impact assessment to ensure the project would not cause any undue environmental harm. However, before undertaking that assessment, SSP began a program of community engagement aimed at winning over the local population: free health clinics, youth soccer tournaments, job training, a beach cleanup day, and computer classes for local residents. In conjunction with these efforts, SSP undertook a public information campaign to "educate" local residents on four key points about the proposed port project: It would create one thousand local jobs, it would be located two

Figure 6   Artisanal fishers in the Bay of Ancón. Photo by Maximilian Viatori.

thousand meters away from the main tourist beach, the company would invest over one million soles in "social responsibility" projects, and the megaport would not "contaminate the beaches" nor would it affect "nautical sports."[5]

Such concern for Ancón's beaches stemmed from the area's history as a resort for Lima's wealthy families. During the nineteenth and twentieth centuries, Ancón was one of the favored getaways for the city's elite, who built summer homes and later high-rise apartment buildings facing the ocean. Although the wealthiest Limeños now favor beaches south of the city, tourism remains a significant source of revenue for Ancón's economy. The beachfront is lined with condominium and apartment buildings that cater to Lima's upper-middle classes. Ancón also occupies a significant space within national historical geographies. It is the site of a famed necropolis, where archaeological excavations in the nineteenth century uncovered a number of mummies, some of them four thousand years old, whose bodies, clothing, and feather ornaments were exceptionally well preserved by the dry climate.

SSP's public outreach focused on assuring Anconeros that the port project would not affect the pristine quality of their beaches and opportunities for marine recreation. However, this approach overlooked the significance of the bay for artisanal fishing. Artisanal fishers have coexisted with the condo owners and tourists that show up in Ancón for the long Peruvian summers. The existing fishing dock in Ancón is quite small and does not take up much of the waterfront. Furthermore, the artisanal fishing dock is located north of the main tourist beaches and is a good bit farther north of the private yacht club. The generally positive relationship between fishers and property owners grew stronger when both saw the megaport proposal as a threat to their livelihoods and property values. Once the concession was announced, the Asociación de Pescadores Artesanales de Ancón (Association of Artisanal Fishers of Ancón) and the Asociación de Propietarios de Ancón (Association of Property Owners of Ancón) initiated concerted efforts to block the construction of new port facilities. On April 4, 2009, fishers and condo owners staged a nautical caravan of artisanal fishing boats, yachts, and jet skis that paraded together around the harbor for two hours in a show of solidarity against SSP's project.

In this and subsequent outings, artisanal fishers highlighted what they saw as the ecologically and historically unique qualities of Ancón, arguing that construction would damage marine resources in the bay and negatively affect the supply of fish to the capital (La República 2009). In concert with these arguments, property owners underscored the ecological impacts of the proposed project, asserting that the extensive construction and dredging required for building the port would scare away birds, disrupt marine mammals, and damage the scenic qualities of the bay that drew tourists to the area. Condo owners also questioned why the megaport project was not slated for any of the ports south of Lima, which had better road access and infrastructure but were the sites of new beach house communities for Lima's wealthiest and most influential residents. By allying themselves with artisanal fishers, property owners were able to adopt an interesting rhetorical class politics. Ancón's property owners did not make the explicit case that they were protesting to defend the value of their condos and summer homes, which certainly would have been impacted by the increased traffic and noise of an industrial port. Rather, they argued that they were fighting to defend the ecology of the bay and the fishers' rights to use it against the desires of elite Limeños.

On November 10, 2010, the loosely organized Colectivo por la Defensa de la Bahía de Ancón (Collective for the Defense of the Bay of Ancón), comprised of fishers and condo owners, protested at and disrupted a public hearing on the port project that was held by SSP and the Ministerio de Transportes y Comunicaciones (Ministry of Transport and Communications). The protestors argued that the majority of the inhabitants of Ancón opposed the construction of the port because it would contaminate the bay. Additionally, the property owners' association had the economic and social capital to hire an outside consultant, Geoconsult SA, to analyze the initial findings of SSP's environmental impact study for the proposed port. The consultant argued that the report was flawed for two reasons: It did not consider an alternative location for the port nor did it specify where exactly the port was to be built.[6]

The case against the port's construction also gained traction at the national level. On a visit to Ancón, President of the Congress Daniel Abugattás Majluf claimed that the port project was an attempt by Chilean shareholders in the Grupo Romero to gain control of a Peruvian port that could compete with Callao. Abugattás Majluf's statements referenced an ongoing controversy that Grupo Romero had engaged in joint ventures with Chilean investors and Chile's state oil company to fund projects in both countries. For example, Inversiones Centenario of Grupo Romero teamed up with the Chilean Corporación Paz de Chile to create Paz Centenario, a Peruvian-based apartment construction company. During the 1990s, Dionisio Romero and the Chilean investor Ricardo Claros jointly created the company Trabajos Marítimos SA, a port administering company that controlled concessions in Paita, Salvaverry, and Callao (La República 2004). Grupo Romero is also part of the consortium that holds the concession to the Chilean port of Arica, which once belonged to Peru but was lost after the War of the Pacific. Opposition to the port project in Ancón became a means for the Humala government symbolically to oppose a project approved by its predecessor and political opponent and to flex its nationalist credentials. During his successful presidential campaign, García portrayed Humala, a former army coronel and founder of the Partido Nacionalista Peruano (PNP, Peruvian Nationalist Party), as a far left radical who would introduce Hugo Chávez-style reforms to Peru and ruin its standing among international investors. When Humala won the presidency five years later, he accused the García government of widespread corruption and favoring multinational corporations over national interests. When he visited Ancón in February 2011, he told residents that their city was "an historic site" and because of this, it would be "counterproductive for a port to be built there with Chilean capital" (La República 2011a). What was celebrated as a Peruvian-based company when the García government awarded the port contract in 2008, became a foreign investor trying to claim historic Peruvian territory in Humala's 2011 speech.

Ultimately, the government blocked the megaport project. On July 26, 2011, the national Congress passed Law 29767, which declared the Bay of Ancón part of Peru's intangible national heritage and proclaimed the government's responsibility to protect the bay and to promote sustainable tourism and artisanal fishing in the name of national interest. The law also established the Parque Ecológico Nacional Antonio Raimondi (Antonio Raimondi National Ecological Park), which enclosed part of the bay and the surrounding hillsides in a protected ecological zone. Finally, the law prohibited "the installation, construction and operation of port, commercial, depositing, transportation, transferring infrastructure and other related activities that affect the natural conditions and patrimony of the protected natural area created by the present Law." This protection did not, the law specifies, apply to the artisanal fishing dock, including its expansion or modernization, as long as the artisanal character of it was preserved.

Two years after Anconeros defeated the megaport proposal, government officials announced that a new port facility and transportation complex would be constructed in Chancay, a small city north of Ancón. The privately owned Peruvian-based company Terminales Portuarios Chancay (TPCh) promised to build ten fully equipped docks in Chancay and a "logistical activity zone" to ease stress on existing port infrastructure in Callao (Gestión 2014c). These facilities were to be dedicated to transporting mineral goods, especially zinc, copper, and lead from Andean mines east of Chancay. TPCh promised that it would create a hub for economic development in the region while protecting "the environment and the intangible cultural heritage of the zone" (La República 2014a). Chancay, like Ancón, is the site of important archaeological discoveries about the Chancay culture, which occupied the valleys north of Lima roughly one thousand years ago. Additionally, Chancay has long supported an economically productive fishery. Chancay is the fifth largest producer of fishmeal in Peru, generating approximately 10 percent of the fishmeal exported by the country each year. There are three artisanal fishers' associations in Chancay. In an average year, these artisanal fishers produce approximately two thousand metric tons of fish for direct human consumption—a significant amount but about half of what the fishers in Ancón produce. Over the past two decades, artisanal fishers have complained that pollution from the fishmeal processing plants has rendered coastal waters unproductive. Nearshore fishers rightly saw the proposed port complex as yet another threat to their livelihoods and staged public protests against the megaport, burning tires and blocking the Pan-American Highway (La República 2013). The protestors accused the port project of being corrupt, arguing that the founder of TPCh was also the owner of a fish processing company located on the site where the port was to be built. The protests, which were dispersed by riot police, garnered little support or attention outside of

Chancay—shortly afterward the government announced that the project had been approved for construction, although at the time of writing, the project has been delayed by financing problems.

The rejection of the Ancón port project and the development of a similar proposal in Chancay underscore the importance of politics for making sense of how capital moves from one space to another as well as how and when it is blocked. In their ethnographic work on roads in Peru, Penny Harvey and Hannah Knox (2012, 523, 525) argue that infrastructure projects "can offer a vital means of tracing the co-emergence of political and material histories" because infrastructures do not just rely on technical knowledge but also on "social and political will which is able to generate and foster the belief that these technologies have a capacity to transform the spaces through which they will pass." Such beliefs are not necessarily a priori but emerge through the disruptions that infrastructure projects create in existing social relationships and their promise for better connectivity, improved access to markets, and economic prosperity (Harvey and Knox 2012, 524–25). However, for fishers in Ancón, the proposed megaport failed to create "powerful affects of social promise" (Harvey and Knox 2012, 525) because it was clear that the infrastructure project would negatively affect them, and for condo owners, the proposed port would have ruined their tourist enclave. In this instance, the interests of artisanal fishers and property owners aligned and provided enough local resistance to thwart an infrastructure project by arguing that the promises would not outweigh the disadvantages. Although fishers have opposed the port expansion in Chancay, they have not had the same kind of elite support that fishers in Ancón were able to draw upon because of Chancay's different history as a fishmeal port—one that was too far outside Lima to serve as an easy resort getaway. Furthermore, fishmeal processing polluted nearshore waters in Chancay, making it difficult for fishers there to oppose port construction on the grounds that it would ruin a pristine bay. While such differences are the result of historical political ecologies and the uneven geographies they have produced, government officials and fishers often talk about them as the outcomes of differences in local, individual responsibility.

Place Value

In one of our interviews with a Produce extension officer who worked with artisanal fishers in Lima Province, he told us matter-of-factly that the fishers' association in Chorrillos was "more suspicious of the state [and] less willing to cooperate" in government initiatives that would benefit them. In contrast, he argued that the fishers' association in Pucusana was "more open [and] willing to collaborate" with state officials. Similarly, one of the Coast Guard officers stationed in Chorrillos during part of our research once explained to us why he thought Ancón was in a better state than Chorrillos. In Ancón, he claimed, there were abundant fish and a number of boats that regularly made profitable ventures to the high seas to catch larger fish because the fishers were well organized and closely monitored each other, unlike other ports. "The Anconero looks after his zone," he told us. "There is more order there; it is cleaner." In contrast, he noted that Chancay had not fared as well because "it's another one of these small ports where there is lots of delinquency and they won't leave you alone."

In a similar vein, Mario once told us, "We have the space, we have the product, we have the geography [in Ancón]." Equally important, he claimed, was that artisanal fishers in Ancón were "modernizing" themselves and learning that the quality of product is more important than quantity if they wanted to get a good price and have a sustainable fishery. As part of this modernization, Ancón's artisanal fishers' association proposed to interested financiers and government officials a new unloading and processing complex with the services that fishers claim they need to advance economically and to get more value from their product by processing it and selling it as dried or canned fish. Mario explained that it would be a large facility, ten or fifteen times larger than the current small dock, which they planned to use for tourism when the second facility was built. Mario argued that fishers in Ancón warranted such investment because "we are entrepreneurs, because in spite of everything we create a large amount of employment, we generate employment, and we pay our taxes." To make his point, Mario compared Ancón to Callao, arguing that the latter "is a place that lamentably, even though it has had its fishing, it has been pillaged, and its people . . . [are] those sorts who live bad lives. They don't know how to value [things]."

Mario asserted that such differences were issues of local mindsets and divergent perspectives on how the world should work. Drawing on popularly circulating discourses of individual responsibility and entrepreneurialism, he noted:

> There are people who are poor because economically they are poor. But there are people who are poor because they want to be poor . . . It's like saying, I am poor but I want to escape from my poverty, right? But there are people who are poor and say, "Alright, I am poor, and the state will take care of me." [They are] living off charity. Then there are many [other] people . . . who are entrepreneurs, people

who have had goals, have had dreams. People without dreams don't have goals. But, there are people who are used [to this] and say, "I'm poor," and that's it.

As Mario made clear, this condition of stasis was a product, in some places, of too much *asistencialismo* (assistentialism), the government's or community's willingness to provide support for people who had not earned it. The fishers' association in Ancón (unlike Chorrillos) did not provide insurance, social security, food for holidays, or other benefits to its members and their families. Mario claimed that this was because such things encouraged people to not take care of themselves and also because the number of fishers in Ancón was too great to do so. Moreover, Mario asserted that the association encouraged fishers to take care of the environment and fish stocks. Fishers in Ancón, he told us, had learned to focus on catching fewer fish and on fishing not for quantity but quality. This meant respecting minimum limits, something that he asserted did not happen in other artisanal fishing ports. Furthermore, he told us that he did not receive a salary for his work as the association leader; he had done it voluntarily because he had a responsibility to the place and to the fishers. Unlike the state and its beneficiaries, "we don't get paid," he said. "We generate."

Mario's statements underscore the importance of local comparisons for informing how individual fishers assert the value of place and fishers' productive practices. In such discourses, Ancón emerges as a success because the fishers there have an entrepreneurial culture and they do not rely on the state for their wellbeing. Such discourses reproduce geographic differences while simultaneously masking the structural inequalities that generate such differences. Callao becomes decrepit not because of its place within unequal coastal geographies but because of a lack of entrepreneurial culture and an overreliance on state beneficence.

Such a dynamic was evident in two interviews we conducted with Brenda and Raúl, who had created a buying cooperative that linked artisanal fishers in northern Peru with wealthy consumers in Lima. The project organized ten fishers in a small port in Tumbes Region—which borders Ecuador on its northern side and Piura Region on its southern—into a cooperative that sold high-quality fish to expensive restaurants in Lima. Tumbes and Piura boast the greatest concentration of artisanal fishers in the country, with an estimated sixteen thousand between the two regions. Paita, the capital of Paita Province, is the rough northern limit of Peru's anchoveta fishery because it is the geographical point at which the Humboldt Current moves away from the coast, allowing warm tropical waters to move in toward shore. This area of Peru's northern coastline has been spared the ill effects of wide-scale anchoveta harvesting and fishmeal production. Since a free trade deal was signed between Peru and the EU in 2012, exports of frozen fish from Piura to Europe have increased steadily. Despite this growth, fishers in Tumbes remain some of the lowest paid artisanal producers in the country.

Brenda and Raúl saw their cooperative as a step toward rectifying this situation by teaching a small group of artisanal fishers how to catch and carefully package fish to meet the high expectations of chefs at expensive restaurants in Lima. Brenda pointed out that the initial economic benefit for the fishers was small—they only got a few soles above local market price for the fish. But, the cooperative gave fishers access to a more stable market for their goods. In one of our first interviews, we asked the two cooperative founders why they had not chosen a location closer to Lima since one of their professed objectives was to improve the sustainability of artisanal fishing in Peru and flying fish hundreds of miles from Tumbes to Lima seemed to run counter to that goal. Brenda responded that the problem with the central coast was the seasonality; during the winter, there was generally only pejerrey. When we asked about Chorrillos as an option, she said that in "Chorrillos there are no fish, just what they sell at the terminal and nothing more" and that while Ancón had enough volume, there was again not enough diversity. In contrast, the tropical waters of northern Peru sustained a greater range of different fish species that were available year-round and new to most Limeños.

It was clear from our conversations that this was not just about volume and diversity of fish but about finding a place that also was far from Lima. An important part of the cooperative's success was Brenda and Raúl's ability to sell chefs in Lima on the place from which the fish were coming. Tumbes offered a location that was far from the industrial and urban contamination of Lima's central coast and that produced fish species that were less familiar to diners in the capital city. The closest port that the duo considered was Pisco, which is a six-hour drive south of Lima. However, Brenda and Raúl claimed that they were drawn to Tumbes because it was the only area in Peru that still had an "affluence of fish" and therefore could provide consumers in Lima with fish that were "exotic."

The emphasis of the project, as Raúl pointed out, was ensuring that chefs and fish buyers for high-end restaurants received the very best quality of the fish. An important aspect of that was place. Raul told us, "When we make the sale, we say to them . . . that it is from this boat and this is obviously the formal owner. It leaves from this site, and from when it leaves to when it arrives, no one breaks the cold seal and no one puts a hand in it, no one sticks a hand in [the cooler] until they receive it. It is as though one were buying it from the same dock." One of the services that Brenda and Raúl provided buyers was information about when their fish was caught and by which boat in the cooperative. As Raul commented, they were not dealing with "any restaurant or any person"—their buyers were picky and had "resources" to choose to buy fish from whomever they liked. In addition to emphasizing place, Brenda and Raúl trained artisanal fishers in the cooperative in how to catch and handle fish to ensure that it was not only fresh but also looked good when it got to the buyers.[7]

Brenda and Raúl saw the buying cooperative as a step toward instituting a region- or country-wide certification project that would be able to "generate protocols of how [the cooperative] should function" in regard to the production of "sustainable," "local" fish—an objective which they considered replicating in other fishing communities in southern Peru through training workshops aimed at certifying artisanal fishers in handling and packing table fish. As Brenda told us, "We are looking into other systems to certify not only why we have arrived at [a certain dock to buy fish or] what boat brought [the fish], but we are thinking about going further. What would it mean to go further? To certify what [kind of] nets, what type of apparatus is used to extract each product." The purpose of doing so, she noted, was to sell elite buyers on the importance of sustainable fisheries. Brenda and Raúl stressed that they were doing their work as inter- mediaries without the expectation of personal gain but as a way to make an "ideological shift" in Peru toward valuing fish that is fresh, which would benefit artisanal fishers who understood the importance of fishing for quality and not quantity. However, emphasizing the importance of individual responsibility has the potential to, on the one hand, reify local differences as the products of com- munity comportment, while on the other hand, mask the different opportunities that fishers in different ports have as a result of their places within structurally unequal geographies. There is only so much demand for high-quality seafood, and most of Peru's artisanal fishers are not able to exploit Lima's high-end fish market because what they fish is considered too common.

Ultimately, the challenges of transporting fresh-caught fish from Tumbes to Lima led Brenda and Raúl to abandon their project. While both worked for Produce at the time, they complained about the absence of the state in artisanal fishing, especially the lack of government-funded infrastructure, not only to connect fishers to markets but also to ensure the proper processing of fish when they were landed. Raúl lamented that the artisanal fishing ports in the north did not have the proper facilities for unloading, processing, and selling fish in a safe and sanitary manner—many did not have running potable water or adequate wastewater disposal. What transportation infrastructure existed was for the bulk export of raw materials, not the transportation of small quantities of high-value products, such as table fish. The only solution they had found to quickly transport fresh fish from Tumbes to Lima was using commercial passenger flights to literally deliver the fish by hand twice a week. In the end, this was more effort than they could invest in the project. When we interviewed Brenda again in 2017, she had moved on to a new project with several former Produce employees. The latest venture was similar in that it was essentially a buying cooperative but this new venture was aimed at linking artisanal fishers with larger domestic and international buyers who had the capital and infrastructure to transport and sell "sustainably caught" table fish in more profitable quantities by supplying them to chain grocery stores in Peru and the United States.

Brenda and Raúl's efforts to create sustainable fish buying cooperatives demonstrate the importance of place for adding value to the fish that wealthy consumers buy. Similar certification programs, which provide conscientious consumers with information about where and when and how their fish was caught, have emerged all over the world and are now considered an important tool for assuring the sustainable sourcing of seafood. As Timothy Bresnihan (2016, 72, 86) argues in his analysis of Irish fisheries, such marketing schemes to "empower" fishers by linking them with "responsible" consumers are fundamentally neoliberal in that they emphasize "the measurement and valorization of the environmental performance of the fishermen, something that is always open to improvement" and that is not bound to the "natural" limits of fish stocks.[8] He rightly argues that such schemas "encourage competition between fishermen in terms of their performance" while ignoring the fact that not all producers are able to participate equally because many lack the economic and cultural capital to engage in certification schemes or market themselves and their products to consumers (Bresnihan 2016, 72). As Brenda and Raúl's buying cooperative demonstrates, fishers' locations within existing uneven geographies also contribute to inequalities in who can participate effectively in sustainable seafood programs, which emphasize the importance of where fish is being caught. While this project represented an attempt to create alternative market links between small-scale producers and distant consumers, it did so by reproducing extant differences in Peru's coastal geography and attributing them to differences in the responsibility of particular fishers.

Conclusion

The geographical differentiation of space is what makes it possible for capitalism to work. In the case of coastal Peru, flexible capital is able to move from one port to another to find the ideal geographic and economic conditions as well as a lack of social or political opposition. And yet, this reality is pasted over by dominant discourses of coastal space in Peru that tend to emphasize local differences as the unique products of the peculiarities of local physical geography or mindsets. Key aspects of these discourses are also produced in local movements to defend artisanal fishing rights, where fishers and association leaders often talk about local differences as the results of differing levels of entrepreneurialism and sustainability, setting up contrasts between ports that have done well and those that have not. Such mappings are significant not only because they offer important commentaries on the geographic disparities produced by ongoing uneven development but also because they provide insight into how discourses of market, opportunity, and self-responsibility reproduce and justify such disparities. In their defense of the Bay of Ancón, fishers and condo owners asserted their right to control what happened to Ancón and how the coast and bay were used and to what ends. Similarly, Brenda and Raúl's buying cooperative attempted to provide artisanal fishers with access to new markets in an effort to help sustain their livelihoods as small producers of seafood. However, these efforts largely reinforced dominant assumptions about development and neoliberalized ideologies of governance and responsibility. While local place-based activism in ports such as Ancón has succeeded in fighting the threats of enclosures in particular places, a lack of regional coordinating has meant that capital has simply moved to other places where it is easier to enact the displacements necessary for new development.

When packaged in the language of local responsibility, geographical disparities appear as the result of fishers in some areas outcompeting their counterparts in other ports because they have been more conscientious and more entrepreneurial in finding new markets, thus moving beyond the limitations of existing markets and ecological constraints. This appraisal of coastal geographies subtly reinforces the notion that extending and expanding markets solves ecological issues and that those who are not responsible eventually go out of business and are forced to move on to other kinds of work. This emphasis on responsibility obscures the reality that geographic inequalities result from the uneven development produced by particular assemblages of nature, capital, and politics. As Brenda and Raúl's buying cooperative demonstrates, such inequalities represent opportunities for individuals with social and economic capital to exploit them. Yet, this is an option not available to many impoverished artisanal fishers who do not have resources to make such links or who live in an area that is not marketable as ecologically pristine and thus not valued as a "place" by consumers. Discourses of individualized responsibility attribute more agency to artisanal fishers than they actually have in the shaping of regional disparities and, in the process, function to draw attention away from the structural role that capitalist ecologies play in producing and reinforcing such disparities. While such discourses appear at first glance to be in support of local fishing communities and their autonomy, in point of fact they correspond quite closely with discourses of neoliberalized self-governance, which have continued to undermine the autonomy of impoverished fishers and fish vendors.

CHAPTER 4

Governance, Responsibility,
and Class on the Wharf

Peruvian officials have framed artisanal fishers' and vendors' access to ocean resources and coastal infrastructure as privileges that should be granted only to individuals who adhere to the authorized parameters of what it means to be a responsible entrepreneur. Thus far, attempts to restrict access to individuals who can demonstrate that they comply with government-sanctioned practices for responsible production have been only partially successful. Nonetheless, responsibility has become an important means by which artisanal fishers and vendors in Chorrillos and in other ports along Lima's coast understand, explain, and critique their situations. Fishers and vendors in Chorrillos often invoke individual responsibility, which dovetails with traditional ideals of work and morality, to explain why certain people do better than others or why their dock is in a state of disrepair. In this chapter, we argue that artisanal fishers' and government officials' discussions of inequality and invocations of responsibility represent important focal points for examining daily struggles over how to account for inequality.

Recently, Produce has undertaken considerable efforts to "formalize" artisanal fishers by conducting a national census of them, initiating a widespread campaign to ensure that all artisanal fishers are licensed and reorganized into local associations. James Scott (1998, 4, 183) describes such efforts as central to modern statecraft—"schemes to improve the human condition" that are primarily attempts to make once-marginal populations more "visible" to state bureaucracies, thus making it easier to control and tax them. As one of Produce's extension officers told us, the goal of programs to document and license artisanal fishers has been to "formalize them first" and then "regulate them" through an expanded system of financial monitoring and taxation.

This governance project has relied upon and in turn advanced a neoliberalized image of "good" artisanal fishers as responsible, self-reliant entrepreneurs whose right to fish and utilize Peru's marine resources is a reward for demonstrating that they can comport themselves according to "best practices." The local fishers' association in Chorrillos has encountered the same logic in its struggle to maintain the right to administer the area's small wharf. As tourism-related development has made the wharf look more and more out of place in Lima's Costa Verde, municipal governments have pressured fishers to make the wharf's space more attractive to local tourism and more similar to its surroundings. This pressure has taken the form of a range of directives—from making improvements to the dock's infrastructure to instituting a more regular sanitation schedule for the fish market—all of which have emphasized the need of the wharf's fishers and vendors to take more active roles in regulating themselves.

Such efforts to reconstitute fishers' rights as rewards for proper comportment have not been entirely successful. Many officials lack sufficient resources to enforce licensing or sanitation schedules. Leaders and members of the fishers' association have wanted to maintain government recognition of their control of the dock and the nearshore fishery and have sought to do so by working through established bureaucratic parameters. However, they simultaneously have questioned the government's moral authority to govern them, arguing that the state has abandoned them and that local officials have been unable to provide them with the resources they need to comply with new regulations. At the outset of Produce's formalization efforts, many fishers continued to fish without licenses, forcing government officials to adjust their plans and make it easier for fishers to obtain licenses. Nonetheless, neoliberalized discourses of governance have had a profound effect on how both government officials and association leaders have established what the problems are with artisanal fishing and the wharf in Chorrillos and what can be done to solve them. In their seminal work on neoliberal governmentality, Peter Miller and Nikolas Rose (2008, 200) argue that governance is constantly failing, ushering in new problems and redefining how something is problematic for new technologies of governance to solve. Even failed governance has an impact on how daily lives are lived because it reorients subjectivities and frames what is possible and what is not (Miller and Rose 2008).

We argue that government projects to promote individual responsibility among artisanal fishers and vendors advance enclosure by reducing complex ecological and social relationships and class relations to a narrow range of individualized economic practices that are easily made visible to state regulators. In her analysis of Mexican fishing communities in Baja California Sur, Nicole D. Peterson (2014, 245) argues that neoliberalized fishing regulations are driven by the ideology that individuals are economically rational actors whose actions are motivated only by "selfishness and incentives." The result is that contemporary environmental management schemes define "environmental issues as economic problems" and in doing so negate other "motives or values" that inform people's behavior and marginalize alternative ecological approaches (Peterson 2014, 246). Similarly, Patrick Bresnihan (2016: 126, 142–45) argues in his analysis of Irish fisheries that processes of "enclosure and 'improvement'" rely upon separations of the cultural and ecological relationships that make the reproduction of a "more-than-human commons" possible from a narrowly defined band of relationships that comprise economic production (see also Federici 2004).

Dealing with such enclosures has become a central challenge for artisanal fishers and vendors in Chorrillos, whose daily work to reproduce a common is invisible to contemporary government efforts to make them demonstrate that they are responsible producers by submitting themselves to new licensing regimes and by following recently established "best practices" for caring for the wharf. Furthermore, we argue that neoliberalized discourses of individual responsibility disable class both as a framework for naming the structural dynamics that have contributed to fishers' and vendors' poverty and as a basis for fishers and vendors to advocate collectively for their autonomy. In her critique of neoliberalized governance, Wendy Brown (2015, 65) asserts that an emphasis on the individual "as the only relevant and wholly accountable actor" undercuts the vitality of collective forms of struggle, while imagining society as comprising "entrepreneurs competing with other entrepreneurs" exacerbates individual inequalities. Dictums of individual responsibility have not undercut the relationships that make up a more-than-human commons in Chorrillos but they have challenged them and contributed to tensions among fishers and vendors about the future of the wharf and their places in it.

We explore these challenges by first analyzing officials' interactions with the fishers' association and our interviews with government officials, which show the degree to which efforts to formalize artisanal fishing have been about class and have worked through historically rooted notions of the racial and social alterity of Lima's fishing populations. For example, an official once told us that the problem with the fishers in Chorrillos was the messy, disorganized nature of their lives and their supposed propensity for broken homes, drink, and irrationality. These beliefs, commonly expressed among the bureaucrats who interacted regularly with fishers and vendors in Chorrillos, masked the reality that fishers' situation was the result of the reconfiguration of Peru's ocean natures and Lima's coastal space to generate value for fishmeal entrepreneurs and the city's wealthier residents and real estate investors. In place of class, neoliberalized governance has emphasized the responsibility that individuals have to demonstrate their willingness to self-regulate for the good of local natural resources and the wharf. This emphasis on responsibility and self-governance has shifted the burden of retaining fishing rights and the dock back onto fishers and vendors, a process that exacerbated local differences.

In the second half of this chapter, we explore this dynamic by tracing discussions within the fishers' association and among fishers and vendors about what was wrong with the dock and who was responsible for it. In his famous work on the historical emergence of England's working classes, E. P. Thompson (1963, 11) contends that class is not a "thing" but rather "social and cultural formation[s]" that arise during particular historical periods. In this vein, Lesley Gill (2016, 7) argues in her study of popular struggle in northern Colombia that class, as a "fluid analytic category," is indispensable for understanding the "centrality of conflict to the formation of social relations." This is particularly critical, she asserts, in the present conjuncture because neoliberalized market politics have led to "recurrent" dispossessions of working people and deepening inequalities, which have spurred the reconfiguration of class by "creating new divisions and labor relations, and forcing people to assess what they can, and cannot, do with each other" (Gill 2016, 9).

In this and the following chapter, we demonstrate the importance of day-to-day discussions and conversations about the wharf and its future for understanding how people who have worked there have made and unmade class solidarities and, perhaps unintentionally, rationalized potential enclosures. Tania Murray Li (2014, 8–9) argues that dispossession often unfolds in the "mundane" interactions of capitalist relations, driven by competition and profit, which rework social relationships and erode the basis of impoverished people's lives in "piecemeal" ways that are often "unexpected and unplanned." Government projects to formalize and improve the wharf, combined with daily struggles to earn a living, created tension among fishers and vendors as they sought to articulate strategies for taking care of themselves and protecting their access to and control of the wharf. The growing importance of the tourism economy and government pressure to renovate the wharf led to discussions about which parts of the dock were failing and which needed to be refurbished. In these discussions, fishers identified the fish market and food kiosks as problem areas that perhaps should be replaced with private restaurants, thus laying the ideological groundwork for the potential displacement of vendors. Similarly, the government's restructuring of the local fishing union exacerbated divisions among fishers, tourist boat operators, and former members who had run afoul of the union, creating new challenges to the local association's right to administer the wharf. These instances reveal the importance of ongoing negotiations about work, responsibility, and the future for understanding how enclosure is contested, stalled, or slowly advanced.

Invisible Commoning

Throughout our research, government officials repeatedly characterized artisanal fishers as being concerned only with the present, with catching whatever they could today in order to get enough money to make it to tomorrow. This mischaracterization often led government officials to conclude that fishers were selfish producers who cared only about landing as many fish as they could and were thus incapable of organizing themselves or planning for their communities' best interests. This ideology of fishers as actors motivated only by their economic drive has extended recently to ecological issues, with some officials and industry advocates arguing that artisanal fishers were despoiling Peru's ocean commons without consideration for the ecological limits of given fisheries.

This misrepresentation of fishers is as widespread as it is wrong because it frames fishers' activities through a very narrow economic lens that ignores the myriad social, cultural, and ecological relationships and work that go into catching and selling fish on a sustainable basis (Acheson 1988; García-Quijano 2007; Orlove 2002). For example, Bresnihan (2016, 124–25) describes the social and ecological encounters that comprise an average day of fishing in the small Irish town where he conducted his research, which involved stopping to have tea with friends, borrowing tools from others, deciding when and where to fish based on recent conditions, gifting fish to friends or relatives, and so on. The persistence of fishing is possible because of "countless acts of gift giving, favors, and loans" that make up a system of daily exchange and community support (Bresnihan 2016, 131). This process of "commoning" extends beyond human relationships to engage nonhuman entities in the production of a "more-than-human commons" (Bresnihan 2016, 128).

These relationships are critical for understanding how fishers maintain and care for the ecological relationships upon which they depend. As James R. McGoodwin (2006, 183) points out in his discussion of fisheries policy, artisanal and nearshore fishers rely upon local ecologies for their livelihoods—unlike industrial fishing boats, they cannot simply pick up and move to another location hundreds of miles away when fishing conditions deteriorate, and thus, small-scale fishers have greater knowledge of the limits of "whole or entire marine ecosystems." Because nearshore fishers depend on fish being there in the future, Bresnihan (2016, 149) argues that they engage in practices of care to maintain ecologies by "respecting their limits." These limits, he notes, are always changing, which requires fishers to rework relationships, a process that not only demands significant social and ecological knowledge but also the collective support that a commons provides and which enables fishers to deal with and persist through uncertainty (Bresnihan 2016, 155).

The same is true of artisanal fishers in Chorrillos. On an average day, a fisher leaves his house—which he may share with his partner and children and perhaps extended family members—on the periphery of Chorrillos and walks or catches a bus to the wharf. At the wharf, he may stop and eat breakfast at one of the food kiosks run by his sister or cousin or friend, where he likely sits next to other fishers and jokes or talks about the weather conditions and recent catches. After eating, the fisher makes his way to the storage room where he keeps his nets, stopping to have several more conversations with friends before heading to his boat. When he goes out, he may be accompanied by his brother or his son or even a cousin, who helps to pull in the nets when it is time to check them and who gets a portion of the catch or a return favor for his work. Depending on the time of year, the fisher lays nets in different parts of the bay, avoiding known spawning grounds for different fish or moving farther out in the warm months when pollution is concentrated closer to shore. Once the catch is loaded—usually a crate or two of different kinds of fish—the fisher makes his way back to the dock, where the fish is stored in the freezer until it is ready to be sold, either to a restaurant owner or at the fishers' evening market.

Not only are fishers limited by the desire to preserve stocks for future catches but also by the relatively small market in Chorrillos, which cannot handle large quantities of fish. After storing the fish, the fisher might make his way to the shaded shipyard to join others who are mending their nets and complaining about lobos tearing holes in them or the lack of government subsidies for fishers. Tools may be borrowed or lent, plans may be made for fishing in the coming night, or money may be exchanged to help pay for some line, a baptism cake, or medicine for a sick child. When the time comes for the evening market, the fisher lays out his catch on a small table, hoping to sell all of it to passing tourists for the best possible price. He takes any leftover fish and puts it back into the cooler for the next day or takes it home for his family or as a gift to a relative or neighbor. These relationships do not exist outside of the economic activity of catching and selling fish; they make that activity possible while also helping to set limits on it.

The same is true for the vendors who work on the dock selling food and fish. At the beginning of a normal day, a vendor likely gets up and makes breakfast for her children before taking them to school or to a relative to watch them or, if school is out, with her on errands to local markets to buy the necessary goods for preparing the day's meals in a food kiosk. The food kiosks in Chorrillos are family affairs, as we discuss in greater detail below. Women work with their mothers, sisters, and cousins to prepare and sell food, often with the help of children, who spend their summer days on the dock working and playing with the kids of other fishers and vendors. A vendor may pass parts of her day shopping for supplies or talking to other vendors about rising food costs or where the best and cheapest fish can be procured. She may also exchange money with other vendors—small loans to help pay back debts, buy supplies, or get through a rough patch. Fishers, some of whom are relatives, may also bring fish to the kiosk to be prepared as ceviche, something that the vendor will do for a small price, much lower than what she would charge one of the tourists. After the evening market, many fishers often join their children and wives or other female relatives at the kiosk they run for an evening meal before closing shop and heading home together.

Webs of kinship and relatedness, both human and nonhuman, underpin and enable the functioning of the wharf's economy. While fishing appears to be a very individualistic endeavor, in reality its persistence as a livelihood is made possible by networks of cooperation and support. Artisanal fishing in Chorrillos is a family affair. Fishers learn to fish from their older male relatives, usually fathers or uncles, and often work with brothers and cousins to do the work of putting out nets, bringing fish in, repairing boats, and fixing nets. The same is true of the wharf's economy, where many of the vendors are sisters, mothers, daughters, and cousins of male members of the fishers' association. These relationships provide critical support networks in times of ecological or economic difficulty. Such relationships also extend to the water. Artisanal fishers rely on a diverse array of fish and shellfish species to maintain small but steady catches throughout the year, both to sell in the market and to feed themselves and their families. To do so, fishers rely on profound knowledge of individual species: when they spawn, when the juveniles are big enough to catch, and when they enter the bay or must be pursued farther from the coast. Fishers often talk about fish species and other sea creatures, especially lobos, as agents—as beings who chose to arrive or depart or who see and avoid their nets and thus thwart fishers' efforts to catch them. Despite the need to pursue these species, fishers also care for them by avoiding areas where certain species are known to spawn at particular times of year or by throwing back juvenile fish that are caught by their gillnets. Such relationships are remade constantly as fishers adapt to the eastern Pacific's fluctuations. As certain species become less abundant, fishers shift to target other species that may be more readily available.

The wharf is not just a space of economic production but a cultural and ecological space where relationships are created and reproduced. It is a place where religious festivals are celebrated among friends and workers and where funerals are observed when fishers die of old age or are taken by the sea. As one vendor remarked, "Here on the beach is my house. I leave all my problems in the sea . . . I will never leave this place." This sentiment was oft-repeated among fishers and vendors. In a similar vein, a fisher commented, "I live for this water; this water is my life." As these comments suggest, many fishers and vendors saw the wharf and the surrounding water not just as a place where they made a living but a place where they made their lives.

This is not to say that the wharf in Chorrillos represents a communal utopia or that it functions outside contemporary market pressures or governance demands. The relationships that comprise the web of commoning in Chorrillos are not all equal. They are riven by inequalities in gender, status, and occupation. These inequalities have been the subject of ongoing discussions among fishers and vendors about the wharf's future and how it should be run. Moreover, relationships of commoning in Chorrillos do not exist outside of market demands and the daily pressures they place on people. As manual workers in Lima's "informal" economy, fishers' and vendors' labor is economically and socially devalued within dominant hierarchies of what constitutes "good" and "formal" work. This—combined with rising costs of living, operating a boat, running a food kiosk, and paying rent in an increasingly expensive city—adds to the constant economic precarity that fishers and vendors face in their struggles to not only get by but also sustain what they consider a culturally dignified life. This precarity is further exacerbated by the fact that because of ecological shifts, the availability of different fish species and the prices that fishers and vendors can get for them fluctuate constantly. While commoning provides people with resources to weather these fluctuations, sometimes it is not enough. Some fishers and vendors are not able to make it, and boats are sold or abandoned, and jobs have to be found working construction, driving a moto-taxi, or doing domestic service in the city. As industrial overfishing and pollution have affected nearshore fishing, as market demands have placed greater stress on fishers and vendors to make a living, and as coastal development has brought the wharf's operations under greater scrutiny, fishers and vendors have faced new limits to their cultural reproduction and have had to renegotiate the relationships that comprise the more-than-human commons in Chorrillos.

This process of renegotiation has been inflected and challenged by emergent regimes of neoliberalized governance and enclosure, which have placed greater pressure on fishers and vendors to demonstrate that they are responsible entrepreneurs and users of the wharf's and the ocean's resources. These regimes are problematic because they identify a very narrow range of economic activities that count as "care" for the ocean, fish stocks, and the wharf and its "community." Officials have justified the institution of new forms of neoliberalized governance on the assumption that a community of accountable citizens does not already exist and must be created to ensure that individual producers are responsibly using natural resources and built infrastructure. This assumption not only separates the economic from the social and cultural but also the economic from the natural. The result is that the already existing more-than-human commons in Chorrillos is invisible to neoliberalized governance regimes. This presents a serious and not easily resolved challenge for fishers and vendors. Since the colonial era, fishers have sought to shelter their lives from state visibility as a means of protecting their autonomy and livelihoods. Many fishers have struggled to maintain that invisibility and resisted recent state attempts to license and register them. However, growing state encroachment has meant that fishers and vendors have had to engage with new regimes of governance or risk losing their right to the wharf or the fishery. This has generated a series of discussions among fishers and vendors about how best to care for themselves and the wharf, discussions that have brought existing forms of commoning into tension with neoliberalized understandings of work, responsibility, and community.

Making Fishers Visible

The artisanal fishing wharf sits at the southern end of the bay, where on a sunny day one can easily see the buildings of Miraflores, one of wealthiest municipalities of greater Lima, just over four kilometers in the distance. Approximately four hundred fishers and vendors make their living from the wharf, supplying residents of southern Lima with fresh fish and tourists with prepared seafood. Most of the fishers in Chorrillos concentrate on nearshore fishing, plying the waters within a few nautical miles of the coast using small wooden boats to pursue a wide range of species that are available at different times of the year. There are also *buzos* (divers), who search for *chanque* (*Concholepas concholepas*, Chilean abalone) or *concha navaja* (*Ensis macha*, razor clam) from shore or from boats. During the summer, a few fishers also venture farther out in larger boats for stints of several days to a couple of weeks to chase species such as bonito or pota. The most economically productive time of the year for fishing is during the austral summer months of November to March. During the winter, some fishers travel to other ports to work on boat crews where the fishing is steadier or take up construction jobs in the city. However, many stay active during the off months, fishing when the water is calm for pejerrey.

Fishers in Chorrillos rely on the small concrete wharf and pier that extend into the ocean for unloading their catches, repairing their boats, and selling their fish. From the bustling center of Chorrillos, there are two staircases that lead down the cliffs to the wharf. At the base, one crosses the busy Circuito de Playas thoroughfare, which provides tourists access to the beach. On the other side of the street is a parking lot full of thirty open-air kiosks and another fifteen stands that serve seafood. Waiting just outside the parking lot is usually a group of eight or ten *jaladores*, hawkers who run after passing cars and shout invitations to tourists to stop and eat at the kiosks. Beyond the shouts of the jaladores is a set of concrete buildings that comprise the physical center of the wharf: a covered fish market attached to a building with a large refrigeration unit for storage, a meeting hall, and the office of the local fishers' association, which sits one story above ground level so that one passes under it to access the concrete pier that juts into the bay.

The Asociación José Silverio Olaya Balandra de Pescadores Artesanales de la Caleta de Chorrillos (Jose Silverio Olaya Balandra Association of Artisanal Fishers of the Bay of Chorrillos) administers the wharf. At last official count, the association claimed 148 members with over 200 *asociados* (associates, many older fishers who were no longer active). Members pay annual dues and in return have the right to vote every two years for the association's leadership in addition to receiving holiday bonuses for their families and the option of buying into group insurance plans. Fishers are almost always gathered in the large hall, just south of the association's office. Resembling an old warehouse, the union hall has a large mural outside the entrance of José Silverio Olaya Balandra, an Afro-Peruvian hero of the War of Independence and a fisher. Inside, there is a small bar that sells beer, soda, and water; a set of bathrooms, which tourists pay to use; a pool table, where anyone can play for a sol; and storage for the tables that fishers use to sell their fish, ambulant vendor's carts, and regalia for festivals to celebrate events such as the Feast of San Pedro. There are almost always a few fishers in the hall reading the papers, talking politics, or playing cards. The association also uses the hall for their monthly assemblies, where 80 or more fishers pack into the open area in the middle to debate issues facing the association, such as how to distribute its revenue.

On March 18, 2012, a group of government officials from Produce and the Instituto Nacional de Estadística e Informática (INEI, National Institute of Statistics and Computing) arrived at the fishers' wharf in Chorrillos to initiate what they claimed would be the first national census of artisanal fishers in Peru. The census lasted for two weeks, with similar scenes unfolding up and down Peru's long coast. The officials set up white plastic tables with blue chairs under the awnings of the shipyard. Soon after this process was finished, fishers lined up and waited to sit across the table from one of the statisticians. The census takers asked fishers about numerous aspects of their lives: how much they made in an average month, how many children they had, what kinds of work they did besides fishing, and if they had access to credit. Among these officials was José Urquizo, the minister of Produce, who was interviewed by local news media. Urquizo asserted that the census was a critical step toward providing the government with a more exact picture of the needs of artisanal fishers and their impacts on Peru's fisheries. According to Urquizo, the census would "make it possible to create measures for promoting and strengthening this important sector" and would "obtain real data" about artisanal fishing.[1]

The national census emerged partly out of interest among some officials in the Humala government for developing a more robust market for domestic fish consumption and partly in response to complaints among fishmeal industry proponents, both within and outside the government, that artisanal fishers were a threat to the sustainability of Peru's fisheries because they lacked oversight. The census was just one of several government measures aimed at making artisanal fishers more visible to state bureaucrats. Perhaps the most extensive of these was an effort by Produce and the Coast Guard to ensure that all artisanal fishers have the appropriate *carnet* (license). As part of the licensing process, Produce offered fifteen-day free courses at the end of which fishers applied to the Coast Guard, who awarded them the license. According to Produce officials, the course gave artisanal fishers training in how to best maintain boats and engines to ensure their continued safety when at sea. This professionalization of artisanal fishers also supposedly guaranteed that fishers were effective self-managers who could adapt flexibly to new markets and produce safe-to-eat fish for consumers.[2] The constitutional right to fish nearshore waters has historically been afforded to all Peruvian citizens. Since the 1990s, this shifted to a privilege given by the state to those fishers who comported themselves as worthy users of the nation's piscatorial resources. As part of its efforts to convert artisanal fishers into free market entrepreneurs, in 1994, the Fujimori government declared that artisanal fishers and divers had to obtain the appropriate *carnet de pescador artesanal* (artisanal fisher's license) or a *patente de buzo* (diver's registration). Following the 1994 regulation, the number of licensed fishers varied from region to region and from port to port within specific regions.

The 2012 census data showed that fewer than half of the fishers in Chorrillos had carnets. Produce officials emphasized that the census and licensing process were critical for helping the government to get a more accurate sense of how many artisanal fishers were active in Peru and what their needs were so that Produce and other government agencies could improve the services they provided to artisanal fishers. However, when we talked to Produce and Coast Guard officials in Chorrillos about the licensing process, they emphasized that it was critical for making artisanal fishers visible to state infrastructures not only as a means of improving the lives of fishers but also as a means of regulating and taxing them more effectively. In justifying these measures, the officials whom we interviewed drew on long-standing ideologies of class, asserting that the licensing process was necessary for imposing order on the disorganized lives of artisanal fishers.

In 2012 and 2013, we interviewed Antonio, a Produce officer who worked with artisanal fishers in Lima Province, to ask him about the formalization process in Chorrillos. When we asked him what the benefits of formalization were for fishers, he responded, "Well, we [Produce] are very interested in the formalization of the fishers' unions and the formal organizations of the artisanal [fishers] and the individual artisanal fishers because it gives them formal recognition, it gives them legal recognition before society, before the Ministry of Production, before the financial organizations, it gives them recognition before the tax institutions." When we asked him again what the specific incentives were for artisanal fishers to formalize, he noted that for the time being there were none. At that point, the government did not require individual fishers to report their finances or to pay taxes on the fish that they caught and sold. However, Antonio noted that this situation was likely to change, that Produce officials not only saw the licensing process as a necessary step toward more effectively taxing artisanal fishers, and thus extracting rent from them for using Peru's ocean natures, but also toward better regulating artisanal fisheries. The formalization of artisanal fishers, Antonio claimed, "is necessary" not only for taxation but also because "the state needs to know" what the "capacity of artisanal fishers [is] to extract resources compared to those small-scale [boats] and industrial [boats], for their impact on the resource."

Esteban, one of the Coast Guard officers stationed at the Chorrillos wharf during our research, identified the large number of *indocumentados* (undocumented fishers) in Chorrillos as a significant problem for the area and his regulation of the bay. According to Esteban, the carnet was evidence that a fisher had earned the right to work in the ocean, demonstrating that he was willing "to study for at least fifteen days" to learn how to be a "good" fisher. He argued that in places where the fishers were well organized, regulated the fishery themselves, and encouraged members of the union to get their carnets, the situation was better. "There are coves where the fishers look after their zone themselves and do not allow fishing with dynamite," Esteban pointed out. But there are also "areas that are abandoned or not organized, where someone could go and fish with dynamite." The role of the formalization process, he argued, was for the government to "facilitate"—a word he used repeatedly—rights and access to deserving fishers, to those who demonstrated that they could self-govern.

Despite Antonio's and Esteban's emphasis on the licensing process for demonstrating that fishers in Chorrillos could be organized and tax-paying producers, at the time of our interviews, these state officials had little power to use fishers' lack of formalization as a means to deprive them of access to marine resources. Although by law no fishers were supposed to leave the dock without registering their carnets with the Coast Guard and despite Esteban's tough talk, in practice this was not the case. It was not as though the Coast Guard actively policed who embarked from the dock. Coast Guard officers only checked carnets for crews of the few larger boats that fished in the high seas. Moreover, the captains of these boats had to go to the Coast Guard office with the carnets to register their crew, not the reverse. Even then, registering the crew was only necessary when a captain planned to unload his catch at a different port. For those who chose to fish only from their home dock, as was the case for the overwhelming majority of Chorrillanos, a carnet was an unnecessary formality.

Moreover, for many fishers in Chorrillos, the benefits of having a carnet were too few to merit using precious resources to obtain one. At the outset of the formalization process, the expense, both in terms of time and money, of the mandatory training course was prohibitive. Fishers in Chorrillos had to travel to Callao to complete a fifteen-day training course. Although the course was free, fishers had to pay for transportation on their own and were not compensated for lost wages. This was significant in that it placed the onus on fishers to use their limited resources to perform the necessary steps to realize what they all considered to be their constitutional right. There were few fishers, especially those with families, who could afford to lose fifteen days of work. Even during the slow winter season, there were rarely more than a few days in a row when fishers did not go out. A number of fishers had debts that they paid on a day-to-day basis and the inability to bring in even a few fish from their gillnets posed a direct threat to their daily livelihood.

The issue of carnets highlighted some of the ways in which ambivalence characterized contemporary governance and fishers' experiences of it. Fishers who did not have carnets occupied a legally hazy position. Technically, they were not "formally" licensed as artisanal fishers but they were not restricted when they fished the nearshore waters of their home bay. These fishers were, in part, responsible for producing this ambiguity in that they made the very logical choice to not give up two weeks of wages in order to receive a license that offered them few tangible benefits in return. Yet, it should be stressed that such ambiguity was not simply a product of fishers' practices, as government discourses of artisanal "informality" would suggest. Rather, such ambiguity was part and parcel of the exercise, or lack thereof, of state authority in Chorrillos. Governmental authority is in part rooted in the beliefs of individual citizens that the state has the legitimate power to act (Bourdieu 1999; Mathews 2008). The choice of many of Chorrillos' fishers, while informed by economic strictures, was an indication that state officials did not have the authority to regulate artisanal fishing—in certain regards, it was an act of ignoring state officials, choosing to withhold belief in their authority to license them. In Chorrillos, as in many artisanal ports elsewhere in the country, fishers saw the force of custom as a greater indication of their right to the sea than the legal requirement of a carnet. In response, Produce officials exerted greater pressure on the fishers in Chorrillos to formalize, backed by the threat of revoking the fishers' right to the dock.

Replacing the Union

In 2014, Produce officials informed fishers in Chorrillos that their union had to become an association in accordance with a shift in Produce's approach to organizing artisanal fishers. What had been a mutual aid association became a union in 1969 to strengthen fishers' relationship to a corporatist state. However, as part of broader decentralization efforts, Produce's officials decided that artisanal fishers should no longer organize as unions through the ministry but reclassify as associations. When we asked Produce officials about this change, they argued that unions were organizations of workers within a company and therefore artisanal fishers could no longer legally be organized as a union. This explanation served to gloss over the political implications of the change. Although some of the weakest in the region, Peru's labor laws allow for workers in the same craft or profession, but who do not work for the same companies, to form unions across local, regional, and national levels as long as they have twenty or more members. Unions are entitled to specific legal protections, such as the right to strike. In contrast, associations are the most common form of social organization and the least regulated. Any two or more people pursuing a common, nonprofit goal can form an association and apply for tax-exempt status. The move from a corporatist union to an association also has created the possibility for fishers to organize into multiple associations, which has meant that Produce and other governing agencies can shift from working with one to another in order to find more amenable administrators.

Produce officials made it clear to fishers that reorganizing as an association was a requirement for them to continue to administer the wharf in Chorrillos. Officials also linked the shift from a union to an association with their efforts to formalize fishers by making licensing a requirement for membership in the fishers' association. Initially, Produce bureaucrats required the union to produce a list of its registered members, whether those fishers had licenses or not. This list constituted the membership of the new association, which the fishers created in 2015 and which retained the organizational structure of the union with a board of directors elected by the members every two years. Government administrators and extension officers required the association to ensure that all members had carnets within two years of its founding. In order to further this process, in 2015 and 2016, Produce officials convened several training workshops for fishers in Chorrillos so that they did not have to travel to Callao for their carnets and set up two events on the dock to process the paperwork for elderly fishers to obtain carnets without undergoing the training course. By late 2016, the vast majority of the fishers in Chorrillos had carnets.

As Produce officials repeatedly stated, this formalization of artisanal fishers was a necessary first step in making these individuals visible to state bureaucracy and accountable to government regulation. As this process neared completion, officials focused increasingly on the association's oversight of the dock, stressing the need for artisanal fishers to do a more adequate job of demonstrating that they could be responsible for self-governing the space as a requisite for holding on to it. For example, Antonio told us that the association needed to take significant steps to improve the infrastructure of the dock and its management. He argued that fishers had to adapt to a new market reality by developing a plan for the investment of the association's funds into the wharf's infrastructure and by instituting best practices for the operation of the fish market and the improved commercialization of the fishing operations.

However, in Antonio's extended commentary on the fishers in Chorrillos, it was clear that his criticisms had as much to do with bureaucratic assessments of effective management as with class and what he deemed the sociocultural inappropriateness of fishers. Antonio made this clear in what he identified as the most serious problems among fishers in Chorrillos. "The low level of income is one of the problems with fishing in Chorrillos," he said, "but we could also talk about the other social problems in the families." According to Antonio, what little fishers made they oftentimes wasted on drugs and alcohol. In addition to this problem and a lack of secondary education among fishers, he claimed,

"On the subject of values in the home, there is a lack of fathers in the house, divorces, [a lack of mothers and fathers] living together, right? [The homes] are a little, we could say, disorganized, very disorganized . . . Extramarital children, right? Unplanned, right? It is more of an issue of values in the home, more than anything else." Antonio compared this presumed situation with the condition of the dock, noting that there were many problems with its management. "This pier lacks a lot," he said. "There is neglect [and] total disorder." There was not, he noted, a coordinated system for the disposal of waste from the fish cleaning or selling areas—the waste was dumped straight into the bay, contributing to the contaminated nature of the water. Antonio attributed the neglected state of the wharf's infrastructure to what he saw as the association's corruption and disorganization, which had stymied plans to reinvest rent from the wharf's operations into physical improvements.[3] These were all indications, Antonio asserted, that the association in Chorrillos needed to ensure that its members became more responsible producers, ones who could more effectively care for themselves and the resources they used.

In his criticism of fishers and their association, Antonio invoked a narrow understanding of class as a moral justification for government intervention, arguing that it was fishers' working-class behavior that had brought about the poor state of their association and wharf. And yet, considerations of class disappeared in Antonio's and other officials' insistence that fishers and their association's leaders take greater responsibility for themselves and their wharf in order to retain control of it. The latter conveniently glossed over the fact that fishers had few resources to undertake significant renovations to the dock because of their status as impoverished producers within broader systems of unequal political power. In short, government officials' efforts to *make* fishers and their association responsible disabled class as a necessary tool for addressing the challenges that fishers faced in caring for the dock and themselves while simultaneously exacerbating inequalities among fishers and vendors as well as between them and the wharf's neighbors.

Made Responsible

On March 16, 2015, the dock was a flurry of cleaning and painting. The association had declared a mandatory cleaning day and everything was closed: No one was working at the fish market, the chairs were up on the tables at the food kiosks, and there were no fishers coming back from a morning at sea. One of the association's directors, Juan, was in the union hall cooking rice and chicken in a big pot so that everyone had lunch waiting for them. The cleaning day was a response to a combined Produce and municipal government review of the dock's operations. The review team was set to present its final report to the association's leadership that day, and the fishers knew that sanitation was at the top of the reviewers' concerns.

Wandering around the dock, we ran into one of the association's leaders, Pablo, who asked if we would like to sit in on the review. We agreed and made our way up the short flight of stairs to the association's office. Soon afterward, the review team arrived and took seats. The team consisted of a representative from the Viceministro de Pesca y Acuicultura (Viceministry of Fishing and Aquaculture, the part of Produce that regulates artisanal fishing), a representative from the Organismo Nacional de Sanidad Pesquera (National Agency of Fisheries Health or SANIPES, an autonomous agency linked to Produce), the Municipalidad Distrital de Chorrillos (District Municipality of Chorrillos), and three individuals from the Municipalidad Metropolitana de Lima (Metropolitan Municipality of Lima), one from the health department and two from the department of economic development.

The leader of the review team, who was from the economic development department of Metro Lima, began by stating that sanitation was the biggest problem on the dock. The association, she argued, needed to do a much better job of ensuring that there was potable water for cleaning and preparing fish and that the drainage system functioned properly so that dirty water did not sit and stagnate, increasing the risk of waterborne disease. The representative from the health department seconded this suggestion and added that the conditions under which food was prepared in the kiosks was deplorable. There needed to be a clear and standardized schedule for more regular cleaning of everything, he noted, such as cutting boards, utensils, tables, and floors. "It must be habit," he said. "Every ten days, every month, every two months." He also argued that the association needed to do a better job of sanctioning those who were not following the proper procedures for sanitation.

At this point the representative from SANIPES chimed in, noting that the tables that the fishers used to sell their catches were in an unsanitary state. He said that although Peru did not have regulations specifically requiring it, most countries mandated the use of stainless steel tables with food-safe plastic bins full of ice for selling fish and that was what the fishers should use as well. He also pointed out that the association should control more closely what kinds of fish were landed at the dock. Most of the shellfish, he argued, were not suitable for human consumption because of the high level of contamination in the Bay of Chorrillos. The sewage collector for much of southern Lima, referred to as La Chira (the name of the beach near where the plant is located), is just a few kilometers south and the prevailing currents push the largely untreated waste from more than three million people up along the coast. Unsurprisingly, the coliform bacteria content in the Bay of Chorrillos is extremely high as are other contaminants common to urban coastal areas. The SANIPES representative summarized what he saw as the major problems in Chorrillos: waste from La Chira; the aging water infrastructure of the wharf, which was built before the newest sanitation regulations were in place; and the lack of clean, potable water. He acknowledged that the first was completely out of the hands of the fishers but asserted that the association could and needed to rectify the second two issues.

In his first statement of the meeting, Pablo quietly asked how the fishers could deal with the latter two, both of which would require updating the drainage and water infrastructure on the dock, the costs of which were beyond the association's revenue. The SANIPES representative responded that the association should ask FONDEPES, the Ministry of Production's agency that provides development loans to artisanal fishers, for money to rebuild the drains. The leader of the review team added that while there were structural problems that presented challenges for the association, it should focus on what it could do: enforce good practices. She noted that on her tour of the wharf, she saw people throw trash on the floor and not adequately clean and sanitize surfaces where food was being prepared. She asserted that it was "worrying" that the association leaders were "not interested" in solving these problems. She finished by adding that the bathrooms in the association hall were in a terrible state. The health director from Metro Lima interjected that "Roky's has good sanitation, the Yacht Club does, [but the] wharf does not." Roky's was a two-story chain restaurant that specialized in rotisserie chicken, which had opened a few hundred yards north of the wharf in 2013 (but had gone out of business by 2018).

As these comments suggest, one of the main objectives of the joint review was to insist that if the association did a better job of administering the dock, then it would not stand out so much in contrast to its neighbors. The fishing wharf is situated at the southern end of the Costa Verde. The city has developed the area as a continuous park space, building beaches and parks and creating

Figure 7 Playing cards and selling fish on one of the portable tables in the fish market. Photo by Maximilian Viatori.

a thoroughfare that serves as a bypass for the congested streets of the central city. In recent years, Metro Lima and individual district governments have installed new sidewalks, walkways over the highway, and play structures along their respective portions of the coast. The Costa Verde officially ends with the wharf's neighbor, the Yacht Club, a large gated compound that has served the recreation desires of the city's elite since its founding in 1875. The Club has tennis courts, swimming pools, a mall, restaurants, indoor basketball and soccer courts, and rows of beach chairs with green umbrellas that look out onto the sea. Members of the Yacht Club have become more and more concerned about the state of the fishing wharf, which stands in stark contrast to its wealthy neighbor. Also, because Club members have to drive through the wharf to get to the Club's entrance and because the Club has been renting part of the wharf to park cars, there has been growing concern among the Yacht Club's administration about security.

Pablo patiently listened to the reviewers' negative comparisons of the dock to its surroundings. He then noted that among those who worked on the dock, there was a "culture of tomorrow," of putting things off, such as cleaning, instead of tackling them sooner. However, he subtly turned this issue back to the government officials, pointing out that people would listen to them more so than the association's wharf administrator. Perhaps, he mused, if the municipality made more visits to the dock and more consistently sanctioned people, things would change and people would more closely follow the regulations. Pablo argued that the association was doing all it could with its limited resources and it was the government, in all its forms, that was not complying with its responsibilities.

In this vein, Pablo brought up the issue of clean water, assuring the officials that he shared their concern about providing potable water to the kiosks and the fish market. The main problem, he suggested, was that the wharf's water supply had been cut off several years ago because the previous administration had not paid the bill. Obviously, this made the problem of sanitation worse and made it harder for the association to comply with Produce's and the municipality's regulations. In the meantime, the association had worked out a deal with the Yacht Club to get water from them so that the kiosks and the market could continue to function. Pablo noted that his administration had paid the outstanding water bill and no longer owed a debt to the Servicio de Agua Potable y Alcantarillado de Lima (SEDEPAL, Service for Potable Water and Sewage of Lima). However, for reasons that no one in the meeting seemed to understand, the previous municipal government of Chorrillos had taken out the old pipes after SEDE-PAL had cut off the water supply to the wharf so that it was no longer possible to resume water service without first installing new pipes. Pablo claimed that the association had asked repeatedly for the Chorrillos municipal government and SEDEPAL to help resolve the issue but to no avail. He wondered out loud if the government of Metro Lima could help them with this problem. To which the leader of the review team replied by changing the subject and asking, "Yes, but how are you going to deal with the waste and other issues?" Pablo responded that access to potable water was a real issue and pointed out that "we have no help" in dealing with an issue that the team leader herself had identified as a central problem. "We've paid all of the fees," he said. "We've done everything. The problem is with SEDEPAL."

The review team leader advised Pablo to stop talking about what the previous association leaders or government officials had done wrong and tell the team what the current leaders would do about the trash, the drainage system, and sanitation on the dock. "Above all else," she argued, the association needed to deal with the antiquated trap for the central drain. She also noted that the association had to dispose of the abandoned boats that lined the beaches around the dock. Removing the boats was a difficult task because while they were abandoned, they still had owners. By law, the association was not able simply to have them hauled away and scrapped. They first had to contact the owner and ask him or her to move it, and if that did not happen within six months, then the association could contact the municipal government of Chorrillos and ask them to put a notice on the boat that if it was not claimed within a month, it would be removed. This was a difficult process that required the active participation of the fiscal department of the municipal government of Chorrillos, which Pablo claimed was not easily persuaded to intervene in these matters. Furthermore, the association often had a difficult time establishing whom the legal owner was of particular abandoned boat, which made it impossible for them to initiate the process of removing them.

The artisanal fisheries representative from Produce confirmed that dealing with this situation was complicated and that the municipality should be able to help the fishers establish where the legal owners were for some of these boats. The leader of the review team agreed that there should be better coordination and suggested people whom Pablo might contact to resolve the issue, although she appeared uncertain about the process and did not make any concrete commitments to help the association with the problem. Pablo responded with frustration that he had tried to work with the municipal government of Chorrillos on the issue of the abandoned boats but he felt that the people in the fiscal office were "prejudiced against" the association and that the fishers could not do anything to change it. There was no comment from the representative of the district government of Chorrillos.

The review meeting represented an important instance for exploring government officials' attempts to make the fishers' association and its members more responsible for maintaining the dock and monitoring their behavior. The event was a show of authority, a moment when officials made their presence felt in an effort to present a unified, strong critique of all that was wrong with the space and the association's management of it. The association responded in kind, shutting down the wharf's operations for a day to show that it was serious about officials' recommendations for improved sanitation. However, the review was also part of ongoing government efforts to make fishers more accountable to state desires and provided an interesting moment for analyzing the ways in which officials framed the association's problems and the acceptable solutions to them. Throughout much of the review, the government bureaucrats discussed the wharf's physical state of ruination, such as the malfunctioning drainage system, which made it impossible for fishers and vendors to comply fully with sanitation regulations. These were projects that, as Pablo repeatedly noted, were too large and expensive for the association to address. Infrastructural renovations were undertakings that required government assistance, which was not forthcoming. Not only was government support lacking, but as the review meeting illustrated, there was often confusion among different government agencies as to whom would be responsible for providing administrative support, instituting regulations, or enforcing best practices.

In the wake of Fujimori's resignation in 2000 and his flight from Peru, federal officials instituted policies of governmental decentralization, a move popular throughout the region, with the goal of increasing bureaucratic efficiency and responsiveness to local populations. Aspects of federal governance were devolved to regional and municipal governments. In the case of the oversight of artisanal fisheries, decentralization resulted in the division of responsibility between Produce and regional governments with the exception of Lima Province, where the Metropolitan Municipality of Lima holds this responsibility. Among the many problems with this process are the lack of local capacity for carrying out additional governmental responsibilities and the often quite vague understandings of who specifically is responsible for what.

For fishers in Chorrillos, government decentralization meant that they were made increasingly responsible for instituting "best practices" for the administration of the dock. Yet, fishers have to negotiate the demands of a multitude of institutions and agents, from federal ministries to municipal governments, each of which oversees a different portion of the wharf or a particular aspect of fisheries management.[4] Because Peru's coast up to fifty meters in from the high tide mark legally belongs to the state, the federal government is responsible for any construction that extends into the ocean. In Chorrillos, the wharf also falls under the jurisdiction both of the District Municipality of Chorrillos, which is responsible for its coastline from the point where federal jurisdiction ends on the beach, and of Metro Lima, which oversees the Costa Verde's transportation infrastructure. Finally, Metro Lima shares responsibility with Produce for regulating artisanal fishing in Lima Province. This complexity was an issue that Pablo raised when he argued that a lack of coordination among Produce and the municipal governments made it more difficult to dispose of abandoned boats.

In response, officials consistently obscured such considerations in their discussions of artisanal fishers' administration of the wharf. Instead, they emphasized that artisanal fishers' livelihoods and access to the wharf were in jeopardy because of the pathologies of fishers' lower-class culture. For example, several times the leader of the review team told Pablo to stop complaining about what the government or previous union leaders had or had not done and focus on what really mattered, what fishers and vendors could do: take it upon themselves to be better dock citizens by cleaning and sanitizing things on a more regular basis. Such comments briefly recognized the limitations of the association to care for the wharf on its own, but quickly reduced the state of the wharf to fishers' individual behavior. In particular, officials drew on long-standing discourses of personal hygiene that equated cleanliness with progress and an apparent lack of sanitation with the squalor of the lower classes. In other words, officials combined seemingly apolitical language about the common-sense aspects of good governance and best practices to outline what fishers and vendors should have done to demonstrate they deserved to use the dock while simultaneously invoking class prejudices to explain why these fishers and vendors were unwilling, and perhaps unable, to comply. Such an approach to governance assumes that the inability to demonstrate personal worth is the result of individual moral failings—an ideology that not only cuts against class solidarity but also paves the way for the future denial of rights or access to certain individuals.

What makes this ideology so insidious is its fusing of neoliberalized discourses of individual responsibility with historically rooted ideas about class, hard work, and achievement. On the one hand, Pablo and his colleagues in the association pushed back against officials' admonitions that fishers invest in improved infrastructure, complaining that the state had abandoned its responsibility to provide fishers with the necessary resources for such projects and that disorganization among different offices had thwarted what improvements the association could undertake. On the other hand, Pablo echoed the review leader's comments about the unwillingness of vendors and fishers to clean their spaces, suggesting that they had a culture of procrastination and would be more attentive if government officials actively enforced the regulations more often. In this manner, discourses of self-governance and responsibility that attributed rights to good individual comportment were smuggled into fishers' discussions about what was happening on the wharf, what they could do about it, and with whom. In the remainder of this chapter, we trace these discussions in order to explore how in attempts to prevent the enclosure of the resources upon which they depended, fishers thought it might be acceptable to displace some of the dock's fish sellers and food kiosk operators if it meant that they could better care for the association's families. Fishers justified such visions of the future by arguing that a renovated dock would enable the association to better meet its social responsibilities by generating more revenue for fishers' families while noting that the poor work ethic of some individuals might have justified their dispossession. Rather than strengthen class solidarity across divisions of gender and types of employment, commentaries about responsibility and hard work accentuated these divisions.

Difference amid Market Ruins

In response to government pressure to demonstrate that they were effective caretakers of the wharf, the association leaders and members discussed ways they could ensure that the area was not only a safe place for neighboring tourists and Yacht Club goers but also that it was a potential site for private investment and commerce. Fishers consistently identified the wharf's food kiosks and fish market as problem areas in need of infrastructural improvements and better sanitation practices. Despite the importance of the kiosks for the dock economy and fishing families, when leaders and members of the association talked about the future of the dock, they almost always prioritized the removal or renovation of the kiosks. The reasons for this are complex and provide important insight into how and why many fishers would have proposed the potential displacement of vendors in their discussions of an improved wharf while imagining that such a change would have benefited all fishers and vendors. These discussions about the food kiosks and fish market represent important sites for understanding how in day-to-day considerations of what is possible, individuals may unwittingly fashion a justification for dispossessing other members of a collective.

The food kiosks in Chorrillos consist of small concrete enclosures that are just big enough to fit a tiny stove, sink, some counters for food preparation, and a refrigerator. The front of the kiosks face seating areas that accommodate five or six plastic tables with chairs and are sheltered from the sun by large umbrellas or tarps. Tourists can also go to the small fish market, pick out a fish, and take it to one of the kiosks to be prepared. Women run the kiosks, which serve seafood dishes such as ceviches and *jaleas* (huge plates of battered, deep-fried fish). During the summer months, the food kiosks bustle with activity and represent an important component of the dock's tourist economy, providing labor for jaladores, kiosk owners, and helpers. They are also a source of revenue for the association because each of the kiosk operators pays a fee to the dock administrator for a two-year lease.

Working in the food kiosks is a family affair. Most of the women who run them are related in some way to one of the association's members and employ relatives and their children, who wait and bus the tables and help with food preparation. The dock administrator, who is appointed by the association but technically employed by Produce, generally awards contracts for the food kiosks to individuals who have (or had) a relative in the association, with the reasoning that this was a way of providing help to the families of the associations' members. The kiosks function as gathering spaces where fishers meet to eat with their families. Among the fishers we interviewed who had long-term partners, almost all worked outside the home, usually in some aspect of Lima's "informal" economy—as street vendors, for example. Running a food kiosk appealed to many women because it offered them relative autonomy in comparison to wage labor, such as domestic service, and made it possible for them to have their children accompany them and help when they were not in school.

While many fishers valued the economic and familial contributions that the kiosks made to the dock, they saw the food stalls as an activity that was ancillary to fishing. Association leaders and members often referred to the women who worked in the kiosks as the "friendly face" of the dock. Most fishers admitted that they could not be bothered with customer service, preferring to be left alone to talk with each other and work on their nets. For many fishers in Chorrillos, masculinity was achieved through hard physical work at sea and was also idealized by the image of the freedom that artisanal fishing allowed a man—the ability, or at least its imagined ideal, of setting off and returning as he liked and not answering to a boss or providing a service to a customer. Catering to tourists violated this ideal for many fishers, who preferred to dedicate themselves to what they saw as the definitive work of the dock: fishing.

In some other artisanal fishing ports in Peru, especially in rural areas, women play an active role in the fishing trade. For example, women are responsible for mending nets, unloading and packing fish for transportation, and the business of negotiating prices for selling fish. This was not the case in Chorrillos, where men were exclusively responsible for all aspects of catching and selling their fish. There were multiple reasons for this. The quantity and quality of fishing in the bay of Chorrillos was not as good as many areas to the north or south of the city, and fishing did not provide enough economic sustenance to support whole families nor did it require much additional labor to manage catches. On an average day, a fisher heading out to check his nets would likely bring in a few kilos of fish. This was not enough to support a family, especially in the city where the cost of living is considerably higher than in much of the rest of the country. While many fishers liked to see themselves as the traditional breadwinners, women, and in some cases children as well, play equally important roles in economically reproducing fishing families. Yet, fishers saw themselves as the owners of the wharf—the wharf was there to support fishing, and it was the fishers' association that had the authority to manage the space.

Dominant ideologies of work and masculinity informed this dynamic, and fishers' thoughts about what could and should be done with the wharf reflected how they confronted changing working conditions and gender relations. In a broad study of urban masculinities in Peru, Norma Fuller (2003) demonstrates the centrality of work, especially manual labor, to working class men's identities. "To enter the world of work," she argues, "signifies the acquisition of the status of adulthood; it is a prerequisite for establishing a family and the principle source of social recognition" (Fuller 2003, 138). Individuals who did not achieve this, who did not find acceptable work, came to represent marginalized "versions of masculinity, such as criminals and those who are lazy" (Fuller 2003, 143). The working-class Peruvian men whom Fuller interviewed believed that they "held the authority within the family" because they were the ones who went out into the public sphere and earned money, as opposed to women who were in charge of the domestic sphere. Working class men saw public spaces (such as the wharf in Chorrillos) as the key sites in which their authority and identity as workers was enacted and recognized among peers (Fuller 2003).

However, profound changes in Peru's urban political economies in recent decades have undermined this idealized representation of working class masculinity, as growing numbers of women have engaged in public wage work (especially in the informal sector), traditional employment opportunities for men have become more precarious, and attitudes about gender equality and work have changed, especially among younger people.[5] This has been clear in the wharf's economy, where artisanal fishers have struggled to earn a living through fishing given the deteriorating state of the local fishery and women vendors have constituted a growing and equally important role not only in the overall economy of the wharf but also in the reproduction of fishing families. Nonetheless, many fishers have continued to see themselves as traditional breadwinners and have viewed their control of the wharf as critical for the social recognition of their status. They have advocated for renovations to the wharf that would have reinforced the centrality of fishing as the main activity and would have helped to reestablish fishers' role as providers for women and children (rather than the other way around).

Such visions of the dock's future reinforced a de facto social hierarchy on the dock whereby fishing was accorded greater status in the dock's governance over other types of labor. Moreover, this hierarchy was gendered, given that most of the individuals who worked in non-fishing roles were women who did not have a say in the official functioning of the association or the dock. Only fishers were members of the association, which made decisions about how the dock's resources should be allocated for the good of the community. Many fishers professed a strong sense of responsibility to the families of the associations' members and couched their discussions of the future within this sentiment, arguing that replacing the kiosks with privately run restaurants would be an improvement for everyone working on the wharf.[6] Were the kiosks to be replaced with privately run enterprises, the dock would not only be upgraded but fishers imagined there would be new jobs created for those who would lose their kiosks. The association's president once told us that such a measure would create more jobs for "the public"—meaning all of those employed in the dock who were not fishers—than the current food kiosks did. Furthermore, he asserted that the association would generate more revenue.

This was a solution that government officials also pushed—private investment in the tourist infrastructure of the dock to ensure a solid base of revenue for the association so that it could maintain and develop the space. For example, officials from Metro Lima encouraged the association to find an investor to help revamp the wharf. There had been interest in creating just such a venture. A renowned chef and owner of an empire of top-end restaurants in Lima scheduled a meeting with the association to discuss the possibility of investing in the wharf through the creation of a new waterfront restaurant. While such a plan drew on growing interest in local food production and gestures at sustainability, it never gained any traction and likely would have only employed a fraction of the fishers active in the dock. The association also proposed a joint venture with the municipal government of Chorrillos and Produce to construct a new boardwalk along the waterfront at the wharf. Pablo told us that the municipality had ignored his proposals. The Yacht Club's architecture contest, which we discuss at the end of this chapter, was the closest the fishers came to securing significant investment in the dock.

Despite a lack of government funding and outside money for dock improvements, association leaders and members continued to talk about possibilities for future investment. In these discussions, fishers almost always commented on the need to remove the kiosks and replace them with nicer restaurants. This topic came up in a conversation we had with three fishers about the dock's economy and its future. The men quickly shifted the conversation from our questions about how the administration of the space worked to their visions for how it should work and what an improved wharf would entail. In particular, they emphasized that the state of the food kiosks was a critical problem. One of them remarked that he brought relatives from Venezuela to the wharf for a meal and they commented on the poor condition of the kiosks and the dock in general. Looking around the wharf, he said that "all of this is broken, all of it is dirty." In contrast, his relatives claimed that "in Venezuela [in] the markets everything is really clean, everyone sweeps and cleans, they sweep every other minute" and "everyone is uniformed." It was clear that this comparison had made the fisher feel ashamed of the wharf. But in its retelling, he used it as a means of identifying an end goal of progress, a more desirable future for the wharf, at the center of which were cleaner food kiosks or restaurants that would attract more and wealthier tourists, thus improving the dock's economy. Gesturing to the car park area that fronted a number of the kiosks, another of the fishers said that he thought it needed to be converted "into something [such as] a tourist fair." Expanding on this idea, he imagined that "you could make an entrance over there [where the cars enter] with a good name" and that there would be kiosks "but bigger" and nicer than the ones that existed. "If you are a fisher and you want progress," he said to us, "you want . . . hygiene and cleanliness with good service" in the kiosks. As these comments suggest, fishers' discontent with the physical state of the wharf sometimes shifted to criticisms of the kiosk operators for not being cleaner or providing more professional service.

Such critiques echoed long-standing elite discourses that associated poverty with poor hygiene and uncleanliness, and fishers adopted them as a guide for identifying what they saw as the negative aspects of the wharf.

Not all fishers agreed with such commentary, especially those whose spouses or mothers worked in the kiosks. Rather, they advocated for a degendering of the public space of the work and emphasized the importance of intra-family solidarity for weathering economic difficulties. They argued that in the process of making plans for the wharf's future, the association needed to be more transparent about its finances and what was done with them. They also stressed that vendors and fish cleaners should be included in the association's decision-making process. In a March 2016 conversation, Marcos, whose mother and sister-in-law ran one of the kiosks, commented that the association needed to change, that it needed to "be for everyone" and "include the concerns of all" those who worked on the dock, not just the fishers. While Marcos usually worked as a fisher with his brother Luis and was a member of the association, he had also worked as a jalador for his mother's kiosk, which was an important economic resource for the whole family. Marcos and Luis expressed their hopes for a renovated wharf with improved infrastructure and new kiosks that would attract more tourists, especially given their belief that fishing was becoming a less reliable source of income. However, unlike other fishers who did not have direct ties to one of the kiosks or the market, the two brothers felt strongly that any plans to renew the wharf should not displace fishers or kiosk operators and that everyone who worked on the wharf should benefit economically. The problem, as they saw it, was that the association's leadership had not done an acceptable job of including fishers, vendors, and their families in the process of deciding how the association's resources could be used to improve the situation on the dock.

Different opinions about the importance of the food kiosks and whether kiosk operators should have a say in the wharf's administration reflected differences among fishers. These differences came to the fore as association leaders and members considered how best to demonstrate that they were responsible administrators of the dock and what should be done to improve the space. The majority of fishers in Chorrillos did the same kind of work: fishing the near-shore zone with small boats and then selling their catches to tourists on the dock or to specific restaurants in Chorrillos where they had an arrangement with an owner. There were also a few larger artisanal boats that were owned and captained by fishers in Chorrillos, who at different points were able to generate enough capital to invest in more lucrative, but also risky, high seas fisheries. These boats employed crews of five to six mostly younger fishers during the summer months. In contrast to the smaller boats, which usually brought in a crate or two of fish, these larger boats loaded up with several tons of ice before going out and, if they were lucky, came back with a ton or more of fish.

The dock in Chorrillos was not built for these types of hauls, but the fishers who owned these boats were from there and preferred to unload in Chorrillos, which was safer than Callao and did not have the same oversight as Pucusana, where there was a Produce officer stationed on the dock. These larger boats had to be loaded and unloaded via a laborious relay using a rowboat and fishers who waded the last few meters to the shore, carrying crates of fish or ice on their shoulders. There were a few fishers who advocated for expansion of the dock to make it capable of handling more of these boats and other larger ships, working on the assumption that there would be more captains who would also prefer to unload in Chorrillos instead of ports such as Callao. According to several fishers with whom we spoke, there was a Chinese firm that expressed interest in investing in an upgrade of the Chorrillos wharf. However, nothing ever came of this, which is unsurprising given that the road in and out of the wharf is often congested and increased shipping traffic would have to contend with this.

Because of the diminishing quality of fishing and Chorrillos' location on the Costa Verde, tourism has become an increasingly significant part of the wharf's economy, which led to tensions between fishers who were better positioned to take advantage of this shift or whose household income depended on it and those who were not able or did not want to serve tourists. This was an issue that came up at a special association meeting in June 2013, which the association leaders called to discuss the future of the wharf. There were about seventy fishers in attendance, crammed into the center of the hall that also housed the food carts and regalia for the wharf's festivals. The main topic of the meeting was how the union could regain its authority on the wharf and could do a better job of making it a more attractive location for local business and tourism—a broad mandate which most of those assembled seemed to support. However, differences emerged among members who had converted boats to give tourists rides and those who continued to fish as their primary work. *Paseadores*, individuals who gave these rides, complained that although they had paid their use fees for years, the dock had not been maintained in a way that made it attractive to tourists. In contrast, those still active in fishing argued that the tourist boats were docked next to the pier, which made it difficult for fishers to unload their catches in a timely manner and thus impaired the central function of the wharf: landing fish.

This was an ongoing issue, one that led to heated discussions at times, and points to how divisions emerged among fishers at a time of considerable change and uncertainty about the future. The cost of converting a fishing boat to one for tourist rides was prohibitive for most fishers who do not have savings or access to low-interest capital. Moreover, some fishers did not own the boats they used to fish but rented from or had agreements with boat owners (sometimes fishers, other times not) for their use. Only a small percentage of fishers could make the transition from earning their incomes through fishing to operating primarily as tour guides. Even if they had the resources, there were many fishers who would have opted to not become tourist guides. For many, the dock's primary function was fishing, and while tourism was necessary for the survival of the wharf, it was not something in which they wanted to be directly involved. For some, such as Luis and Marcos who had family working in the food kiosks, tourism was an important aspect of their family's revenue and provided good work for their family members. For this reason, they questioned the necessity of removing the kiosks or converting them to private restaurants. Others who did not have close family working on the dock were less concerned about who ran the kiosks or fish market as long as they were well run and generated revenue for the association, which could then be put back into the community and the dock's infrastructure, enabling them to continue to fish.

This was an issue that also emerged at the special meeting of the association. According to the association's leaders, the previous administration had done an inadequate job of managing the association's finances. They had not kept close accounts of how much the vendors and food kiosk operators owed the union. This caused two interrelated problems. First, the association had not been generating as much money as it should have been, which meant fewer benefits for members and upkeep on the dock. Second, individuals who paid to use the dock had become lax not only in paying their dues but also in doing their part to keep the area clean and follow good sanitation practices. This made it seem to visitors, whether they were tourists or government officials, as though the association was not putting the area to good use and taking care of it. The assembled fishers agreed that the fish market was the most egregious example of the deterioration of the wharf's operations.

The covered fish market could house about twelve fish vendors, although in recent years the number had dropped to three or four, each of whom paid a daily fee to the association to use the space. Unlike the women who ran the kiosks, those who sold fish in the market did not always have ties to the association through a family member. Many fishers looked down upon the fish vendors as schemers who were using the dock for their own good and with no regard for the reputation of the wharf. There were several occasions when consumers bought bad fish from the market vendors and then complained to the association and the local press. Many fishers referenced these instances as evidence that the market vendors had done more to hurt than help the dock's economy.

Fishers' criticisms of the dilapidated state of the food kiosks and the low standards of the fish market vendors were not widely publicized but emerged in association meetings behind closed doors or in conversations among small groups of fishers. Kiosk operators or vendors did not have opportunities to address or confront them publicly. However, in daily conversations, some of them expressed their frustrations at being excluded from the wharf's operations, a topic to which we return in the following chapter. Ana had worked in Chorrillos as a jaladora for eleven years when we interviewed her in 2015. Her husband was a fisher as was her uncle, and her mother-in-law used to sell fish at the market in Chorrillos.

Ana, like most of the other women who worked on the dock, did so to help support her family and because she was not able to find better work elsewhere. Although she worked on the dock most of the year, during times when business was slow, she also took on work in Lima as a house cleaner. In contrast to fishers' claims that they were the primary providers, Ana noted, "The life of a fisher is very risky and quite tough, because as you see, in summer there is money and all that, but during the winter there isn't any, and the winter is longer than the summer. So when there isn't any [fish] in winter, what are you supposed to do if you have a family and you have to feed your family and help support your mother?" This was why Ana did not want her sons to go into fishing and it was also why she had to work on the dock—because her husband did not generate enough money to take care of their family's needs. Yet, she did not receive any direct financial support from the association the way that fishers did. "The people from the association say that they will help us [the jaladores and vendors], but in the end they don't," said Ana, adding that this was unjust because "the majority of us who work here as jaladores are children of fishers." She expressed the belief that the association needed to change: "I would change the association. They should involve working women from here more because the majority have spent many years working here . . . They are involved only with the members, they have nothing to do with women, as always." Ana said that at one point the association leaders had promised to help the jaladores, to perhaps help them get access to health care "but then nothing" happened. Josefina, a younger woman who had worked for a year as a *fileteadora* (filleter) in the fish market, echoed this sentiment when we spoke with her, arguing that "all fishers and fish cleaners should be treated equally. At the very least" everyone who worked on the dock should have the access to the same benefits.

Other women found subtle ways of questioning the legitimacy of the fishers' association to govern the dock while avoiding any public confrontation that would jeopardize their access, via family relationships, to the resources they needed to make a living. For example, although the kiosk operators would prepare fish that tourists bought from the fishers, they generally used fish that came from Lima's biggest fish market in Villa Maria. The vendors made their reasoning clear: Fishers in Chorrillos charged too much for their fish—it was twice or sometimes three times as much as the fish in Villa Maria. It did not make economic sense for them to buy from the fishers. Kiosk operators made the same argument, although some also added that buying fish from Villa Maria had the extra benefit of not having to do business with family who were members of the association and thus they could avoid any complications or disputes over the prices of fish or money that would negatively affect them. By choosing to not buy their fish from the fishers, vendors were able to assert autonomy in their business.

Because of the political organization of the wharf, vendors did not have the same official say in plans for the space's future development. Yet, as the above examples demonstrate, vendors found indirect ways of calling into question the association's legitimacy to govern the space. One visible exception to this was a vendor whom the fishers accused of squatting on an area of beach for which the association was responsible. Previous association administrators had granted her permission for one summer to sell beverages and food from a small stand.

However, the woman had never left and each year added on to her ramshackle stand to the point where it took up considerable space—equivalent to three or four of the food kiosks. She would not pay a fee to the association nor pay for her utilities because she claimed that she inhabited a public space. In contrast, the association leadership argued that she was occupying a space deeded to the fishers and that her shack was an eyesore that negatively affected tourism. The association leaders had not been able to evict her. In fact, the local police who used the beach to train came to favor the spot and they were often there drinking. She had refused to leave, and the issue arose in the 2015 government review of the wharf, with officials noting the rundown state of the structure and asking association leaders what they had done to address it. In response, the association leader at the time complained bitterly that he had petitioned both the municipality and Produce officials to evict the vendor but he quipped that none of the officials whom he contacted could be bothered to deal with the situation. The association leaders and the fishers who supported them saw the dilapidated, makeshift bar as a clear marker of the wharf's poverty and informality in a more egregious manner than the food kiosks and the fish market. And yet, they were powerless to do anything about it, providing at least one clear indication to officials that the fishers' association had limited authority to ensure that they were administering the dock effectively and responsibly.

Renovation and Division

In 2015, the fishers' problem of coming up with sufficient resources to renovate the wharf and bring it in line with tourist development in the rest of the Costa Verde appeared to have been solved. The administration of the neighboring Yacht Club announced an architecture contest with a winning cash prize of $7,500 for a plan to rebuild the fishers' wharf and make it more "sustainable" and amenable to tourism. According to the call for proposals, the total estimated budget for the renovation project was reported to be over $5 million. In an article for *El Comercio*, Jorge Ruiz de Somocurcio (2015), a prominent architect who was involved in helping to discuss and plan the contest, wrote that the competition was evidence that the club had "decided to satisfy its share of social responsibility." While noting the beauty and history of the area's beaches, he proclaimed that the dock's "facilities are deplorable." Ruiz de Somorcurcio wrote that the winning plan had to consider the needs of existing fishers, such as a dock for unloading, but had to also improve tourist services and leave space for "private initiative," and he stated that among the options he had discussed with the club and fishers were a hotel and the "conversion of the food kiosks into gourmet restaurants with reasonable prices." The panel for the contest consisted of seven judges: the president of the Yacht Club, the club's architect, representatives from the governments of Chorrillos and Metro Lima, architects from the School of Architects of Peru and the Association for the Study of Architecture, and one member of the fishers' association.

The winning plan was a sanitized version of what the wharf could look like. The submission included a computer-animated video of the dock converted into double-tiered concrete and wood walkways for tourists. Although the written plan made references to (albeit much reduced) space for fishers and restaurants, the video mockup showed no food vendors nor food stalls and a few recreational sailboats (compared to the dozens of fishing boats usually in the harbor). The only people represented in the video were tourists in bikinis and swim trunks and almost all of them were white—a stark contrast to the fishers, vendors, and beach goers of color present on the wharf most days during the summer.

When we spoke to fishers about the plan in late 2015 and again in spring 2016, they expressed support for it. Many saw it as their only opportunity to modernize the dock and ensure a decent future for themselves and their children. None of the fishers with whom we talked had seen the winning plan's video and were surprised when we told them that it did not depict any vendors or fishers. As one fisher argued, though, they needed to think about the future: The number of active fishers continued to decline and the association had to do something to provide support to the growing number of older fishers. Given their shrinking numbers, he told us that someday the Yacht Club would simply take over the dock because there would not be enough fishers to claim it, and so it was better to work with the club now so that fishers would get some immediate benefit. The important thing, he and others noted, was that fishers and their association maintain control of the wharf and had input in how it was developed. Fishers assumed that they would continue to control the wharf, which meant they would continue to fish, and with the proposed renovations, could earn more money, which they would then be able to divest to their members and their families. Even if the food kiosks and the market were removed or reduced in number and size, fishers believed the community would benefit as a whole.

When the contest was announced, the president of the Yacht Club speculated that construction would be done by the end of 2016. The project never made it past the proposal stage. No one we spoke with was sure why. Several fishers speculated that it was because the Yacht Club member who initially had promised to fund the project as a tax write-off had changed his mind. By the time of our 2017 visit, fishers had written off the contest as another broken promise that would never happen. In the meantime, fishers had made some changes to the wharf. A Produce employee told us that the fishers finally had accepted that they had to do something to improve their area. With funding from FONDEPES, the fishers' association built a gate around the area where they landed their catches so that they could better control it and charge tourists to go down onto the landing, which is what they had been doing with the pier. The idea was that the gate would not only make the area look nicer but that the association would also be able to generate more revenue by charging tourists to access both areas. The association hall had been reroofed, and the association office had been painted. Furthermore, the fishers had taken down the old awnings that hung over the area they used for their evening market. The space was now open and easier for tourists to move through. While the fish market had been only half full in previous years, there were now fishers using it to sell their catches. This marked an attempt by fishers to reassert their control of the market. There were still two women selling fish from Villa Maria in the covered space. However, the fishers had taken over the prime area through which tourists passed when going from the parking lot to the dock. The fishers used the permanent tile banks that had been for the filleters, who moved to the steel tables at the other end of the market. Fishers were selling on the four banks plus four more at tables. There were also plans in the works to spend money to enclose the market so that it would no longer be open on three sides, thus bringing it closer to compliance with sanitation regulations.

While government officials looked upon such changes favorably, they earned fishers and vendors only momentary respite. Once the licensing campaign had been completed, Produce officials began a process to register all boat owners with the hopes of being able to tax them in the future. As of 2018, only a few boat owners in Chorrillos had been registered through this new process. While these efforts to register fishers and boat owners had yet to have any immediate impacts on the wharf, Produce's reorganization of the fishers' union as an association had had an impact. A second fishers' association had emerged to vie with the existing association for control of the pier, landing area, market, and refrigeration unit—the areas of the wharf that generated the most income for the association. In 2016, retired fishers as well as former members of the

Figure 8 A view from the bow of an artisanal fishing boat of the Yacht Club's new restaurant. Photo by Maximilian Viatori.

old union created the Gremio de Pescadores Artesanales San Pedro de Chorrillos (Association of Artisanal Fishers "San Pedro of Chorrillos") and argued that they could do a better job of administering critical areas of the dock. The members of this rival group all had carnets and went through the legal process of registering themselves as an association. There were also discussions about the potential formation of a third association of paseadores to advocate for the development of the wharf to their benefit. This situation was a direct result of Produce's breaking up of the union, which created the possibility for the emergence of various associations competing for control of the dock.

At the time of writing, it was not clear how this situation would be resolved. This was not something that the fishers' associations appeared to be able to settle on their own, which reinforced Produce's power to deem who would be granted the authority to oversee the wharf's operations. The active fishers whom we spoke with were concerned about the gremio taking control, because if the association was not running the dock, they would have to pay use fees to the gremio for the fish market and the freezer. On a broader level, a change in who managed the wharf would also potentially undermine existing systems of patronage and support that depended on the current association's foundation in kinship networks that linked fishers and their families to benefits. Many speculated that Produce would continue to support the larger association, which was comprised of active and retired fishers, because it represented more people and had a history of running the wharf. Another possibility, though, would be that Produce would make a public call for bids to manage the wharf's resources, which opened the chance for a private entity, rather than one of the two associations, to win the concession to run the pier, market, and refrigeration unit. Even if the association were to hold onto the concession, the presence of more than one interested party could mean that Produce would issue the contract on a short-term basis with a formal process for evaluating the association's performance and whether it warranted further contract extensions.

This situation provided government officials with more opportunities to curtail fishers' autonomy on the dock. It also placed greater strain on fishers to deal with a new threat to the existing conditions of their access to the dock while increasing tension and divisions among the people who have used the wharf to make a living. In the long term, this poses as much, if not more, of a threat than encroachment by the Yacht Club. The potential of making the concession for the wharf public and the division of the union into multiple associations represents a subtle and seemingly apolitical way in which fishers could lose their ability to administer key parts of the wharf.

Conclusion

Official campaigns to introduce neoliberalized regimes of governance and self-regulation have stumbled repeatedly in their implementation. Nonetheless, projects to license and reorganize fishers have emphasized the ideology that fishing is an economic activity and that fishers are individuals who care only about extracting as much fish as they can. Based on this ideology, government officials have implemented programs aimed at making fishers and vendors more responsible for creating a functional, sustainable wharf "community." Such neoliberalized regimes of individual responsibility have marginalized and obscured artisanal fishers' and vendors' roles in sustaining cultural and ecological relationships that comprise a more-than-human commons in Chorrillos. This separation of the economic aspects of fishing from the cultural and ecological relationships that make it possible has enabled government officials to put increasing pressure on fishers and vendors to demonstrate they are economically responsible users of the wharf in Chorrillos or face the possibility of its dispossession. This pressure has created tensions and exacerbated divisions at a critical moment in which workers in Chorrillos have been forced to think about what they can do with each other.

Fishers have considered their options and discussed possibilities for retaining control of the wharf, increasing the association's revenue, and providing stable jobs for their family members. In doing so, they have reinforced the centrality of fishing to the wharf's economy and social makeup while bracketing out work done primarily by women as something that is ancillary and at times harmful to the dock's reputation and therefore a good candidate for proposed changes. While women have been excluded from these conversations, they still have found ways to assert their autonomy by, for example, subtly withholding recognition of the association's legitimacy. Recently, a group of former union members contested the association's legitimacy openly and officially by forming their own association in an attempt to administer the limited revenue that the wharf generates each year. This is a direct result of a neoliberalized reorganization of artisanal fishers around the country, which has aimed to break up corporatist unions and replace them with community associations with fewer legal and labor rights. These divisions and tensions provide a window into how local differences have been articulated at a moment of considerable change in a manner that both challenges dispossession and potentially undermines class solidarity among the men and women who work on the dock.

CHAPTER 5

Dignity, Abandonment, and Agency

O fficial governance projects, such as licensing fishers and inspecting the dock's administration, were aimed at making the lives and work of artisanal fishers more visible to state bureaucrats while also promoting the ideology that fishers had to demonstrate that they were entrepreneurial and responsible for themselves and the resources they used. In response, leaders and members of the fishers' association in Chorrillos dragged their feet, complying with licensing regulations only once the government made it a requirement for reorganizing the union as an association, and complaining to officials that state and municipal agencies had not provided them with the resources they needed to administer the local wharf. However, fishers did not reject officials' assertions that the wharf was in poor shape and needed major improvements. Members of the association often discussed their desire for private investment to fund significant renovations aimed at making the wharf and pier more attractive to tourism. While fishers justified these visions of the future as improvements that would benefit everyone, such plans usually included the removal or replacement of the existing market and food kiosks and thus laid out the discursive groundwork for the potential displacement of vendors. Such instances underscore how neoliberalized understandings of responsibility made their way into seemingly run-of-the-mill deliberations about how to improve the dock and retain fishers' right to administer it.

In this chapter, we explore the daily commentaries of fishers, fish cleaners, kiosk operators, and vendors about their lives and work, and we argue that these commentaries represent important avenues for thinking about how they experienced and analyzed their situations and came to understand their political subjectivities. Fishers and vendors often talked about their daily economic precarity and the difficulties of making it in an increasingly expensive urban area, where competition for dwindling resources, customers, and decent wages made it harder to earn a living. Reflecting on their situations, many individuals identified broader structural inequalities and injustices as the root causes of their poverty. For example, fishers repeatedly blamed industrial fishing boats that violated state regulations for over-harvesting the bay, leaving artisanal fishers to compete with lobos for the remaining fish. Such expressions of resentment, argues Ann Laura Stoler (2013, 29), are an "active, critical force in the present" that is "about the possibility of naming injuries for what they are, a demand that the conditions of constraint and injury be reckoned with and acknowledged." Fishers' and vendors' resentments emerged out of their economic difficulties— their daily struggles to get by and hope that things would improve. Yet, their resentment was about more than just making ends meet—it reflected a feeling that they were losing the ability to fulfill their desires to be full cultural citizens in Lima's urban landscape, individuals who could buy their children the things they wanted and hope for a better future.

In his discussion of small producers, James Scott (2012, 88–89) underscores the dream that many have of owning some property, such as a business or a boat or a plot of land, because it provides individuals with the "minimal rights associated with small property." More than "income security," Scott (2012, 90) argues that property confers upon individuals "freedom from close supervision and autonomy of the working day" as well as the all-important resources for "full cultural citizenship." The long hours of work that often result in little pay are worth it for many people if they can feel a sense of dignity not only through autonomy but also by producing just enough wealth to be able to "give expression to their worth and social standing" through participation in significant aspects of cultural life (Scott 2012, 90). For many fishers and vendors, work at sea and on the dock represents a life of toil and long hours but one that affords them greater autonomy than low-paid and socially demeaning wage work in the city. This emphasis on personal dignity is something that ran through fishers' and vendors' explanations for why they continued to work on the dock and it presents a direct counter to neoliberalized accountings of the proper workings of markets and human capital, which have excluded dignity as a critical foundation for ensuring people's basic social welfare. Fishers' and vendors' resentments stem in large part from the frustration that as their economic situation has become increasingly precarious, it has become harder and harder for them to escape the status of what Scott (2012, 90) calls "second-class cultural citizens."

However, in fishers' and vendors' commentaries, resentment about structural inequalities and the importance of dignity often existed in tension with the commonly stated belief that some had fared better than others because they had made smarter financial decisions or were willing to do more to get ahead than others. Diego, a boat mechanic in Chorrillos, once told us that the blame for diminishing fish stocks lay with the state because "governments did not know how to take control of something as straightforward as natural resources." But, he argued, the blame for the poor economic state of the dock in Chorrillos lay with the fishers. "They don't take care of things," he said. "They don't have any culture, any reading, any [knowledge] of books, [of having] educated themselves in order to understand what it means to have the dock, what it means to be a fisher, in order to value themselves more."

We argue that the tension between these attributions of structure and agency suggests how important struggles over accounting for harm unfolded in the interstices of everyday life on the dock and how depoliticized understandings of individual responsibility made their way into daily considerations of inequality and its causes. This dynamic is key for thinking about what Philip Mirowski (2013, 58) calls "everyday neoliberalism" and the actualities of how neoliberalized modes of subjectivity emerge in daily struggles for material wellbeing. Fishers' and vendors' day-to-day explanations of poverty both challenged enduring class inequalities and laid the ideological foundations for accepting some dispossessions as potentially beneficial. Furthermore, analyzing how fishers and vendors connected experiences of poverty with feelings of abandonment and moral responsibility is critical for understanding why feelings of resentment toward the state and industrial fishing boats did not transform into a rejection of individualized explanations of poverty but the reverse. Despite the proliferation of different forms of localized accounting and governance, fishers and vendors repeatedly asserted that powerful actors at both national and local levels had abandoned their social and moral responsibilities to care for artisanal fishers by, for example, protecting artisanal fishing grounds from industrial depredation. While fishers aimed their resentment at a state they felt had abandoned them, fish cleaners and vendors expressed ire at the local fishers' association for not complying with their duties to take care of the wharf and the people who relied upon it to make a living.

Fishers and vendors felt they had no other option than to care for themselves, to do whatever they had to do to ensure that they and their families had some chance of coming out ahead. Individual fishers and vendors asserted that, despite the challenges they faced and suffering they endured, they complied with their social and moral responsibilities to care for themselves, their families, and their children by working hard, saving money, and taking advantage of whatever opportunities they could find. These articulations of individual agency emerged in part as a critique of powerful actors' failure to comply with their responsibilities and stemmed from historically rooted notions of family, gender, and state corporatism. However, such discourses of moral responsibility dovetailed and often neatly overlaid neoliberalized notions of entrepreneurial agency and responsibility to local communities, both of which quietly reinforced the feeling among many fishers and vendors that if hard work and individual willingness were the only options for moving forward, then those who were worse off had themselves to blame.

We trace the tension between competing ways of accounting for poverty and responsibility by first examining fishers' discussions about the autonomy that fishing and working on the wharf offered them. Despite the growing risks and difficulties of making a living as artisanal fishers, the sense of dignity that accompanied the work continued to attract a small group of young fishers. However, most fishers felt that the diminishing quality of fishing in Chorrillos and beyond imperiled their ability to make a living with dignity, and most older fishers told us that they hoped their sons would stay away from fishing. Fishers blamed dwindling fish stocks on state protections for lobos and boliches, repeatedly complaining that such protections existed because powerful actors were able to pressure the state to their advantage. In their commentaries on this situation, fishers often expressed the feeling that they were slipping backwards because they did not earn enough to guarantee their personal dignity, which they articulated as their inability to ensure that their families had what they needed to be full cultural citizens in Lima's urban society. In these commentaries, fishers often emphasized individual choice, noting that if they had made better decisions or been more responsible with their finances, they might have done better. Many fishers also noted that the impoverished state of the dock was due in part to a lack of work ethic and responsibility among some of its users.

Vendors and kiosk operators expressed similar feelings, noting the autonomy that came with working on the dock but also the growing challenges that came with trying to make a living from the local fishing and tourist economies. In contrast to fishers, vendors argued that the run-down state of the dock was due to the fishers' association, which had not complied with its responsibility to take care of the area and guarantee good working conditions for the women who worked there. Given the difficulties of making a living and the lack of support, vendors asserted that they had to take care of themselves and to be willing to do anything to get ahead. Taken together, the commentaries of young and old fishers and women vendors illustrate the ways in which ideas of dignity, choice, and responsibility existed in tension with their recognition of structural inequalities and feelings that they could only rely on their individual hard work if they had any hope of coming out ahead.

Lisa

We sat on the dock one warm March afternoon with Luis. The dock was crowded with beachgoers looking for fish to buy, beer to drink, and rides around the harbor. The three of us sat on large bundles of fishing nets that fishers had mended for their next trips into the bay or the deeper waters beyond. Luis said that it was time for him to go and check his nets and asked if we wanted to come along. We agreed and headed to the water, where a fleet of small, brightly painted boats slowly bobbed in the waves.

At the side of the dock there were three men, each with a pile of black mussels. They broke the mollusks open with ball-peen hammers and put the meat in baskets. Later, they would carry the baskets to a nearby stand and sell the bait, along with hooks, lines, and lead sinkers, to tourists interested in fishing. Up and down the dock there were men, some with rods, others with simple hand lines, engaged in the same rhythmic motion of slowly jigging their baited hooks up and down in the hopes of enticing a fish to hand. Luis's son, who was probably six or seven at the time, gingerly stepped around the men and onto a small rowboat, which the fishers used to go to and from their individual boats anchored in the harbor. In no time, Luis's son brought back one of his father's two boats, a wooden rowboat of about four meters in length that weighed a couple of tons. The boat's hull was painted a bright green, and the gunwales were covered in white paint, which had chipped in places revealing the strata of paints that had been layered one over the other through years of use. Luis hopped into the boat and grabbed the oars to steady it as we carefully climbed over the bow. He then deftly turned the boat and moved away from shore until he found a place where the pier was high enough for us to pass under, navigating the dock's pilings. We headed out into the harbor moving toward its southern edge where Luis had left two sets of nets.

Unlike the small rowboats used for pleasure trips around a pond, in which the rower faces the back of the boat, Luis and the other fishers stood up and faced forward as they rowed. This gave them the advantage of seeing where they were going and helped them row with more force since they could lean forward and push their bodies against the thick wooden oars. Luis looked as though he was barely working when he rowed. His hands jabbed forward in unison. As he rowed, he talked about how when he was a boy, he and his brother would row north toward La Punta in Callao to access other fishing grounds, a trip that would take them the better part of a day. Luis learned how to fish from his father, who at the time was in his mid-seventies and still regularly fished the bay. During the summers when school was out, his children were always on the dock, helping their father, swimming out to the boats, or playing on the beach.

As we moved farther out, Luis pointed to a school of juvenile lisa (mullet) that were active on the surface. As the lisa swarmed near the surface, they made a crackling sound as the water's surface fizzled with their activity. In his field guide to fish of the eastern Pacific, Gar Goodson (1988, 133) writes that "also called 'jumpers,' mullets leap from the water to escape nets or predators, or seemingly for the joy of jumping. At certain times of the day, coastal shallows, bays, and inlets come alive with leaping mullets." Soon enough, the languid pelicans, who usually looked for handouts at the fish market, started to move in, their ungainly beaks plunging into the ocean to scoop up mouthfuls of fish.

It was not long until the floats of Luis's first net were in sight. They were gillnets with floats on the top end and weights on the bottom so that the net formed a rectangle suspended in the ocean. Luis had positioned the net along the southern edge of the bay, near a breaker that formed the beginning of the Yacht Club. Fish of a catchable size were able to enter the net—their heads just fit through but they could not get out because their gills got caught on the nylon. When we got to the net, Luis grabbed the top and began to pull it up from the dark water to see if there were any fish. There were none in the first few meters, only some seaweed and a few jellyfish, which Luis tried to avoid lest he be stung. He continued to work, pulling the boat along by tugging on the net. The first fish that Luis brought up was a little flat fish, a pinkish-white lenguado. The fish was too small to keep, so Luis quickly worked it free from the net and tossed it back. A few minutes later there was a flash of silver in the water, a sure sign of a fish. It was a lisa, a good-sized one of maybe a foot or more, not like those we had seen feeding earlier. Luis pulled the fish from the net and tossed it into the boat.

The mullet had a long, teardrop shaped body with a gently forked tail that shaded to darker gray. Its head sloped to a small upturned mouth and a large eye. In pictures or even in a market on a pile of ice, mullets have the basic coloration of many fish—a dark back, silver sides and a white belly. This muted color scheme belies what the fish looks like when it first comes from the ocean. The mullet's back was a deep, metallic cerulean mixed with midnight blue and cobalt. Rather than a pale gray, the sides bristled silver with purple stripes, hints of turquoise, lavender, and pink. These are things to which the fisher is usually the only witness as the fish crosses that brief threshold from sea to boat. As the fish began to die, the colors quickly faded to the gray-scale familiar to fish consumers around the world.

Luis pulled one more fish, smaller than the first, from the net. That was it for the afternoon. He checked the second net, but there were no fish. The water had been turbulent that day and stirred up seaweed and algae, which had clung to the nets and made it easier for the fish to see and avoid them. There were also large tears in the second net—a sign that a lobo had found what few fish may have been caught and had torn them out. Luis turned the bow of the boat so that it faced toward shore. In no time, we were back at the dock, and Luis was mooring the boat. It was the last night of our trip, and he invited us to come to his wife's kiosk for a special farewell dinner. In the meantime, we meandered and talked to some other fishers. Then, we made our way to the row of kiosks that lined the edge of the wharf.

We sat down in Juana's kiosk with Luis just as the neon light in the parking lot and those in the kiosks' kitchens came on. Out over the ocean, the sky had begun to turn a deeper blue. Juana had prepared a ceviche with the mullet that Luis had caught. We drank beer and slowly ate. Luis's one-year-old daughter sat and stood on his lap the whole time. He was proud to show us that she liked to eat raw onions and chew on some of the fish. The fact that his children loved the strong tastes of ceviche and fresh fish were clear signs for Luis that they were from a fishing family. As we talked, the conversation shifted to Luis's future and his family's. When he talked about fishing, it was clear that Luis loved it: being on the water, the independence of the work, all of it. However, it was harder and harder for him to make a living with the rising cost of operating, the shaky prices for fish, and the declining quality of the fishing in Chorrillos, which Luis claimed had gone down noticeably in the last decade. He said it would be better for his sons to get good educations, stay in school, and become professionals with reliable wages rather than fish. Luis brought his son out with him so that he would at least have the skill and know how to fish in case he needed to make some extra money. But, he didn't want his son to be a fisher because fishing, in his words, was "not profitable." Despite the difficulties of artisanal fishing and parents' wishes that their sons find other work, there were still a small number of young men who chose to become artisanal fishers in Chorrillos in the hopes that they could take care of their new families in a way that offered them some respect and dignity.

Young Fishers

Enrique did not look like the other fishers, who tended to be powerfully built after years of rowing. He was tall and lanky and, in his early twenties, one of the youngest fishers in Chorrillos. He wore a ball cap turned sideways, hip-hop style, baggy jeans, and skater sneakers. He was a capable fisher, though, and a good boat hand. Enrique learned to fish from his father and another older fisher who mentored him and then employed him on his boat when Enrique was twelve. He was the only one of his siblings to go into fishing: "My father did not want us to work as fishers because fishing is a kind of work that gives [you something] some days and others takes [from you]. And now, in these times, it's difficult to survive from fishing because there isn't much fish. Before, yes. Twenty years ago [Chorrillos was] full of fish." And yet, there were a handful of young fishers, such as Enrique, who still tried to make a go of it. For these young men, artisanal fishing provided an alternative to the often demeaning and unstable work that was available to Chorrillanos with little social capital. Although they made roughly equivalent to what they would earn working in construction or manufacturing, they retained more control over what they did and when and worked in a place where they felt they were afforded a modicum of respect.

These were all things that Augusto, a twenty-three-year-old fisher, told us in 2015. He had worked on the wharf for fourteen years in one capacity or another. As a kid, he helped his mother sell breakfasts on the beach. Later, he cleaned fish and got to know the fishers. "They took me out and that is how I learned," he said. Eventually he made enough money fishing that he decided to drop out of school. For a while, he fished the high seas because the money was good, but once his daughter was born, he chose to fish the bay instead. "With fishing, I survive," he said. "It provides a daily wage, daily food, not much, but enough." Sometimes when the fishing was not good, he made twenty or thirty soles a day mending nets.

Claudio, another young fisher who was the same age as Augusto, shared similar reasons for working as an artisanal fisher. Claudio completed secondary school and was part way through advanced studies when he got his girlfriend pregnant and decided that he needed to find a way to support his daughter. His father was a fisher, and "the people [on the wharf] knew me since I was just a little kid," he said. Despite having "the [fishing] blood" in his family, he was the only one of his parents' six children to take up fishing. The rest studied and found work in the city as laborers or security guards. As with Augusto, Claudio worked in construction and did other odd jobs in the city when his family needed the money. He once tried to take a longer-term job "on land" as a welder but left after a few months and returned to fishing. He said he was "glad to be here [in Chorrillos] . . . it's relaxed here, you de-stress, the problems that you have some-times at home or other problems, you come here and de-stress." Working on the dock meant that fishers could escape the surveillance and drudgery of wage work in construction or the service sector. This was not to say that the work was easy. Early on, Claudio fished the high seas because the money was good, but he talked about the dangers that went with it. The first time he went out, the boat he was on was caught in a storm and tossed by huge waves. He said that water "entered [the boat] from all sides, we were like that for three days . . . without being able to do anything, you are there waiting for the storm to pass . . . one hundred and fifty, two hundred [nautical] miles out" from shore.

Fishing the high seas is one option for young fishers to make good money in a short period of time. During the summer, there are several larger boats in Chorrillos that head out on a weekly basis to pursue bonito, which often fetch good prices in Lima's main fish market in Villa Maria. However, as Claudio's comments suggest, fishing the high seas is dangerous work that is full not only of physical risk and hard manual work but also of significant financial risk. Bonito, one of the primary targets of high seas artisanal fishing, are most active near the surface during the night. For almost a week, a boat's crew stays up from six in the evening until about five in the morning, searching for signs of the fish. When they do find and catch them, the boat hands have to unload the catch, which hopefully is heavy, and move it into the hold for storage on ice. During the day, members of the crew take turns navigating and watching for other ships to avoid collisions. While fishing high seas holds the promise of big catches, it is a promise that is not always realized. Deep waters are the loosely regulated zone of industrial fishing, where large boats can scoop up massive amounts of fish in a short period of time. As one fisher told us, "There is scarcity also in the high [seas]." And there are no guarantees of good pay since what the crew and captain make are determined by the catch and its sale price. In Chorrillos—and this is a common arrangement in many other ports—after the captain pays the costs of the expedition, the profit is split fifty-fifty between the boat owner and the rest of the crew. From their fifty percent, each of the crew members receives an equal share. If the catch is good, this can be upwards of one thousand soles—two to three times the amount that one could usually make in a month of nearshore fishing in Chorrillos. However, if the catch is bad, then the pay is lower or it could be none at all, leaving the captain and crew in debt and gambling that the next foray will be better.

Despite the attraction of potentially big pay days, young fishers such as Enrique, Augusto, and Claudio eventually decided to give up fishing the high seas and chose instead to try their luck fishing nearshore waters in the Chorrillos area. These young fishers noted that deciding to fish the bay meant they could be close to home, which allowed them to help take care of their children, and they were also more independent in their work. However, the disadvantage was that they had to try and make a living as the quality of the fishing in Chorrillos declined. Augusto said that the fishing in Chorrillos "has declined, and one does not earn what one would have before." Because of this, he and his wife, who worked for a local business, were doing all they could to "save a little" and perhaps get into one of the food kiosks. Augusto claimed that the fishers who had done well were the ones who knew how "to save in order to create their business." Similarly, Claudio commented that the pay was not nearly as good as high seas fishing but he wanted to continue fishing in Chorrillos in the long term. "I think a lot about the fact that sometimes one earns," he said. "[But] sometimes one loses, and I have to give my daughter a good future." He lamented that "the buyers are paying us less because the fish are small." Claudio did not mention saving, perhaps because it was not a possibility given that his partner's primary job was taking care of their daughter. He was working toward becoming a member of the fishers' association, which would afford him some support in the form of subsidized insurance and extra food at the holidays. He also expressed hope that the government would more closely monitor the boliches and regulate catches so that the fish would not get smaller and smaller as the stocks were depleted. "Wouldn't it be better for all of us to only take big fish?" he asked.

Enrique, Augusto, and Claudio struggled and took significant risks in the present to support themselves and their families, enduring with the hope that things would stay the same or get a little better in the future. The only other option they had was menial labor in the city, which was perhaps less dangerous than fishing but no better paying or predictable, given that construction and other trades often hired men on short contracts. At least fishing in Chorrillos provided some dignity and some slim hope for a better future. But, as Claudio reminded us, a fisher had to be able to "do everything" to survive.

Dignity at a Cost

As the experiences of young fishers show, artisanal fishing offered individuals the chance to earn a living while still maintaining control over themselves and their work. Most fishers did not have to answer to a boss, and their hard work garnered the respect of other fishers. The wharf was a critical aspect of this, a cultural space that fishers saw as a second home, a place that they felt they owned and where they could go and not experience the humiliation of constant supervision and oversight of wage work in the city. Augusto, one of the young fishers, once told us that when there were no fish or the waters were too rough to go out, "one has to work on land." That was something he only did begrudgingly. Augusto much preferred to work on the wharf and in the bay fishing because it was "tranquil" and he liked working as a fisher because "here practically no one orders you around; it's not like in a company where they order you around." However, declines in the quality of fishing pressed artisanal fishers to their limits. Many fishers told us that autonomy was coming increasingly at the price of dignity, as they were not able to earn enough to support their families and make ends meet, especially since government support for artisanal fishers had, in their opinions, not been forthcoming.

Without exception, fishers commented that the fishing in Chorrillos was not as good as it had been in previous decades. In a 2013 interview, Luis and his brother, Marcos, talked about what fishing used to be like. Both had spent their lives living in Chorrillos and were descended from a long line of fishers. Marcos said he learned to fish with his family: "I went out with my father, with my brothers, with my uncles from my mother's side." Luis added, "I went out with my father, and my father went out with his father." Both remembered a time when the fishing was consistent enough during the summer season to make good money fishing. Luis reminisced, "[There was] money in all quantities . . . during the season for lisa, we would make three trips out. We would leave at three in the morning, four in the morning. By eight or nine in the morning, we would already be loaded and back with the boat . . . We would disembark [and then] we would go back out. We would enter [the bay] at three or four in the afternoon, unload, and we would head back out at eight or nine at night and we would already be here again." The lisa fishing had not been that good for a decade or more. For a while, Marcos said he had gone after crabs when the fishing deteriorated because the crabbing was good in the bay. Now, he said, there were not many crabs either. In 2015, the lisa were finally back in good numbers. It was the beginning of a strong El Niño and unusually warm water, which lisa favor, pushed up along Peru's central coast. Luis and other fishers initially were happy to be catching mature fish in good numbers, but soon with the market flooded, the price for lisa dropped to the point where fishers were selling a kilo of fish for a few soles. Beleaguered fishers got little reprieve. As climatic changes and overfishing have made the business of catching fish increasingly unstable and uncertain, artisanal fishers have felt a growing economic and social strain.

César, a fisher who was then in his sixties, told us that he had started fishing during the 1960s when he was a young boy because his father had died and "there were few economic resources in the home." For César, fishing was a means of taking care of himself and his family. During the 1960s and 1970s, he claimed, "When you went out fishing, you earned. The next day [there were] more fish, more money . . . There were fish, enough product, everywhere." According to César, that had changed for the worse because of overfishing. Another older fisher told us that "never would we have imagined that from one night to the next morning, the fish would leave in a way that left us with nothing—before one earned money." This fisher used to have three boats and employed other men to fish out of two of them, which meant that during the high season, he earned well. Now he only had one good boat: One was broken and the other he had to sell because "the fishing had turned so bad." In his opinion, "People don't want to head out to sea because they don't earn anything."

There was undoubtedly a tinge of nostalgia in fishers' discussions of the past and the quality of fishing in Chorrillos—the good days when the fishing was better. However, their stories of decline were not just products of longing for a past that faintly existed. Fishers in Chorrillos were acutely aware of changes in their bay's ecosystem and fish stocks—most were on the water as many days of the year as they could be, and given that their livelihood depended on it, they were tuned in to the ways in which the bay had changed not only over recent decades but in recent years as well. Government statistics on the number of tons landed in Chorrillos over the past fifty years corroborate these claims of declining fish stocks, indicating that the average tonnage of fresh fish landed has gone down.[1]

One big problem fishers faced was a lack of viable alternatives for earning, given that most of the men were not well educated and lacked social capital that translated into other types of good jobs. One of the options, which some engaged in from time to time, was construction. While work in construction was not hard to come by, especially during Lima's building boom in the early 2000s, it was low-wage and short-term. Fishers who had worked construction complained that they only got minimum wage and contracts for three months or less so that their employers did not have to pay them benefits. This, combined with the fact that the fishers were working for a boss and therefore had little autonomy in their work, made it a last resort and not a good one at that.

Furthermore, the government provided little support for artisanal fishers that would enable them to fish less and still be able to meet their families' basic needs. This was clear in the data for Lima Province from Produce's 2012 census of artisanal fishers. Of the 2,107 fishers interviewed in the province, thirty-two percent made on average less than five hundred soles a month, and sixty-nine percent made less than one thousand soles a month, with none making over two thousand soles a month. To put this in perspective, in 2012, the official minimum wage in Peru—the lowest among surrounding countries in the region—was seven hundred fifty soles per month. In other words, roughly half the fishers in Lima Province were making less than the national minimum wage. Even if one considers that fishers may have underreported their income to avoid telling government officials exactly how much they made, this still indicates a high degree of poverty among artisanal fishers, which was reflected in other indicators. Echoing what we heard from fishers in Chorrillos, the census reported that for 99.7 percent of the fishers interviewed, fishing was their principal economic activity and 64.1 percent noted that they had no other way of making money. Only 28.2 percent reported receiving any kind of third party financing for their fishing, and few received benefits from the government. Out of 2,107 fishers interviewed in Lima, only 410 had health insurance, 143 had life insurance, and a scant 27 individuals reported to have a pension. Yet, almost five times that number reported that they had suffered injuries related to fishing in the previous six months.

In other words, a slim margin separated making it as a fisher from sliding into abject poverty. This was important context for considering two issues that were constant and significant points of anger for all of the fishers with whom we spoke in Chorrillos: the lobos and the boliches. While fishers generally attributed declining fish stocks to overfishing by the small- and large-scale fleets, they felt that their immediate situation was made increasingly worse by lobos, who stole fish from them and broke their nets, and by the small-scale boliches that entered the harbor from time to time when they needed more fish to fill their holds. Artisanal fishers saw themselves as being in direct competition with lobos and boliches for dwindling nearshore fisheries but complained that the competition was stacked against them. Fishers in Chorrillos believed that lobos and boliches received special protections from a corrupt state that favored powerful interests over artisanal fishers' work of trying to feed *el pueblo* (the people) of Chorrillos. Artisanal fishers' commentaries about these two topics provide insight into how they recognized and discussed political and socio-economic inequalities and why they often concluded that they were on their own and could rely only on their individual hard work to prosper and live in a dignified way.

Lobos

Several centuries of extensive hunting and culling to ease competition with regional fisheries has left South American sea lions threatened up and down the continent's southern coasts.[2] In Peru and Chile, there have been government bans on killing lobos since their population numbers dropped dramatically following the 1997–98 El Niño. In her comparative work on fishing communities along South America's Pacific coast, Sarah Keene Meltzoff (2013, 12) argues that the relationships between lobos and fishers "underscore environmental tensions and difficulties" related to shifting oceanic conditions, conservation, development policies, and tourism. Meltzoff (2013, 12) describes the many ways in which fishers "see themselves in the sea lions" since both have to "weather" the difficulties of environmental changes. She also notes that fishers sometimes talk about "vying with sea lions for limited fish" (Meltzoff 2013, 12). This latter sentiment dominated fishers' discussion of lobos in Chorrillos. Fishers identified lobos as a significant threat to their livelihoods.

Lobos, which can grow to three hundred kilograms and depend on fish as their main source of nutrition, often damage fishers' nets. They swim into them to prey on trapped fish and follow fishers' boats, diving into and breaking the nets as fishers attempt to pull in their catch. Not only do damaged nets result in lost fish and therefore lost revenue for the fishers, but after boats, nets are the costliest and most important of the fishers' gear. Fishers spend hours mending the breaks in their nets caused by lobos, using large spools of nylon to painstakingly hand weave the nets back together. While he was repairing a net one day, César said in disgust that the lobos "break your tools for work." "How much do you earn?" he asked rhetorically. "You don't earn anything; it's more like you lose." The issue for fishers was not just that the lobos cost them fish and money but that government bans on culling lobos indicated that the state was not attentive to the fishers' needs and their economic suffering. For fishers in Chorrillos, the ban on killing lobos did not serve a solid environmental purpose because from their perspective, there was an overabundance of lobos. Fishers saw the ban as evidence that the state was more responsive to transnational environmental lobbies that had pressed for the animals' protection and to tourist industry since foreign tourists, in the fishers' experience, were drawn to the cuteness of the animals. As Pablo, one of the former leaders of the association, told us one day, environmentalists always made artisanal fishers out to be the bad guys but the fishers had to fish to eat and had no other options. He said indignantly, "Animals don't have kids to feed, a family to take care of, we do." At the very least, fishers felt the state could permit them to haze lobos as a means to protect the livelihood of fishing communities, an issue that Luis and Marcos explained in this exchange:

> LUIS: Do you know how to improve the fishing? There are two or three options. One of them is to cull the lobos. That's not to say exterminate them, just to do it once [because] there are too many . . . They come, the lobos come here at night to eat . . . and they eat through the net.
> MARCOS: The fish that's in the net, the few fish that are in the net, they come and eat them. But everyone has a reason, just like the big ships.

Such commentaries revealed the degree to which fishers' complaints about lobos functioned as proxy narratives about what they saw as state neglect. As Marcos said, "everyone has a reason," meaning that the lobos, the artisanal fishers, and the industrial boat captains were all trying to make it, trying to get enough fish to live. As he and other fishers in Chorrillos often pointed out, it was only the lobos and boliches that were really protected by the state—artisanal fishers felt largely ignored and forgotten.

Boliches

In addition to the lobos, fishers identified boliches as a constant threat to their livelihoods. Looking back on previous decades, César said that "what did us the most harm were the industrial boliches that came in closer to the coast . . . They took all the product." Similarly, Marcos claimed, "The big ships, bigger than this one [pointing to a boliche in the bay], which is small, they prey on all of the fish, [not just] the ones that are key for making fishmeal, [but] they capture all of them. Even if there is lorna, pejerrey. They throw all of them into the meal, [even] bonito. Everything that they catch in their nets, they throw into the meal. Besides that, they are taking food. The anchoveta is the most important food for all of the other fish." Two fishers in their sixties, Silvio and Alejandro, asserted that the fishing in Chorrillos had been in precipitous decline because "there had been an over-exploitation of it, an irresponsible exploitation, and this was made worse by poor [government] supervision . . . [and a] lack of control." They noted that there used to be anchoveta in Chorrillos, but they had been wiped out years ago by the industrial boats, which continued to enter the harbor to take out whatever they could for the fishmeal processing plants. One of the younger fishers, Claudio, echoed these concerns when he told us that "the boliches come and lift out whatever . . . small fish, big fish, everything." The result, he claimed, was that there were "fishes that are now going extinct."[3] The passage of Law 005 in 2012 prohibited boliches from the small-scale fleet from fishing for anchovies closer than five nautical miles and larger industrial boats from entering closer than ten nautical miles. Fishers in Chorrillos saw this legislation as a positive turn, an indication that Humala's administration had taken a stand against powerful commercial interests in the country and tried to do something for artisanal fishers. However, according to the fishers at the local level, little was done to protect artisanal fishers, reinforcing the feeling that a distant state had abandoned them.[4] "The law is given," Silvio said, "but they [the boliches] do not respect it, and that is what the Ministry of Production needs to do—[it is] responsible for being in charge of regulation."

Boliches entered the bay from time to time, despite the fact that there was a pair of Coast Guard officers stationed in Chorrillos. Fishers told us that you could file a report to the Coast Guard when a boliche entered the harbor, but nothing would happen. One day in March 2014, when we were visiting the wharf and having lunch with a fisher, a boliche anchored within clear sight of the dock and the Coast Guard office. After watching and waiting to see if the boat would leave, two of the fishers made their way to the Coast Guard office and asked the officer to sanction the boat. What followed was a routine worthy of the Keystone Cops—the Coast Guard officer took over an hour arranging and rearranging his equipment, his life vest, and his boat in an epic display of foot dragging. By the time he was ready to head out, the boliche had pulled anchor and headed back to open water.

We raised the issue of boliches with Esteban. If a boliche entered the harbor, we asked, was Esteban responsible for going out and notifying the captain that the boat had to leave. While the Coast Guard was responsible for the bay, for what goes on in the water, Esteban noted that the dock belonged to Produce and was administered by the association. Therefore, the dock administrator had the authority to decide which boats were allowed to unload at the dock. Esteban insinuated that if larger boats were a problem for fishers in Chorrillos, they should do a better job of self-regulating them. What if, we asked, a boliche crossed the five-mile line to fish the harbor? Would it then be the responsibility of the Coast Guard? Esteban replied, "Yes, if one of these boats appeared in my jurisdiction, I have the obligation to go and, how would you say it, intervene . . . The industrial boats are prohibited, they cannot fish closer than five miles, but the artisanal [boats] can. And also the problem that has emerged is that the [industrial] boats enter the coast, and all of the fish that was [for the] artisanal [fishers] in the sea is taken out." Esteban did not mention any instances in which he actually cited boliches, although he did note ambiguously that "various things have been done." However, rather than interpret the actions of the state as embodied in local Coast Guard officers, the fishers saw the officers as petty bureaucrats acting out of personal disinterest in the enforcement of the law in a manner that would have protected fishers. As one fisher told us, the "Coast

Guard is like having nothing." He said that once when a fisher was lost, all the Coast Guard officer did was "make a call and say 'send me a helicopter' that arrive[d] four weeks later after we found him [the lost fisher]."

Corruption

Fishers in Chorrillos saw the disjuncture between what they thought the state should do to protect them and what Coast Guard officers actually did as evidence of corruption. They assumed, for example, that boliche owners were not ever fined or regulated because they had connections—for example, a cousin in the government who could protect them. This sentiment echoed broadly circulating discourses of corruption in Peru. Politicians, pundits, and citizens regularly point to presumably insidious corruption at all levels of government (and often social life) as both evidence of and explanations for the apparently dysfunctional nature of the country's political and economic systems.[5] Such discourses provide insight into how individuals experience governance and their relationships to the state (Gupta 1995). Many individuals feel that they can only glimpse the power and capital that apparently flow through the state but that they are diverted by petty bureaucrats, business owners, police, and others before they reach those who are politically, economically, or geographically marginalized (Aretxaga 2003).

This was certainly the case among fishers in Chorrillos. Marcos, for example, told us that he had heard in Chile "if there is a closure, [if] there are no fish, they subsidize him [the fisher] and pay him his monthly salary." Regardless of the veracity of this claim, fishers made such comparisons in their discussions of the Peruvian state to assert the state's responsibility to take care of them and prove that it had not done so. Another fisher complained that the state had never worried about artisanal fishers. In support of this argument, he noted that the government gave them no health insurance or burial benefits. Fishers paid into a fund managed by their association so that they could have limited benefits. Such feelings of abandonment in the present were sometimes coupled with nostalgia for previous governments in fishers' commentaries. Numerous fishers, especially those over forty, argued that the governments of the leftist Velasco and the right-wing Fujimori created tangible benefits for small-scale fishers. For example, Velasco organized artisanal fishers into unions and gave the fishers in Chorrillos the right to administer the dock. Under Fujimori, the five-nautical-mile limit was created to protect artisanal fisheries with the neoliberal goal of converting artisanal fishers into self-reliant producers while wharfs such as the one in Chorrillos were built or expanded.

This idealized vision emerged in no small part through fishers' contrasting previous governments with what they saw as their current predicament in which they were left to fend for themselves against other better positioned actors. This dynamic was clear in a recent problem with the local police and their illicit expansion of a training ground on the beach in Chorrillos between the wharf and the Yacht Club. The police had a small storage facility that abutted the Yacht Club property, which they used to store equipment for rescue training exercises in the water. Over the course of several years, the police slowly expanded their building and took over a portion of the beach and parking lot that the fishers' association officially controlled. This land was part of the space that extended from the freshwater spring approximately one hundred meters north of the dock to the border with the club south of the dock. The police had not asked permission from the fishers' association to use the space. Although legally the association had clear grounds for challenging the police, they did not for several reasons.

First, and perhaps most obviously, the fishers did not want to cause problems with the police and risk drawing increased attention to any of the fishers' practices that could be interpreted as falling on the wrong side of the law. Second, many—including the fishers, but especially the wealthy Yacht Club goers—considered the dock to be a dangerous place after dark. Thus, the Yacht Club administration implicitly supported the presence of the police in the area, and the association did not want to mar its complicated relationship with the Yacht Club. Numerous fishers expressed concern that powerful members of the Yacht Club were working behind the scenes to force the fishers out and develop the area for tourists. Yet, the club's managers provided water for the restaurant kiosks on the dock because the municipality had cut off the water. The third issue facing the fishers was that they felt they lacked clear justification for challenging the police. Despite their legal right to the land, association leaders believed that they had to make a case that they needed the area so that they could put it to some productive use. Much of the land between the dock and the club was filled with old, dilapidated fishing boats. The association leaders wanted to clean up the area and make it more attractive for tourism, a move that at least rhetorically was supported by Produce and the municipal governments of Metro Lima and Chorrillos. However, the association had not been able to convince the municipal governments to invest in a revitalization project because the fishers had not been able to convince the local government that they had a clear and compelling plan for turning the parking area and beachfront into something that would attract more tourists.

As this example suggests, fishers' images of a once-paternalistic state existed in tension with the experiences of local state agents, such as the police and Coast Guard, as disinterested at best and direct threats to fishers' livelihoods at worst. Among fishers in Chorrillos, the result was not just a general feeling of state absence but also dysfunction. In their nostalgia for a paternalistic state, fishers evoked a better past when the state provided basic resources and rights for the reproduction not only of fishers but also of their association's authority. In their discussions of government agents and projects, fishers criticized the state as an agent of elite power and wealth that had abandoned them. They felt they no longer had a direct, clear channel to the state nor did they have concrete resources or backing from the government, which they believed they had in the past.

In this regard, fishers' discussions of state abandonment represented important critiques of structural inequality in Peru. They also made it clear that declining fish stocks and artisanal fishers' slow displacement from productive resources were not authorless but the product of decisions and actions taken by powerful actors. Such commentaries served as implicit critiques of what fishers saw as the state's abandonment of them to decreasingly productive fish stocks and increasingly competitive markets as well as an implicit recognition that alternatives existed to the status quo. However, the critical force of such critiques was countered by the work that narratives of state abandonment did to reinforce the idea that fishers had no other alternative than to do things for themselves. Fishers' commentaries about state abandonment subtly reinforced notions of self-reliance and entrepreneurialism as the only possible solutions to the problems they faced.

Backwards

Complaints about lobos, boliches, and the state's apparent unwillingness to do something about them highlighted fishers' beliefs that they were slipping backwards and that progress had become a chimera—something to which they were no longer able to aspire. This was a dominant theme in fishers' discussions of their lives and their characterizations of the dock in Chorrillos. Fishers' laments about being excluded from progress served as pointed critiques of pervasive political and economic inequalities. Such laments also drew on discourses of responsibility and self-help, which indicated the tensions and ambiguities that existed between fishers' explanations of why they were poor and threatened with dispossession. This suggests some of the ways in which fishers both recognized their dispossession and the unjustness of it while at the same time at least partially accepting responsibility for it. This apparent contradiction is critical for understanding how the enclosure of the wharf was potentially advanced through the naturalization of dominant logics that functioned to contest, muddy, or soften critiques aimed at the agents of dispossession—state actors, industrial captains, and private investors.

One afternoon in 2013, we conversed with a group of fishers about fishing and how it had changed. One fisher complained that state officials only showed up in Chorrillos for photo opportunities such as Produce's 2012 census of artisanal fishers or the annual Feast of San Pedro. The only time anything was done or any regulations were enforced, he argued, was when journalists did a story about food poisoning from people eating bad fish. The boliches, he said, continued to "kill the sea." The result, he complained, was that artisanal fishers were "like *campesinos* [peasants] now . . . We are poor. Everyone talks about economic growth, Peru's rapid economic growth, but we don't see it. Where is it? We are poorer than ever." This critique drew on and simultaneously criticized dominant social geographies and images of progress in Peru. In a country where the coast has been the seat of economic and political power as well as metropolitan culture, elites have long imagined campesinos as an Other: primarily Indigenous, rural, poor, and from the politically marginal highlands. The campesino was the object of state redemptory projects throughout much of the twentieth century—a subject to be overcome in the push to abolish "backwardness." This fisher's complaint signaled the degree to which fishers saw themselves as being of a different class than rural peasants. Fishers in Chorrillos were urban, they were autonomous, and to a large degree, they identified with dominant narratives of progress, imagining that through hard work and earning they would move forward. To many fishers, this meant that they would be able to aspire to a more comfortable working-class existence in the city. While Peru moved forward, many fishers felt they were not only being left behind but they were moving backwards and becoming more like campesinos.

Some articulated this feeling as shame that they were not able to provide what their family needed to be able to participate in the kinds of consumption that had become tied to notions of what it meant to be a citizen in Lima's urban life. Marcos, for example, said, "My daughters have suffered because many times there were many things I could not buy for them," such as the kind of notebooks or shoes that they wanted for school. Similarly, César commented that the waters in Chorrillos were changing and full of "*malas aguas*" (bad waters) that entered and drove the fish off. The water, he claimed, changed "from one moment to the next." The result, he said, was that sometimes fishers went out into the bay because they thought the fishing would be good, only to find that there were no fish—"we go out happy and return sad." He added, "At least I don't have children . . . the ones who do arrive at their house and the children [say] 'Papa, I want bread, papa' . . . [And the father has to say] 'There is none, child.'"

While fishers often directed their anger for not progressing economically at the absent state, they also directed these frustrations at themselves and other fishers, ruminating about their economic hardships in ways that framed poverty as the product of bad decisions. Talking about the better days, César said, "Before, yes, we earned money. I remember that I earned a lot of money . . . There was so much product, well, one earned, one earned . . . Lamentably, the old fishers, the fishers, did not know to save, well . . . one or two have known [how] to save [and] have their good house, good cars, [a] good position [in life] . . . a few but not all." It is hard to imagine how fishers could have seen the downturn coming, but many noted that had they been smarter about saving, they could have moved forward.

While some mulled over what they could have done better, others made more pointed commentary about what they saw as the shortcomings of other fishers and dock workers, whom they blamed for restricting the development of the wharf. For example, two older fishers, Silvio and Alejandro, had the following exchange about why they believed Chorrillos was in such a bad state:

SILVIO: This beach does not progress because the [association] leaders take all the money; they steal the money.

ALEJANDRO: Because of ignorance, old man, ignorance.

SILVIO: This is the worst dock that exists here [in this part of the coast].

ALEJANDRO: What tourist would come down here? What does a tourist see here? Nothing.

SILVIO: Dogs, crazy people.

ALEJANDRO: The whole beach is filthy.

Another older fisher, Patricio, echoed these complaints: "Look around, there are no tourists here, and it's close to the city. There should be people here but there aren't any." He believed that a lot of this had to do with the fact that people were afraid they would get robbed at the dock because, according to him, "no one works here," there is just "*vicio*"—drugs, people looking to steal from others, and few honest, working fishers.

Such statements suggest how traditional ideas about hard work intermingled with neoliberalized discourses of self-responsibility in fishers' narratives about what they saw as the deteriorating nature of life on the wharf. Fishers' identity as urban, working-class men was rooted in doing manual labor in a public space where they were recognized by their peers for their hard work, capability, and autonomy. Growing economic precarity, diminished catches, and a lack of state support threatened fishers' ability to realize this ideal of masculinity. This was clear in Silvio's, Alejandro's, and Patricio's complaints that the wharf was becoming too closely associated with criminality and laziness—marginalized masculinities that were signs that men had failed to find good, socially recognized work (Fuller 2003, 143). In their critiques of this situation, fishers recognized and named structural inequalities that they felt negatively affected their livelihoods—inequalities in political power, class disparities, and government corruption.

They also made it clear that there was not much they could do about these broad structural problems, such as government corruption, the unequal power that industry had to influence government policy, or the enforcement of regulations. In contrast, in discussions of their decisions and behavior, past and present, fishers focused on what they could have done better: They could have made better decisions about how to invest their money or saved it so that they would be in a better position. Such discourses relied on a selective remembrance of the past—the good fishing and the money that was made. However, the financial crises of the 1980s and 1990s—which brought with them runaway inflation and which impacted fishers' abilities to save even when the fishing was good—oftentimes did not factor prominently in fishers' accounts of the past.

The result was that through discourses of individual agency, morality, and choice, fishers acknowledged local inequalities—the fact that some had done better than others and were able to move away or buy better houses or a car—while belying the role that inequalities in market relationships played in producing these differences. The fact was obscured, for example, that a few fishers may have had access to capital through family members or arrangements with a local merchant that allowed them to do a little bit better and outcompete other local fishers. Such discourses stemmed in part from fishers' traditional valuing of personal autonomy, hard work, and the responsibility of caring for one's family. These beliefs also dovetailed with neoliberal tenets of entrepreneurial agency that were promoted by government agents and which emphasized that people had what they did because they "earned" it while others suffered because of poor choices. This dynamic was evident in vendors' commentaries about their struggles to make a living from the wharf and care for their children, although women's discussions of individual responsibility highlighted important differences in their experiences of and engagement with notions of neoliberalized agency and responsibility.

The Market

Graciela had been working on the wharf for over thirty years when we spoke with her in 2015. She was born in Apurimac, a region in the southern Andes. Her family sent her to Lima as a young girl to work as a servant. "I passed my whole youth [working in the city]," she said. "In four years of working, I earned nothing." Graciela met her husband in Lima, and her sister-in-law, who worked on the wharf, brought Graciela with her one day to help sell earrings. Later, Graciela switched to selling vegetables before working for decades as a fish cleaner and then, with failing health, as a vendor. She said bluntly, "I don't have anywhere else to work and I have to work." However, this was not easy for Graciela, who suffered from paralysis in the left part of her face and arm and did not hear well. Explaining her challenges, Graciela told us:

> I have family. I have five children, but my five children have their [own] diffi-
> cult[ies]. That's why I have to work, to give them [what they need]. I have one who
> is fifteen years old who has not yet finished high school and another daughter who
> did not finish. She did not want to study. Now I am [here] again to see if I can
> achieve something because of that [my children's situations]. [My injuries] gave
> me paralysis, and my ear is bad when I don't have this [hearing aid]. I suffered a lot
> to be able to work, [but over and over] clients left [my table]. I would say, "How?
> What?" And they would leave. And there are other vendors who take advantage of
> this. One here and another out front. And they each work with their daughter, and
> I [work] alone. Sometimes they ask, [but other times], they just take the customer.
> Since I don't hear well, [the customer] leaves, and I lose the sale.

Despite this, each day Graciela went to Chorrillos with the hope of selling a kilo or two of fish so that she could provide her two youngest daughters with money. She bought the fish from the market in Villa Maria because the fish in Chorrillos were too expensive. Graciela no longer cleaned fish because she said there were not enough fish in Chorrillos to make money doing it and because she was no longer physically able.

Two years prior to our conversation, she had been robbed and hurt. She had money on her because she had lent to someone who needed a small loan and she had just been repaid. The mugging left her partially paralyzed. She was out of work for six months after the attack. "One has to suffer to [move] forward," she quipped, but "instead of getting better, I sink more." While she was recuperating, she took out a thousand soles in loans from other vendors, who charged twenty to thirty percent interest. Graciela paid the loans back in daily installments of forty soles. When business was bad, there were days when she could not pay it. The women who had lent her the money were understanding and let Graciela miss some payments, but she still had to come up with the money, and it was difficult to do that when she was selling only a little bit of fish each day. She tried to get her children to help her sell so that she could increase her profit. She told them to "come and study here, come and help me and that way we will be able to pay [the debts]." However, her daughters did not want to have anything to do with the dock or fish selling. Graciela earned what she could selling fish and told us that in the meantime she would have to "suffer until God takes me, [because] what else is there to do?"

This stark characterization of life on the wharf reflected the particularly difficult challenges that Graciela's health and family responsibilities presented her. In contrast, another long-term vendor who had retired once told us that she still liked to come to the dock when she was "feeling worried" about something because on the dock, she could "relax, clear my mind, see my friends, and I forget my problems." Like the fishers, many women saw the wharf as a space where they had autonomy and could work with dignity. However, aspects of Graciela's comments about the difficulty of making a living on the dock resonated throughout our conversations with other women. Many highlighted the challenges of work as fish vendors, jaladoras, or kiosk operators and noted that working on the dock had not been among their first choices for employment. All of the women whom we interviewed had started out doing another kind of work or had studied with the hopes of establishing a career in a profession with greater social prestige. Some had lost more prestigious jobs and turned to the wharf as an alternative to other forms of informal, unskilled work in the city. Others noted that they started to work on the wharf after they had children. Within traditional gender roles, women were expected to care for children and maintain the home through labor such as daily cooking, cleaning, and food shopping. However, most could not afford to stay at home and had to find wage work outside the home in order to provide for their families given precarity in the local fishing economy and the devaluation of manual labor in Lima's economy. While this was critical for maintaining their families' livelihoods, it increased the overall amount of labor that women performed on a day-to-day basis. For some women, working on the wharf provided a means for balancing the demands of their daily labor routines. Women often commented that the benefit of work on the dock was the flexibility of choosing not to work if they had to care for children or the ability to have their children with them while they worked.

These were some of the issues that Luisa, who had only been working on the dock for a year when we spoke to her, raised in her comments about making a living as a fish cleaner. She was trained as a jeweler and had worked for a jewelry company for seventeen years when she lost her job because of "personnel reductions." Her mother had worked on the wharf for years as a fish cleaner, and so when Luisa found herself without a job, she joined her mother. For Luisa, the benefit of cleaning fish was that it was "independent work . . . you decide what hours you work and if you work or not," although she noted that she usually worked "all day." She said, one did not clean fish "because you like it, that's not important, but because you need to work." Luisa hoped to find another job as a jeweler, but for the time being, working on the wharf paid her bills.

Like Luisa, Josefina had family ties to the wharf. "Practically all of my life" was spent on the wharf, she said. As a child, Josefina worked on the beach with her mother, selling beer, crackers, and refreshments to tourists. "I have suffered a ton since I was a child," she told us. "I have known what it is like to be hungry, cold, [to have] problems . . . because I have never had my father with us, I grew up with my mother only, and she taught us a lot about life." When her mother stopped working as a vendor on the beach, Josefina worked for a while cleaning bathrooms in the Yacht Club next door, then she studied to be a receptionist and worked as one for five years before losing her job. She had no option but to return to the dock, where she worked as a filleter to help support her young daughter. The benefit of working on the dock, she explained, was that "this work is an independent job. Here they do not control you. Of course, you come and work, you pay for your table every day. [But] it is flexible. When I have had appointments or when I needed to be with my daughter, I did not come . . . you decide what hours you work and if you work or not." Josefina told us that she worked on the dock because it enabled her to earn so that her daughter could have a better life. More than anything, Josefina wished that her daughter would study so that she would have the ability to change careers when she wanted.

In addition to hopes for greater mobility for their children, women's desires for a better future were motivated in part by the belief that fishing was not as good as it had been in the past. This was a sentiment that Juana, who worked with her mother-in-law in a food kiosk, expressed in one of our conversations. Juana knew fishing and the Chorrillos wharf well. Her father was a fisher who still worked giving tours around the bay, two of her brothers were active fishers who worked up and down the coast, and her husband, Luis, made his living as an artisanal fisher. Before getting married, Juana had studied to be a nurse but then stopped because with "the babies, it was almost impossible to work." When her oldest son turned sixteen, she started working in her mother-in-law's kiosk because "here [in the wharf] I can have them with me, I can see them, and I can be here with my mother-in-law." Describing her daily work, Juana said, "I get up at six in the morning [and] attend to my children early. I give them their breakfast and from there, I come to work on the beach with my mother-in-law in the kitchen, cooking, preparing [food]. Also, I attend to my children and my husband [on the dock] . . . We all eat lunch here together including my mother-in-law, that is the easiest . . . In the mornings, I have my baby here, and my oldest son watches her until he has to go study." Despite the benefits of being able to be with family while working on the dock, Juana wanted her children to study and to find other work and to not go into fishing because "it is difficult and sometimes there are no fish." Furthermore, Juana talked about the tragedies of fishing, of men lost at sea and nearly dead from dehydration and others who drowned in rough waters. She said two of her brothers worked in a pharmacy and offered her husband a job, one that would likely have provided him steadier, less risky work. He turned it down, she said, because he was "used to fishing." Juana did not criticize her husband's decision, but she did note that fishing was not only dangerous but also inconsistent. She and her husband had to combine their income to have any hope of coming out ahead.

Ana, who had worked for eleven years as a jaladora for a boat that gave tourist rides, expressed similar sentiments. Her husband worked in a factory for a while but returned to fishing because his contract in the factory was up. "Because there are no fish," she told us, "fishers have to risk more. They have to go farther out, into rougher water." Ana had two children and she wanted neither to work on the dock. They were studying, and Ana worked on the dock to be able to take care of them and ensure they could finish school.

Echoing other women, Ana emphasized the advantage of the flexibility of work in the wharf: "For example, if I want to miss tomorrow, I say to the boat owner, 'Look, tomorrow I am going to miss because I have things to do,' and there is no problem. It gives me the option of dropping my kids off at school." However, with this flexibility came inconsistency and unpredictably. Business was often slow during the winter, so Ana had to do small jobs, such as cleaning houses, in Lima to make enough money to help support her family. Furthermore, even during the high season, it was harder and harder to make a good living because of increased competition for tourists' dollars. When she started working on the dock over a decade ago, "there were only five [tourist boats], now there are fourteen" during the tourist season.[6] The issue of competition among individuals who worked on the dock was something that emerged, albeit in often subtle ways, in women's commentaries, suggesting the strains and tensions that arose from trying to eke out a living from selling fish or attracting tourists to a food kiosk or tour ride. As Graciela mentioned above, she felt that other market vendors took advantage of her poor hearing to lure clients away from her. In a similar vein, Juana told us that there were sometimes tensions among the women in the kiosks and even fights. In her opinion, many of the women who ran the kiosks did not work well together because of the competition. "The pressure of the clients [to find a better deal] is terrible," she said. In the face of such challenges, many women emphasized the importance of hard work and individual responsibility for getting ahead.

Mercedes, for example, had worked on the wharf for forty-five years as a fish cleaner and vendor, although at the time we spoke in 2015, she was semi-retired, working only a few days a week when she felt up to it. She was born in Arequipa but moved to Lima when she was twenty-two because she had family in the city and was looking for work. Initially, she worked as a domestic servant, washing clothes for wealthy families and military officers, but then a neighbor brought her to the wharf, where she found work as a fish buyer. Mercedes had six children, one of whom was still financially dependent on her because of his ill health. She raised the children herself because her husband, a fisher, was an alcoholic. "I have been mother and father to my children," she said. "[I] confronted my problem and [began] to work . . . for my children." For her, the fish market in Chorrillos was a means of doing that. When we interviewed her, Mercedes cleaned fish sometimes, but there were few pejerrey so she was not working. Sometimes she also brought fish to the market to sell. Mercedes never invested in a food kiosk because she said she did not have the capital to get started in one and pay the rent. She said of her situation, "I cannot complain, when one knows [how] to work, [one] knows [how] to earn and . . . how to move ahead." People on the dock needed to "learn to be responsible" if they wanted to prosper, she commented.

Mercedes offered her son as an example of someone who had accepted his responsibilities and was doing what he should to get ahead. He and his girl-friend had children when they were young and had to leave school. "They have not had a youth," Mercedes commented, but thankfully, they were "responsible parents." Mercedes said her son stayed away from drugs and he learned how to fish "by necessity" so that he could support his family. He started out cleaning fish and then shifted to fishing in the high seas to make better money. Mercedes worried about him, noting that "sometimes I say, 'My God, look after my son.' There are many fishers who go out to sea and who never come back. Too many fishers met this fate, but then, what is he to do?" After returning from one two-week fishing trip empty handed, he had looked for work elsewhere and for a time was employed in a nearby paneling factory. Once he had finished his contract, the company let him go. At the time we spoke with Mercedes, her son was back on the dock working as a fisher so that he could take care of his family.

In contrast, Mercedes argued that the fishers' association was anything but responsible. She noted that while the fishing in Chorrillos had deteriorated as a result of contamination, things were doubly worse for fish sellers and clean-ers because "there is also no cleaning, no hygiene, because there is no water." Instead of fixing such problems, Mercedes commented that the leaders of the association:

> They do not do anything with the money; with the income from here, they do nothing. Right now the [current] administration has already left, they're gone, [and] new ones are coming in [who are] the same. They are people who have not even studied; sometimes they don't even know what a thing is, for example, like the five vowels [of Spanish]. And one would think that to enter an institution, to become a leader, you have to prepare, you have to know the regulations [and] what they are. So suppose you enter and as a novice, you don't know anything, and there is another [person] who is more ambitious, and they inculcate you and they whisper in your ear and tell you to do this and do the other thing, do it like that.

Mercedes asserted that the fishers in Chorrillos were "legal in [how they do] their work," but "there is also much corruption." She framed this as part of a generational shift, one that she claimed to have noticed over the course of her almost half century of working in Chorrillos. "Before fishers were very respectful, well mannered," she said. In her estimation, though, the younger fishers were "*malcriados*" (brats) who "say many rude things." According to Mercedes, in the past, fishers were not only more respectful, but women were also more involved in the fish trade as buyers. Each fisher worked with a woman, sometimes his wife, who was responsible for negotiating and selling his catch, as Mercedes had done when she first started working in Chorrillos. This was no longer the case since fishers sold their own catches or contracted other men to do it for them.

Mercedes' commentary highlighted her and other women's feelings that although there were considerable resources circulating on the dock, they did not have access to them nor were they benefiting from them. Although many, but not all, of the women working in Chorrillos had connections to members of the association, for many, these connections were not very strong since they were through a deceased father or an uncle. These women did not receive the same benefits that the nuclear families of active members did. Few had health insurance. However, all of them had to pay daily or annual use fees to the dock administrator to be able to operate a kiosk or sell or clean fish. For Mercedes and other women, their acknowledgment that it was more difficult to make a living on the dock was paired with the feeling that perhaps that was due in part to the association's neglect of the space and of them.

These discussions suggest the complex ways in which discourses of entrepreneurial agency and responsibility circulated in the wharf. Rather than directing their frustration at an absent state that had abandoned them, as fishers generally did, vendors who worked on the dock expressed their frustration with the fishers' association. Vendors had never been formally included in the official state organization of the dock and so, unlike the fishers, did not have a nostalgic sense of a once beneficent state. Rather, for fish cleaners, vendors, and jaladoras, it was the fishers who were the most visible agents of local governance and, especially in the case of the association, had failed to include them in the dock's workings. Fish cleaners and vendors argued that the association was not complying with its responsibility to care for other workers on the dock—a responsibility that they not only framed both in terms of political fairness and equality but also in terms of the social and moral obligation that men had to support women who had taken on the responsibility of caring for their children and extended families. Women reinforced the latter point in their commentaries by noting that they were not working in their preferred profession but had taken work on the dock because it allowed them to earn when there were few other options and take care of their children. In this vein, women's commentaries on work in Chorrillos reinforced notions of hard work and individual responsibility as a necessity for getting ahead because of diminishing fish supplies and the strains of competing with other vendors for tourist dollars. This aspect of vendors' commentaries paralleled fishers' discussions about the importance of individual responsibility and entrepreneurial agency for explaining some of the disparities among individuals who worked on the dock.

Such discussions also indicated the tension that existed between vendors' and fishers' recognition of their positions within broader inequalities and the lure of individual agency for explaining such disparities. Despite the difficulties of trying to make it through work on the dock, many women and men expressed the feeling that at least the work provided a modicum of individual autonomy and dignity that one could not find in other low-status jobs around the city, such as construction or domestic service.[7] And yet, when it became inflected with notions of individual responsibility, such autonomy could turn into isolation, the feeling that Graciela expressed that she was on her own in her struggle to keep working and provide for her daughters. Moreover, this indicates how it was possible for fishers and vendors to both recognize the impact that structural inequalities had on their livelihoods while regarding specific local cases of poverty and misfortune as a lack of individual planning and initiative.

Conclusion

The belief that fishers had to do anything it takes to survive was shared by older and younger fishers as well as vendors working on the dock, and it was a sentiment that emerged out of a complex mix of feelings, perceptions, and ideologies about dignity, abandonment, and agency. Discussing the challenges that fishers in Chorrillos faced, Marcos once noted that "some have emigrated, they live in another place. [Others] they no longer devote themselves to fishing." When we asked what he and his brother planned to do, Luis answered that for now they would keep going "until things improve, until there is something else to go out for." César claimed that he had no choice but to stay; he was getting old and he said, "We have to die here in the sea." These were not expressions of resignation or despondency but subtle ways in which fishers staked their claim to the wharf as a cultural and economic space. César had spent most of his life working on the wharf in Chorrillos, and his declaration that he would die there was a way of asserting his personal connection to the place. César was not alone in making such assertions.

On May 18, 2013, we arrived at the dock in Chorrillos just as a funeral procession made its way through the parking lot. The funeral was for an older fisher who had died the day before. Six fishers carried the white coffin covered with flowers out of the meeting hall to a car waiting on the street. There were forty or so people dressed in black watching as the coffin was loaded into the car, which then made its way up the hill toward the city. As we watched, we talked to a woman who worked as a walking vendor selling cigarettes, gum, and candy on the wharf. She said that the old fisher was called Carlos. For the past twenty years or so, Carlos had slept in his boat, which he could no longer afford to repair and did not have the strength to take out and keep fishing. Two days before, as a result of a government order, fishers had been working to clean up the beach between the dock and the Yacht Club. They moved some of the big old boats, including Carlos' boat, from the beach to the far end of the parking lot where they could be stored until the owners could move them or the abandoned ones could be hauled away. It was not clear if Carlos had died before the boat had been moved or during the move. The woman told us that she would not want to be buried but would rather have her ashes scattered along the routes she walked as a vendor. Mercedes, a long-time fish cleaner and vendor, told us something similar. She said that she had told her children that when she died she wanted to be cremated and have her ashes scattered on the sea in Chorrillos so that she "would be kept company by the fish."

These statements of personal connection and belonging indicated the importance of the wharf for many of the people who used it as a space where they had been able to express some degree of autonomy and dignity—both of which, fishers and vendors felt, were imperiled by growing inequalities. Individuals who made their livings on the wharf recognized and named structural inequalities, commenting on the difficulties that they faced because they were poor. Furthermore, fishers and vendors expressed anger that individuals with greater power and mobility did not do enough to aid fishers and vendors, a sentiment that was most evident in fishers' resentment toward the industrial boats for depleting fish stocks and toward the state for abandoning them as well as in vendors' criticisms of the fishers' association for not doing more to take care of them.

These were significant critiques of economic and political inequality, and fishers and vendors openly named these factors as the direct causes of the precarity that they faced. However, in response to this situation, fishers and vendors invoked individual responsibility and hard work as the only viable solutions for getting ahead.

Commenting on ideologies of work and laziness in a Mexican fishing community in the Colorado River delta, Shaylih Muehlmann (2013, 115) notes that people "did not highlight structural determinants in order to obscure their own responsibility as individuals" but to "underscore their own agency despite these wider forces." The same was true in Chorrillos, where individuals stressed that, notwithstanding the difficulties and inequalities they faced, they were willing to do all they could in order to get ahead and take care of their families. These assertions of defiance were largely individual—they were personal expressions of what particular people said they were doing to get ahead despite the many challenges they faced. When these proclamations of individual agency ran up against the realities of daily poverty, they often slipped into discussions about what other individuals were not doing as a means of explaining why some failed and why the dock was in bad shape. It was through these discussions about the irresponsibility of certain individuals or groups that dominant ideas about poverty and agency were incorporated into local discourse.

Tensions between structure and agency in fishers' and vendors' narratives of their personal struggles reveal what is at stake and the discursive terrain upon which daily struggles over dispossession unfold. Such narrative tensions underscore the importance of the mundane ways in which the possibility of dispossession is considered, undermined, and sometimes justified. While dispossessions sometimes take the form of dramatic relocations or visible evictions, just as often they are less-visible processes whereby impoverished people are slowly deprived of their rights or access to productive resources or property that they rely upon to live a life of dignity. Paying attention to how people talk about these slow processes and to what or to whom they attribute responsibility or blame for their progression is a critical aspect of thinking about how dispossession works or is potentially blocked.

Conclusion

C laudio was twenty-three years old when we interviewed him in 2015. He was one of several young men trying to make a living by fishing in Chorrillos, where he had spent his adolescence learning the trade from older fishers. Claudio, like most of those fishers, used a small wooden boat and hand-drawn gillnets to fish within a few nautical miles of the shore. Claudio was quick to point out that the bay hosted significant spawning grounds for a number of different species, which meant that the fishing had been very good, and he believed it could be good again if there was greater government control of industrial fishing. As fishers, Claudio argued, "We have to take care of it [the ocean] because it provides our sustenance, and if we don't take care of it, who will?" We asked him what he thought the future held for the bay's fishing. "I hope that it improves," he said, commenting that he wanted to be able to keep fishing in order to create a decent life for himself. The ultimate mark of this was, in his words, "to have something of one's own"—to be "the owner of something" such as a new boat so that he would not have to rent one to fish each day.

Claudio's comments make critical connections that are often absent in broader discussions about environmental issues, both in Peru and around the world. He clearly linked the ecological crisis in Chorrillos' fishery with class politics, both in the form of unchecked industrial exploitation and in his desire for autonomy—to have just enough economic freedom to control his labor and to reproduce himself culturally by creating what he considered to be a decent life. For many of the fishers and vendors we came to know in Chorrillos, this meant being able to send their children to school with good clothes and note-books with the hope that education would lead them to a good future in which they could participate as full citizens in Lima's life. Within contemporary envi-ronmental politics and discussions of climate change, this desire for dignity is sometimes mistaken as evidence of humans' inherent capitalist drive and their need to always have more and expand, which has led to the present global eco-logical crisis. Rather than reveal anything inherent, this assertion discursively hides the class politics of environmental crises and the specific histories of who bears responsibility for them and who shoulders the unequal burden of their consequences. In contrast, Claudio's comments keep these politics in view, mak-ing visible the indelible connections among nature, class, and value.

In this book, we have argued that artisanal fishers' and vendors' lives and the way they have been entwined with the development of Peruvian fisheries provide insight into the challenges they face in maintaining more-than-human collaborations that are sufficient to sustain a living. The history of artisanal fishing in Peru reveals how nature, class, and politics are actively bundled in dialectical relationships of coproduction at particular historical moments. The contemporary state of Peruvian fisheries is the result of successive attempts by the fishmeal industry and the state to reorganize ocean natures to generate sur-plus value. Beginning in the mid-twentieth century, state efforts to territorialize the ocean and coastal spaces served as a means of claiming anchoveta stocks for the burgeoning fishmeal industry. This particular way of organizing ocean natures, which relied upon cheap labor and easy access to anchoveta to overcome technological inefficiencies, created a crisis in production as fish stocks declined and costs increased. This led to subsequent rounds of reorganization whereby the state took over the fishmeal industry in order to save it from bankruptcy, in the process cutting the labor force and encouraging laid off workers to move to the artisanal fishing sector. State officials sought to ameliorate the social impact of this move through profit-sharing programs whereby the development of artisanal fisheries would be funded by fishmeal profits, but resources for this never really materialized given ongoing crises in the industry and the state's prioritization of fishmeal exports. In the ensuing decades, the artisanal food fish sector absorbed growing waves of surplus labor and boats as the fishmeal industry became more efficient and monopolized in order to extract greater value from diminishing stocks. This was also accompanied by new waves of state territorialization of the ocean in ways that reinforced the fishmeal industry's all-but-free access to anchoveta stocks.

A similar dynamic has unfolded in the urban coastal space occupied by artisanal fishers in Chorrillos. Throughout much of the colonial era, fishing settlements existed on the margins of the city, both geographically and socially, functioning as sites to escape the oversight of colonial governance. With the advent of the Bourbon Reforms, the colonial government exerted greater efforts to reign in the autonomy of fishers and sought repeatedly to erase the place-specific rights to fishing grounds that different guilds had established during previous centuries. In the late eighteenth and early nineteenth centuries, wealthy urbanites began to use the beaches for recreation, providing an additional source of income for Indigenous fishers, but also slowly encroaching upon fishers by constructing summer homes and then the Yacht Club along the coast. As Lima expanded during the twentieth century, the city's rich chose to spend time at more exclusive, environmentally pristine beaches to the north and south of the city. Lima's neglected beaches became recreation areas for the growing number of poor urban residents and also became areas where city waste could be dumped without consequence, a way of cheaply dealing with sewage from the growing city. Sewage collectors dotted the city's coastline, dumping raw effluent onto the beaches or into the ocean. Since the 1990s, projects of urban renewal in Miraflores and the city center have reshaped those spaces to make them more amenable to tourism as well as private investment and real estate speculation. The Costa Verde became part of this as both a site beautified for tourism and an important expansion of the city's transportation infrastructure. This has led to increased pressure on fishers to renovate Chorrillos' wharf to bring it in line with recent development in the zone—a process most clearly exhibited by the neighboring Yacht Club's proposal to revamp the fishing wharf and turn it into a tourism destination rather than a functioning hub for the local fishing economy.

One of the central arguments of this book is that enclosure has played a critical role in these reorganizations of ocean and coastal spaces—securing free and exclusive access to ocean natures, the right to dump waste into coastal spaces, or the appropriation of desirable real estate for the production of surplus value. To put it more bluntly, new configurations of nature, capital, and politics rely on the ongoing enclosure of commonly or locally held resources to ensure the production of wealth. This process depends on political discourses that separate nature, class, and politics to disguise these enclosures as "natural" and enable the continuation of inequalities in access to productive resources or the continuation of the accumulation of harm.

Throughout Peru's history, changing regimes of governance have highlighted the alterity of fishers and vendors and the spaces they occupied in changing languages of civilization, ethnicity, race, and class. Such discourses made possible the legal invisibility of traditional fishing grounds and territories under late colonial and later republican law, and they laid the groundwork for the state's claims that Peru's ocean belonged to the nation. Most recently, neoliberalized discourses of responsibility and entrepreneurialism have threatened to wrest access to the wharf from fishers and vendors. Within official programs of neoliberalized fisheries regulation, government officials have framed artisanal fishing communities as comprised of individual, competing entrepreneurs who must demonstrate their responsibility to a "community" and their desire to expand existing markets. These narrowly defined notions of what it means to be a responsible citizen—framed in technical terms of whether fishers follow government-sanctioned, economically oriented "best practices"—have made artisanal fishers and vendors more visible to emerging regulatory and tax regimes. In other words, they represent new forms of enclosure through which state officials have sought to extract value from artisanal fishers in new ways.

These regulatory regimes have failed to recognize the active, collective projects of "commoning" (Bresnihan 2016) that artisanal fishers and vendors have engaged in to reproduce themselves economically, culturally, and ecologically. Intricate and constantly renewed human and nonhuman relationships enable artisanal fishers and vendors to live in dignity, to weather ups and downs of the economy and the fishery, and to set limits on how much fish is extracted in a given season. Government officials claimed that making artisanal fishers more responsible was a necessary step in ensuring the ecological and economic sustainability of fisheries. By extending market principles of entrepreneurialism and competition to natural resources, officials asserted that artisanal fishers would be able to more effectively generate value from marine resources. Yet, we have argued throughout this book that neoliberalized fisheries projects worked to the opposite effect by reinforcing nature as external to economic relationships, as something that responsible entrepreneurs access and use and from which they extract value. Neoliberalized approaches to natural resource management fail to recognize the intricate coproduction of nature, culture, and capital in historical "world-ecologies" (Moore 2015). In so doing, they lay the groundwork for "enclosure-through-separation" (Federici 2004) by making it seem as though fishers exist separately from the fish they catch, as though ecological and economic knowledge are not entwined, and as though cultural relationships and systems of human and extra-human care are not critical for making economic exchange possible.

Ideologies of entrepreneurial responsibility undercut the more-than-human commoning that artisanal fishers and vendors engaged in on a daily basis by threatening an increased enclosure of fisheries or the dispossession of vendors from the wharf if they did not do more to demonstrate that they were good entrepreneurs. While framed in the language of good resource stewardship, government officials' commentaries revealed that such threats were motivated by the assumption that artisanal fishers and vendors were low-class denizens who were out of place in spaces such as Lima's Costa Verde. The challenge of resisting such framings has been that they have wound their way into day-to-day understandings of life on the wharf, dovetailing with traditional ideals of hard work and caring for one's family. While fishers and vendors criticized the government for its threats of enclosure and dispossession in attempts to identify ways forward, they also drew on and reinforced key aspects of neoliberalized responsibility to explain the inequalities that existed among fishers and vendors.

In a similar manner, geographic comparisons recognized inequalities among fishing ports in regards to the amount of fish landed and the overall economic wellbeing of the people working on specific wharves. However, such discourses attributed these inequalities to differences in the physical geography or the culture of work in each place, thus naturalizing such inequalities and erasing capital and class politics as necessary means for understanding the disparate geographies that comprise Peru's coastline and make the ongoing accumulation of capital (and thus the production of new differences) possible. For example, fishers and government managers often commented on the poor quality of fishing in Chorrillos in comparison to Ancón to the north and Pucusana to the south, attributing such disparities to differences in the physical geography of the places and the natural productivity of fish stocks, while also noting that such disparities were conditioned by differences in work ethic and local responsibility. Such explanations helped to justify dispossessions that are necessary for new configurations of nature, capital, and politics by obscuring how the historically specific configurations of the three enabled the accumulation of wealth in some places while concentrating harm and degradation in others.

Critical aspects of this dynamic parallel broader climate politics that reconnect people to nature in neoliberalized ways that not only obscure the role of capitalism in organizing life but also overlook the complex more-than-human relationships that comprise and sustain many ecologies. The idea of the Anthropocene has become ubiquitous in popular and academic discourse on global warming, emerging as the preferred conceptual framework for addressing contemporary climate change. The Nobel-winning atmospheric chemist Paul J. Crutzen and the biologist Eugene F. Stoermer (2000, 18) promoted the term to name "the current geological epoch" in a manner that emphasized the "central role of mankind in geology and ecology." As Jason Moore (2016, 3) points out, this was a bold proposal because it established humans' role in contemporary climate change, made it clear that human and geological history would be intertwined in the long run, and emphasized the need for people to act to ensure that the planet remained a livable place. However, the idea of the Anthropocene fails to recognize capitalism as the driving force of climate change and the ways in which class has shaped not only who has contributed most to global warming but also who suffers most from it (Moore 2016, 4–5). Donna Haraway (2016, 47–49) argues that the concept tells a "story of Species Man as the agent of the Anthropocene," which ignores the "networks of sugar, precious metals, plantations, indigenous genocides, and slavery, with their labor innovations and relocations and recompositions of critters and things sweeping up both human and nonhuman workers of all kinds" that are at the very core of contemporary climate change. Similarly, Andreas Malm (2016, 390) argues that global warming is a direct product of a "fortunate few" appropriating "the bulk of the atmospheric carbon sink through massive emissions which by distinction cannot be extended to humanity as a whole." Malm (2016, 391) asserts that the rich and powerful will find ways to insulate themselves from experiencing a shared climate catastrophe while the situation of the poor will become more and more precarious—"more than ever class distinctions will become matters of life and death."

The current situation of the eastern Pacific Ocean, Peru's fisheries, and Lima's coastal spaces is the result of organizing life at multiple scales for the benefit of a few. The ocean has been appropriated as a free sink for absorbing excess carbon produced by industrialized countries. Peru's most productive fish species are being overexploited by industrial fishing to feed populations of the Global North and now China, who demand increasing quantities of animal protein. The irony of Peru's industrial fishery is that most of the fish are not even being caught for consumption—since few people around the world find anchoveta a desirable table fish—but as feed for preferred fish (in the form of farmed species, such as trout and salmon) and livestock (chicken and pork) proteins. And, Lima's coastal spaces are being reconstructed to facilitate tourism, real estate speculation, and the expansion of the country's export markets. These reorganizations of coastal lives for the purpose of capital accumulation have repeatedly burdened ocean natures *and* subaltern coastal populations. While contemporary global environmental discourse tends to draw our attention to the former, the latter is largely ignored, erased by visions of ocean wilds or lumped into an undifferentiated humanity that is threatening ocean species and chemistry. However, this book demonstrates that this is a mistake. Just as with the ocean species upon which they depend, impoverished fishers and vendors have been thrown into increasingly precarious states and face mounting challenges and struggles to reproduce themselves in culturally meaningful ways.

This situation is not unique to artisanal fishers in Lima. Fisheries around the world have been characterized by successive maritime enclosures as increasingly monopolized fishing corporations have sought to capture dwindling reserves of cheap ocean natures, usually at the expense of artisanal, small-scale, and Indigenous fishers (Bresnihan 2016; Menzies 2016; Muehlmann 2013). One result of this has been that many of these fishers have been pushed out of the trade and those who remain face increased precarity. In one of its recent annual reports on the state of the world's fisheries, FAO (2016, iii) analysts note that "small-scale fisheries provide work to 90 percent of the people employed in capture fisheries." Yet, such fisheries continue to be economically and ecologically vulnerable, despite their important role in local food production, subsistence, and food security. The report's authors assert that this is because small-scale fishers are often left out of management schemes, which are oriented to regulating industrial production. To address this issue, they call for measures to strengthen small-scale fisheries by instituting means to make fishers more responsible and sustainable—a neoliberalized solution that emphasizes greater regulation combined with better access to regional and global markets as the solutions for crises in artisanal fisheries around the world. Such solutions frame fishing as a primarily economic activity and imagine fishers as individuals who are trying to maximize their economic gain and who need to be regulated to ensure that they do not overfish and destroy the commons they utilize.

We have shown that these approaches continue, rather than ameliorate, the enclosure and dispossession of artisanal fishers because such schemes for improvement fail to recognize the cultural, social, and ecological relationships that make fishing possible and the fact that people fish for cultural and social reasons, not just economic ones. As Claudio's comments at the beginning of this conclusion indicate, for artisanal fishers in Lima, cultural dignity and the integrity of local ecologies are just as important as making money. Moreover, the act of artisanal fishing not only is an economic exchange but also relies upon and helps to sustain a dense set of multispecies relationships that comprise coastal life-worlds. Recognizing and promoting these relationships is critical for addressing fisheries crises and climate change because emphasizing that fisheries are embedded in and rely upon the production of more-than-human commons represents a critical alternative to capitalist world-ecologies. In proposing a radical climate politics, Donna Haraway (2016, 99, 109) argues that we need to learn to find new ways of "making kin" through processes of "worlding on a wounded terra" that construct new relationships among species and in the process make the reproduction of life possible. Similarly, Anna Lowenhaupt Tsing (2015) argues that our current era is one that is characterized by human disturbance of the atmosphere and ecological systems around the world. This situation requires new ways of thinking about and approaching biological diversity that do not privilege pristine spaces but rather focus on instances in which, out of the ruins of capital, humans have collaborated with other species to create diverse biological and cultural assemblages (Tsing 2015; Kirksey 2015).

In Chorrillos, fishers have drawn upon and revised their knowledge of ecologically compromised fisheries to eke out a living from an increasingly degraded coastal environment. The area's fishery has been transformed by widespread urban pollution, coastal gentrification, and the fishmeal industry's dramatic reconfiguration of ocean natures and labor. Despite these transformations, several hundred men and women have managed to extract a living from the bay's highly compromised nature. They have done so by adjusting when, how, and what they fish for in attempts to deal with growing water pollution from sewage and more erratic fish yields. Moreover, artisanal fishing families have diversified their strategies for earning a living to deal with ecological and economic precarity. Such strategies represent vital ways in which people have sought to create alternatives that enable them to sustain culturally dignified livelihoods. Capitalist world-ecologies have thrived by obscuring the multispecies networks that make industries, such as industrial fishmeal exports, possible by appropriating nature and labor—life—cheaply and then creating new cheap nature and labor through enclosures and dispossessions (Moore 2015). In contrast, artisanal fishers and vendors have sustained culturally meaningful livelihoods by underscoring and constantly helping to remake multispecies life-worlds. As such, artisanal fishers in this and other Peruvian ports represent critical examples for thinking about life and possibilities in compromised ecologies.

The experiences of Lima's artisanal fishers and vendors show that ecological crises are always at the same time economic and social crises. Class politics and struggles for the dignity of impoverished fishers and vendors are necessary components of an effective strategy against ecological destruction. Any just environmental politics must deal with the enclosures, dispossessions, and appropriations both of nonhuman and human natures that make capital accumulation possible. This is a task that is impossible without careful attention not only to how humans are connected to nonhuman entities in broader ecologies but also how different humans are connected to each other and nonhumans in different and unequal ways and how such inequalities are at the core of contemporary world-ecologies and the crises they face.

Acknowledgments

This book would not have been possible without the support, input, help, and patience of countless people over the course of years of research and writing. Because we chose to follow standard ethnographic convention and protect the anonymity of our research subjects by giving them pseudonyms, we cannot thank by name the many individuals who opened their lives to us and who spent countless hours talking to us about fishing and who showed us the challenges of making a living with the ocean. Our most profound debt is to the fishers, vendors, and other members of the wharf "commons" in Chorrillos. Numerous other individuals made our research in Peru possible, from representatives of fishers' associations in other ports who talked to us in great depth about changes in their local fisheries, to officials in the Ministry of Production who made time in their schedules for interviews, to colleagues in Lima's universities who were always willing to discuss different aspects of our research, to friends who made us feel at home each time we returned to Lima. We are grateful to all of these people for their time and help.

We have received support at Iowa State University that has been crucial for the success of this project. Funding for numerous research trips to Peru and research assistants was provided by the former Department of Anthropology, the Department of World Languages and Cultures, and the College of Liberal Arts and Sciences. We also benefited from the constant support of colleagues, both in our home departments and around campus, who talked through various aspects of the project at different stages, read proposals, commented on chapter drafts, and provided encouragement when it was needed. We owe special thanks to Clare Cardinal-Pett and Marwan Ghandour for serving as long-term interlocutors on Lima and for helping us to think about the role of space in the changing nature of Lima's fisheries. We are also grateful to our colleague Grant Arndt for reading multiple drafts of research proposals related to this project and drafts of each chapter in the book. Additionally, Chad Gasta, Nell Gabiam, Mark Rectanus, and Elisa Rizo read and commented on earlier prospectus and chapter drafts.

Over the course of researching and writing this book, we received invitations to present at events both on the Iowa State University campus and around the country. The organizers and participants of these events provided helpful feedback on some of our early attempts to think through our ongoing research on the lives of artisanal fishers and their places both within Lima's urban geography and broader dynamics in Peruvian fisheries. We are grateful for input and encouragement from Cristina Dreifuss-Serrano, Juliet Erazo, Daniella Gandolfo, Larry Nesper, Suzanne Oakdale, and James Scott.

We owe sincere thanks to Allyson Carter at the University of Arizona Press for her support of this project and work to get it published. The staff of UAP have made working on this manuscript a real pleasure. Thanks go to the two external reviewers for the University of Arizona Press who provided thoughtful suggestions for strengthening the final manuscript. We are also grateful to the editors of the Critical Green Engagements series for their interest in this book: Jim Igoe, Molly Doane, José Martínez-Reyes, Tracey Heatherington, Melissa Checker, and Bram Büscher. Special thanks go to Molly Doane for her detailed and insightful feedback on an earlier draft of the manuscript. We owe thanks to Yibo Fan as well for his work on the maps of Peru and the wharf in Chorrillos and we are grateful to Allison Mills for her careful editing of the final manuscript.

Finally, special thanks go to our friends and families whose constant encouragement and support helped us through the long and often challenging work of writing this book. Max would like to express his deepest gratitude to Anneke Mundel and Elio and Nico Viatori for their constant love and support, without which his work would not be possible. He would also like to thank Anne and Max Viatori for helping to make several research trips to Lima (among other things) possible and to Ben Viatori and Melissa Patterson for being there. Héctor is deeply grateful to his mother, Cecilia Medina Rincón, for her unconditional support and generosity; his father, Hector Antonio Bombiella Sossa, for his advice and inspiration; and his sister, Maritza Cecilia, for her constant encouragement and motivation.

Notes

Introduction

1. Recent research suggests that global warming, specifically in the form of rising ocean temperatures, is creating the conditions for more intense El Niños, such as the "super" El Niño that occurred from 2015 to 2016. On this issue, see e.g. Cai et al. (2014) and Johnson (2014). See Broad and Orlove (2007) on the social and political impacts of Peru's El Niño events.
2. Among other issues, the image of Peru as an "Andean" nation obscures the reality that sixty percent of Peru's territory lies east of the Andes in Amazonia, while more than half of the nation's population live in the thin ribbon of desert coast between the Andes and the Pacific Ocean. On this issue, see Greene (2006).
3. On the subject of "audit culture," see Strathern (2000). For a critical analysis of the concept of community, see Joseph (2002). On the cultural and symbolic aspects of dispossession, including the denial of agency and selfhood, see Bhandar and Bhandar (2016) and Butler and Athanasiou (2013).
4. Existing literature on "commons" demonstrates that powerful actors repeatedly have appropriated resources, wealth, labor, and the knowledge of peasants, workers, and Indigenous peoples for their own gain (Hay et al. 1975; Linebaugh 2008; Thompson 1991). This work has also shown how oppressed peoples have tried to resist such appropriation through day-to-day resistance and social mobilization (Scott 1985).
5. See Moore (2015, 291) on this politics of (un)bundling.

Chapter 1

1. For example, in their analysis of Peru's fishmeal industry, Smetherman and Smetherman (1973, 340) argue that "fish are a 'common property,'" which means

that "no one collects economic rent for use of the resource." They assert that "the economic rent which in other resources is collected by 'owners' whose welfare demands conservatism, is simply divided among all fishers exploiting the resource." Without effective regulation by an "owner," such as the state, each newcomer to the fishery causes rent to be "dissipated in higher costs and lower catches and the basic stock is depleted to a low level." For an updated, but not greatly different, version of this argument about Peru's lack of fisheries regulation, see Aranda (2009).

2.   Numerous critiques have been written of Hardin's idea of the "tragedy of the commons," such as Ostrom (2008), Linebaugh (2010), and Peterson and Isenhour (2014); Longo et al. (2015) examine this idea extensively in their discussion of world fisheries. See Pálsson and Durrenberger (1990) on the cultural politics of support for or against individual boat quotas. See also Moore (2012) on the ways in which fisheries crises and management science frame fishers and fish in particular ways. A number of works in maritime anthropology have argued against the notion that the ocean is a commons, stating that such an idea erases traditional use-tenures and opens up the space and its resources for corporate exploitation. See Acheson (2003), Alexander (1980), McCay (1987), and Menzies (2016).

3.   In his early study of Peru's fishmeal industry, Michael Roemer (1970, 82–3) details how the coalescing of several scientific and technological developments made Peru's anchoveta fishery possible.

4.   Marine legal scholar David Loring (1971, 400) notes that "the figure '200 miles' was somewhat arbitrary, although it was considered approximately the distance covered by land-based whale catchers." On the role that Peru's territorial declarations had in the "Tuna Wars," see Wolff 1980. In 1982, the United Nations passed its Convention on the Law of the Seas, which established a 12-nautical-mile territorial limit for all coastal states as well as a 188-nautical-mile exclusive economic zone (United Nations General Assembly 1982). While this did not support Peru's ongoing claim to expanded territorial waters, it did support its control of economic resources in this area.

5.   These laws were the 1969 General Law of Waters; the 1970 Law of the Public Company for the Commercialization of Fishmeal and Oil Produced in the Country, Decree no. 18253; and the 1971 General Fisheries Law, Decree no. 18810.

6.   In 1968, at the outset of the Velasco government, of the leading twenty-six fishmeal producers, seven were owned by foreigners (five of them U.S.-based) and two were jointly owned with Peruvian partners (Smetherman and Smetherman 1973, 346). Commenting on the integral nature of foreign capital in the industry, Thorp (1983, 40) states that "much Peruvian capital entered the [fishmeal] sector, but most of it entered indirectly via the banking system and always in conjunction with foreign capital."

7.   In an attempt to benefit fishers, the state also gave some boats to laid-off workers as severance (Ros-Tonen and van Boxel 1999, 13). However, many out-of-work fishers could not afford to maintain the boats.

8.   As with many government initiatives aimed at protecting artisanal fishers, this privileged a small cohort of quasi-industrial boats. For example, the boats built with FONDEPES money were sold to fishers for $10,000 each—a price that only a portion of more well off small-scale fishers could afford.

9.   In order of revenue generated, these companies are: Tecnológica de Alimentos (Lima-based, acquired by Brescia Group, a large Peruvian conglomerate); Copeinca (Norwegian capital); Pesquera Diamante, Austral Group (Norwegian capital); Pesquera Hayduk SA (a subsidiary of the Peru-based Bamar Group); Pesquera Exalmar (Peruvian owners, the Matta Curotto family); CFG Investment (a subsidiary of Hong Kong-based Pacific Andes International Holdings); and Pesquera Centinela (a subsidiary of Peruvian Grupo Romero).

10. In March 2018, Kuczynski resigned from the presidency amid corruption scandals that implicated him in vote-buying and receiving bribes from the Brazilian corporation, Odebrecht. Martín Vizcarra Cornejo, the vice president, replaced Kuczynski Godard as president. At the time of writing, Vizcarra had only been in office for a few months. At the outset, however, his administration appeared to be willing to support expanded protections and rights for artisanal fishers, who protested for, demanded, and received consultation meetings with officials from his administration to discuss improved social welfare benefits for artisanal fishers.

Chapter 2

1.   Arroyo Aguilar (2003) provides an interesting analysis of the Feast of San Pedro in Chorrillos, arguing that it incorporates and maintains key aspects of Andean cosmology.

2.   Lima's process of urbanization in the second half of the twentieth century has been the subject of a rich and extensive literature, a complete discussion of which is beyond the scope of this chapter. See Aguirre and Panfichi (2013) for different historical and sociological aspects of Lima's urbanization. For a look at the history of city planning and development in Lima, see Turner (1977) and Mangin and Turner (1968). Blondet (1991), Dietz (1998), Driant (1991), and Riofrío (1991) examine the development of community political organizations in poor neighborhoods. Chion (2002) examines the role of real estate investment in changes to Lima's social geography.

3.   The one exception to this appears to have been fishers in Callao, where there were two fishing settlements, Piti-Piti Viejo and Nuevo, located outside the walls of the city, although a colonial census indicates that close to seventy fishers lived inside the city as well (Charney 2001, 24).

4.   Spanish colonial society in the Viceroyalty of Peru was divided into two republics, one for Spaniards and Creoles and the other for Indigenous peoples. Within this system, *indio* (Indian) was a legal category that required Indigenous people to pay tribute (an important source of colonial revenue) and provide compulsory *mita* labor (a significant source of unpaid labor that went to Spanish mines and

landowners) in return for legal protections from slavery and the preservation of communal land holdings.

5.   Specifically, Lima's elites were concerned with threats to their power that were posed by José Carlos Mariátegui's Partido Socialista Peruana (Socialist Party of Peru, later the Communist Party of Peru) and Víctor Haya de la Torre's Alianza Popular Revolucionaria Americana (American Popular Revolutionary Alliance). On Mariátegui's thought and his influence on both Peruvian and international politics, see Becker (1993). Of particular significance to this discussion is Mariátegui's emphasis on an organic approach to class organizing in Peru, one that highlighted the positive contributions of Indigenous peoples. For a discussion of APRA and state repression of the party during significant portions of the twentieth century, see Nugent (2010).

6.   Briggs and Mantini-Briggs (2004) provide an in-depth examination of the racial politics of Venezuela's cholera outbreak during 1992–93 and highlight how the social stigma associated with the disease enabled it to spread.

7.   Anthropologists working on race, class, and environmental contamination have shown that elites often dismiss the structural factors that concentrate ecological degradation in impoverished areas by claiming that poor residents could simply move or make other choices (Blanton 2011). "By not recognizing structural dynamics that stack the deck of economic and environmental advantage against a significant portion of the population," Bonnie Urciuoli (2011, 115) rightly argues that "elites can frame poor residents as individuals responsible for their own problems." Furthermore, impoverished people often lack the economic or social resources to move and thus suffer "displacement without moving" (Nixon 2011, 19) as their homes or use territories become increasingly uninhabitable (Checker 2005). Ann Laura Stoler (2013, 7) refers to this process of continually binding "human potentials" to socially, ecologically, and economically "degraded environments" as "ruination."

8.   As Gandolfo (2009) notes, aspects of Andrade's urban renewal were blocked by Fujimori, who saw the mayor as a political rival and moved to recentralized aspects of the city's governance, especially the provision of services.

Chapter 3

1.   Harvey has long argued that crises of overaccumulation drive contemporary capitalism. Capitalists generate surplus products in order to create surplus value, which then must be reinvested somewhere in order to generate more value. If there are not sufficient outlets for capital reinvestment, then entrepreneurs risk the devaluation of their assets, stagnation, and ultimately, recession. In order to avoid crises of overaccumulation, capital seeks "spatial fixes" in order to not only tie up capital through investment in the construction of physical spaces, such as ports or real estate investment, but also to find competitive advantages by searching for areas where there are lower transportation or labor costs (Harvey 1982, 444).

2.   In his work on Newfoundland's cod fisheries, Gerald Sider (2003, 24–25) underscores how merchant capitalism produced local differences among "many small and

separate communities scattered over so long a coastline." When, with government subsidies and the appearance of transnational corporations searching for unexploited fish stocks, the Newfoundland fishery modernized in the 1960s and 1970s, local disparities were exacerbated and led many small communities to collapse after the cod stocks crashed in the 1990s due to overfishing.

3. Recently, Tecnológica de Alimentos Somos (TASA), the largest producer of fishmeal and fish oil in Peru, expanded a plant on the outskirts of Pucusana to supply omega-3 fish oil to growing markets in Europe and the United States. In a reverse of the historical trend, this means fish will be shipped from Callao to Pucusana for processing.

4. Peru's economy remains export-driven and depends on the production of natural resources, yet the country's aging and limited transportation infrastructure has strained to keep pace with demand for natural resources. In response, government officials have proposed the creation of expanded and modernized port facilities that would not only handle greater volume but also serve as new sites for multinational investment. In 2003, a new National Port System Law opened Peru's ports for private investment, which shifted the government's responsibilities to the oversight of public ports and the planning of public-private partnerships for investing and reconstructing the country's ports.

5. This information comes from the blog that SSP created to promote its port project in Ancón: http://puertodeancon.blogspot.com.

6. The report, "La Sostentabilidad del Balneario de Ancón: el Puerto y sus stakeholders," was posted on the consultant's website (http://www.esan.edu.pe/conexion /actualidad/2011/02/16/la-sostenibilidad-del-balneario-de-ancon-el-puerto-y-sus -stakeholders/) on February 16, 2011.

7. See Griffith et al. (2013) for an analysis of the ways in which artisanal fishers in Puerto Rico have used the notion of freshness and locally sourced fish to distinguish themselves from industrial producers.

8. A number of recent anthropological works explore the complex ways in which place and food consumption are coproduced in marketing the *terroir* of particular foods or their organic, ethical, or traditional qualities. For a survey of this literature, see Foster (2007), Paolisso (2007), Paxson (2010), and Tracy (2013). García (2013) examines how cosmopolitan discourses surrounding Peru's recent gastronomic boom simultaneously obscure and reproduce critical aspects of colonial social relations and violence against different humans and nonhumans.

Chapter 4

1. Urquizo's quotes come from the Ministry's press release, which included excerpts from his comments to reporters while on the dock in Chorrillos: http://www .produce.gob.pe/index.php/prensa/noticias-del-sector/150-ministro-urquizo -primer-censo-de-la-pesca-artesanal-del-ambito-maritimo-de-la-historia-del -peru-se-realiza-con-normalidad; a video of part of his interview is also available online at https://www.youtube.com/watch?v=4V85CfUzk_s.

2. Government discourses of "formalizing" artisanal fishers clearly situated those fishers who had not undergone the process of obtaining a carnet as "informal"—as subjects whose practices had to become more visible to state intervention. For example, in January 2014, six Peruvian fishers were lost at sea for a total of twenty-one days until the Navy discovered and rescued them. After the incident, officials from the Navy and Produce claimed that the incident was the result of the informality of the rescued fishers. Regional Director of Produce Lizardo Ayón noted that several of the six fishers did not have carnets and the crew was one of many that were heading out into the high seas to fish for squid without radio transmitters, a requirement for boats passing the fifteen-nautical-mile mark but a piece of equipment that few small-scale fishers can afford (El Comercio 2014).

3. The issue of the supposed mismanagement of the dock demonstrates the degree to which the boundary between the state and association were blurred and at times ambiguous, especially in the role of the dock administrator. The fishers' association was responsible for appointing an administrator, who was officially an employee of Produce and was in charge of regulating boat traffic. The administrator was also responsible for coordinating services such as the large refrigerated unit in one of the buildings where fishers could store their catches and the provision of ice for boats heading for extended trips. He collected fees from the vendors who used the wharf, such as the individuals who bought and cleaned fish for local restaurants and who paid a daily fee of a few soles for use of the cleaning tables and the water. Women in the market kiosks had an agreement to pay a daily fee as well to sell their fish, as did the arts and crafts vendors who spread their goods on blankets along parts of the dock. The operators of the food kiosks also paid rent and utilities to the association. And, recreational users of the pier paid a half sol fee to stroll to the end or fish. These fees were the only source of revenue for the association to operate the dock and to provide services, such as water, that benefited fishers and vendors. In 2015, we interviewed Paulino, who had just taken over as dock administrator, and he pointed out that he had to report his daily intake and expenses to the "Ministry of Production and FONDEPES." When we asked him what relationship he had to the association, he commented, "I do not have to report to them, but they verify that I am doing well and nothing more."

4. In a similar vein, Christopher Krupa (2010, 337) notes that Indigenous citizens in Ecuador are expected to comport themselves in state-defined categories of limited cultural citizenship that do not challenge the existing political order. However, while such measures reinforced the state as the official validator of such rights, recent waves of decentralization and the reduction of state institutions "downscaled the governmental sphere in which such rights can be conferred and activated, effectively dispersing and diversifying the locations where reciprocal recognition between 'state' and 'citizen' can occur" (Krupa 2010, 338).

5. For analyses of changing masculinities in Latin America, see Gutmann (2003, 2007), High (2010), and Ramírez (2009).

6.   For example, one of the association leaders told us that each year, the associa-
     tion had provided food baskets with "good turkey, good chicken, good provisions,
     good Christmas bread, all name brand" for each of the member's families. In 2014,
     the association also began a program to provide assistance to members for their
     children's schooling and started to pay into a private fund so that members could
     access lower-cost health insurance. The association leader explained the impor-
     tance of these services, noting that without them fishers and their families had little
     aid in times of crises. He noted that in the previous year there had been two fishers
     who had drowned in an accident, and the younger of the two had no insurance or
     savings and so left his widow and baby with nothing.

Chapter 5

1.   According to surveys conducted by IMARPE, in 1970, fishers in Chorrillos landed
     2,900 metric tons of fish, the vast majority of it for sale as fresh fish with a small
     percentage sold for canning (Vasquez et al. 1970). By the turn of the new mil-
     lennium, that number had dropped to 200 metric tons per year with a moderate
     uptick in the late 2000s, when fishers were landing around 400 to 500 tons per year.
     By 2010, things had improved somewhat, with landings of 1,300 and 1,788 tons in
     2010 and 2011, respectively. However, the following year, the total was back down
     to 603. These numbers are from Produce's online statistical database: http://www
     .produce.gob.pe/index.php/datosabiertos#. Given fishers' suspicion of the state and
     reluctance to tell government auditors too much, as well as government officials'
     reluctance to spend much time earning the trust of artisanal fishers, these numbers
     may be at best approximations, and some of the fluctuations in them could most
     certainly be chalked up to reporting errors, willful or not. However, even when one
     accounts for such uncertainties, a picture of decline in the number of fresh fish
     being landed each year in Chorrillos still emerges.
2.   Maria Rostworowski (1981, 112–14) notes that during the colonial era, hunting sea
     lions was a vibrant and important aspect of Lima's coastal economy. During the
     twentieth century, successive Peruvian governments banned and then reauthorized
     the culling of sea lions to protect the fishing industry.
3.   In his sociological novel of artisanal fishers in Chimbote, Braulio Muñoz's (2008,
     20) narrator provides an interesting and somewhat different commentary on boli-
     cheros, noting that ". . . to be honest, the bolicheros did not belong to Tancay. They
     went around everywhere together in a group and hardly ever talked to us. And the
     truth is, too, that we felt sorry for them. They were like peons. Or, worse, like the
     workers in the damn factories. They would work their hearts out for the owner,
     a fat many who would stay behind sitting in a truck. So, all things considered, it
     was not good to be a bolichero." This notion that the men on a boliche have been
     reduced from autonomous fishers to mere wage laborers is one that resonates with
     artisanal fishers' disdain for them in Chorrillos, since both commentaries on the

boliches reinforce the notion that the boliches are tools for the accumulation of wealth not by fishers but by wealthy bosses.

4.   In his book about artisanal fishers at Lake Titicaca, Benjamin Orlove (2002, 11–13) provides an interesting discussion of the historical significance of discourses of state abandonment and forgetting in Peru and their resonance among poor, rural citizens.

5.   During the past two decades, the United States government and other global powers, multinational lenders, and political analysts branded the countries of the Andean chain as hotspots of political instability, often with Peru taking center stage given its severe economic crises, the bloody civil war with Sendero Luminoso, and Fujimori's self-coup in 1992. This criticism, which obscured the role that hemispheric powers played in the economic and military upheavals of many Latin American countries, dovetailed with dominant neoliberal ideologies, which framed issues of Andean instability as emanating "from malignant political cultures rooted in corruption and nepotism, and entrenched in national state governments" (Viatori 2015, 193). The supposed solution was increased transparency, privatization, and the decentralization of government responsibility, all with the end goal of improving private domestic and foreign investment in the Peruvian economy. Since Fujimori's fall in 2000, when evidence of bribery and embezzlement in his administration publicly emerged, Peruvian political discourse has been dominated by discussions of corruption and its eradication. Quiroz (2013) is an interesting example of how corruption has been deployed as a critique of Peruvian politics. For a thorough examination of Peruvian politics in the 1990s and the Fujimori government, see Conaghan (2005). For analyses of state politics in the Andes, see Krupa and Nugent (2015).

6.   Interestingly, she noted that there were more women than men who did this work because they were better at convincing tourists to take rides than the men.

7.   In his ethnography of crack dealers in East Harlem, Phillipe Bourgois (1995) underscores the significance of dignity for young men who did not have the social capital to work in the city's licit economy and for whom the drug economy, despite its low pay and high risks, provided some modicum of local social respect.

References

Acheson, James. 1988. *The Lobster Gangs of Maine*. Lebanon, N.H.: University Press of New England.

Acheson, James. 2003. *Capturing the Commons: Devising Institutions to Manage the Maine Lobster Industry*. Lebanon, N.H.: University Press of New England.

Adams, Ryan Thomas. 2015. "Neoliberal Environmentality among Elites: Becoming 'Responsible Producers' in Santarém, Brazil." *Culture, Agriculture, Food and Environment* 37, no. 2: 84–95.

Agrawal, Arjun. 2005. *Environmentality: Technologies of Government and the Making of Subjects*. Durham: Duke University Press.

Aguilar Ibarra, Alonso, Chris Reid, and Andy Thorpe. 2000. "The Political Economy of Marine Fisheries Development in Peru, Chile and Mexico." *Journal of Latin American Studies* 32, no. 2: 503–27.

Aguirre, Carlos, and Paulo Drinot. 2017. "Introduction." In *The Peculiar Revolution: Rethinking the Peruvian Experiment under Military Rule*, edited by Carlos Aguirre and Paulo Drinot, 1–24. Austin: University of Texas Press.

Aguirre, Carlos, and Aldo Panfichi, eds. 2013. *Lima, siglo XX: Cultura, socialización y cambio*. Lima: Fondo Editorial de la Pontifica Universidad Católica del Perú.

Alexander, Paul. 1980. "Sea Tenure in Southern Sri Lanka." In *Maritime Adaptations: Essays on Contemporary Fishing Communities*, edited by Alexander Spoehr, 91–111. Pittsburgh: University of Pittsburgh Press.

Aranda, Martin. 2009. "Evolution and State of the Art of Fishing Capacity Management in Peru: The Case of the Anchoveta Fishery." *Pan-American Journal of Aquatic Sciences* 4, no. 2: 146–53.

Aretxaga, Begoña. 2003. "Maddening States." *Annual Review of Anthropology* 32: 393–410.

Arroyo Aguilar, Sabino. 2003. "Hierogamia cósmica: culto a Lamarqocha y a San Pedro." *Revista de Antropología* 1: 141–50.

Autoridad del Proyecto Costa Verde (APCV). 1995. "Plan Maestro de Desarrollo de la Costa Verde." Municipalidad de Lima. http://www.apcvperu.gob.pe/index.php/plan-maestro.

Auyero, Javier. 2012. *Patients of the State: The Politics of Waiting in Argentina.* Durham: Duke University Press.

Bailey, Connor. 1985. "The Blue Revolution: The Impact of Technological Innovation on Third-World Fisheries." *The Rural Sociologist* 5, no. 4: 259–66.

Baletti, Brenda. 2014. "Saving the Amazon? Sustainable Soy and the New Extractivism." *Environment and Planning A: Economy and Space* 46: 5–25.

Bavington, Dean. 2010. *Managed Annihilation: An Unnatural History of the Newfoundland Cod Collapse.* Vancouver: University of British Columbia Press.

Becker, Marc. 1993. *Mariátegui and Latin American Marxist Theory.* Athens, Ohio: Ohio University Center for International Studies.

Biehl, João. 2013. "The Judicialization of Biopolitics: Claiming the Right to Pharmaceuticals in Brazilian Courts." *American Ethnologist* 40, no. 3: 419–36.

Bin, Daniel. 2017. "Rio de Janeiro's Olympic dispossessions." *Journal of Urban Affairs* 39, no. 7: 924–38.

Bhandar, Brenna, and Davina Bhandar. 2016. "Cultures of Dispossession: Rights, Status, Identities." *Darkmatter* 14: 1–15.

Blanton, Ryan. 2011. "Chronotopic Landscapes of Environmental Racism." *Journal of Linguistic Anthropology* 21: E76–E93.

Blondet, Cecilia. 1991. *Las mujeres y el poder: Una historia de Villa el Salvador.* Lima: Instituto de Estudios Peruanos.

Bourdieu, Pierre. 1999. "Rethinking the State: Genesis and Structure of the Bureaucratic Field." In *State/Culture: State-Formation after the Cultural Turn*, edited by George Steinmetz, 53–75. Ithaca: Cornell University Press.

Bourgois, Phillipe. 1995. *In Search of Respect: Selling Crack in El Barrio.* Cambridge: Cambridge University Press.

Brecht, Bertold. 1947. *Selected Poems.* Edited and translated by H. R. Rays. New York: Harcourt Brace Jovanovich.

Bresnihan, Patrick. 2016. *Transforming the Fisheries: Neoliberalism, Nature, and the Commons.* Lincoln: University of Nebraska Press.

Briggs, Charles, and Clara Mantini-Briggs. 2004. *Stories in the Time of Cholera: Racial Profiling during a Medical Nightmare.* Berkeley: University of California Press.

Broad, Kenneth, and Ben Orlove. 2007. "Channeling Globality: The 1997-1998 El Niño Climate Event in Peru." *American Ethnologist* 34, no. 2: 285–302.

Brooke, James. 1991. "Cholera Kills 1,100 in Peru and Marches On, Reaching the Brazilian Border." *New York Times*, April 19, A3.

Brosius, Peter, and Lisa M. Campbell. 2010. "Collaborative Event Ethnography: Conservation and Development Trade-offs at the Fourth World Conservation Congress." *Conservation and Society* 8, no. 4: 245–55.

Brown, Wendy. 2015. *Undoing the Demos: Neoliberalism's Stealth Revolution.* London: Zone Books.

Büscher, Bram, Wolfram Dressler, and Robert Fletcher, eds. 2014. *Nature Inc.: Environmental Conservation in the Neoliberal Age.* Tucson: University of Arizona Press.

Butler, Judith, and Athena Athanasiou. 2003. *Dispossession: The Performative in the Political.* Cambridge: Polity.

Bustamante Cueva, Alba, and Marco B. Borda. 1970. "La pesquería en la caleta de Chorrillos." *Serie de informes especialies* No. IM-60. Lima: IMARPE.

Cai, Wenju, Simon Borlace, Matthieu Lengaigne, Peter van Rensch, Mat Collins, Gabriel Vecchi, Axel Timmermann, Agus Santoso, Michael J. McPhaden, Lixin Wu, Matthew H. England, Guojian Wang, Eric Guilyardi, and Fei-Fei Jin. 2014. "Increasing Frequency of Extreme El Niño Events due to Greenhouse Warming." *Nature Climate Change* 4: 111–16.

Caravedo Molinari, Baltazar. 1977. "The State and the Bourgeoisie in the Peruvian Fishmeal Industry." *Latin American Perspectives* 4, no. 3: 103–23.

Caretas. 1991. "Insalubre Lima." April 29, 1991.

Castree, Noel. 2001. "Socializing Nature: Theory, Practice, and Politics." In *Social Nature: Theory, Practice, and Politics,* edited by Noel Castree and Bruce Braun, 1–21. Malden, Mass.: Blackwell.

Charney, Paul. 2001. *Indian Society in the Valley of Lima, Peru, 1532-1824.* Lanham: University Press of America.

Checker, Melissa. 2005. *Polluted Promises: Environmental Racism and the Search for Justice in a Southern Town.* New York: NYU Press.

Chion, Miriam. 2002. "Dimensión metropolitana de la globalización: Lima a fines del siglo XX." *EURE* 28: 71–87.

Choy, Timothy. 2011. *Ecologies of Comparison: An Ethnography of Endangerment in Hong Kong.* Durham: Duke University Press.

Conaghan, Catherine. 2005. *Fujimori's Peru: Deception in the Public Sphere.* Pittsburgh: University of Pittsburgh Press.

Congreso de la República del Perú. 2002. "Proceso de privatización de Pesca Perú 1992–2001." *Comisión investigadora de delitos económicos y fiancieros 1990-2001.*

Coronil, Fernando. 1997. *The Magical State: Nature, Money, and Modernity in Venezuela.* Chicago: Chicago University Press.

Córdova y Urrutia, José María. 1839. *Estadística histórica, geográfica, industrial y comercial de los pueblos que componen las provincias del departamento de Lima.* Lima: Entre Nous.

Crean, Kevin, and David Symes. 1995. "Privatization of the Commons: The Introduction of Individual Transferable Quotas in Developed Fisheries." *Geoforum* 26, no. 2: 175–85.

Crutzen, Paul J., and Eugene F. Stoermer. 2000. "The Anthropocene." *IGBP Newsletter* 41: 17–18.

Cruz-Torres, María Luz. 2004. *Lives of Dust and Water: An Anthropology of Change and Resistance in Northwestern Mexico.* Tucson: University of Arizona Press.

Cruz-Torres, María Luz, and Pamela McElwee. 2012. "Introduction: Gender and Sustainability." In *Gender and Sustainability: Lessons from Asia and Latin America*, edited by María Luz Cruz-Torres and Pamela McElwee, 1–21. Tucson: University of Arizona Press.

Cueto, Marcos. 2001. *The Return of Epidemics: Health and Society in Peru during the Twentieth Century*. New York: Routledge.

Cushman, Gregory T. 2013. *Guano and the Opening of the Pacific World: A Global Ecological History*. Cambridge: University of Cambridge Press.

de Arona, Juan. 1894. *La Línea de Chorrillos: Descripción de los Tres Principales Balnearios Marítimos que Rodean a Lima*. Lima: Librería, Imprenta y Encuadernación.

de la Cadena, Marisol. 2000. *Indigenous Mestizos: The Politics of Race and Culture in Cuzco, 1919–1991*. Durham: Duke University Press.

Dietz, Henry. 1998. *Urban Poverty, Political Participation, and the State: Lima, 1970–1990*. Pittsburgh: University of Pittsburgh Press.

Doane, Molly. 2012. *Stealing Shining Rivers: Agrarian Conflict, Market Logic, and Conservation in a Mexican Forest*. Tucson: University of Arizona Press.

Dosh, Paul. 2010. *Demanding the Land: Urban Popular Movements in Peru and Ecuador, 1990–2005*. University Park: Pennsylvania State University Press.

Driant, Jean Claude. 1991. *Las barriadas de Lima: Historia e interpretación*. Lima: Instituto Francés de Estudios Andinos.

Drinot, Paulo. 2011. *The Allure of Labor: Workers, Race, and the Making of the Peruvian State*. Durham: Duke University Press.

El Comercio. 1991. "Ya no pescan, ahora pasean por el mar." March 4, 1991.

El Comercio. 1991b. "Tanto nadir para morir en la playa." March 4, 1991.

El Comercio. 1991c. "Quien va a Barranco arriesga su Salud." March 26, 1991.

El Comercio. 1991d. "Males intestinales y a la piel puede ocasionar Costa Verde." March 26, 1991.

El Comercio. 1992a. "Anuncian pronta privatización de Pesca-Perú, Epsep y Cerper." September 3, 1992.

El Comercio. 1992b. "Es indispensable participación privada en el sector pesquero." September 12, 1992.

El Comercio. 2014. "La informalidad originó el drama de los pescadores perdidos." February 26, 2014.

Elmore, T. 1904. "Regimen de aguas filtrantes del Rímac." *Boletín del cuerpo de ingenieros de minas del Perú* 7, no. 1: 105–28.

Escobar, Arturo. 2008. *Territories of Difference: Place, Movements, Life, Redes*. Durham: Duke University Press.

Escudero Herrera, Luis. 1997. "Encuesta estructural de la pesquería artesanal del litoral Peruano." *Informe Progresivo* no. 59. Callao: IMARPE.

Evans, Yvonne, and Sigbjorn Tveteras. 2011. "Status of Fisheries and Aquaculture Development in Peru: Case Studies of the Peruvian Anchoveta Fishery, Shrimp Aquaculture, Trout Aquaculture and Scallop Aquaculture." Food and Agriculture Organization of the United Nations (FAO).

Federici, Silvia. 2004. *Caliban and the Witch: Women, the Body and Primitive Accumulation.* New York: Autonomedia.

Fielder, Reginald H., Norman D. Jarvis, and Milton J. Lobell. 1943. *La pesca y las industrias pesqueras en el Peru: con recomendaciones para su futuro desarrollo.* Lima: Libreria e Imprenta Gil.

Fischer, Brodwyn, Bryan McCann, and Javier Auyero, eds. 2014. *Cities from Scratch: Poverty and Informality in Urban Latin America.* Durham: Duke University Press.

Fletcher, Robert. 2010. "Neoliberal Environmentality: Towards a Poststructuralist Political Ecology of the Conservation Debate." *Conservation and Society* 8, no. 3: 171–81.

Flores Galindo, Alberto. 1991. *La ciudad sumergida: aristocracia y plebe en Lima, 1760–1830.* Lima: Editorial Horizonte.

Food and Agriculture Organization of the United Nations (FAO). 1992. "Informe preparado para el Gobierno de la República del Perú sobre la Ordenación y Planificación Pesquera y la Reactivación del Sector Pesquero en el Perú." *GCP/INT/466/NOR Informe de Campo.*

Foster, John Bellamy. 2000. *Marx's Ecology: Materialism and Nature.* New York: Monthly Review Press.

Foster, Robert. 2007. "The Work of the New Economy: Consumers, Brands, and Value Creation." *Cultural Anthropology* 22, no. 4: 707–31.

Fuentes, M. Atanasio. 1866. *Lima, or Sketches of the capital of Peru: historical, statistical [sic], administrative, commercial and moral.* Paris: Firmin Didot, Brothers, Sons & Co.

Fuller, Norma. 2003. "The Social Constitution of Gender Identity among Peruvian Males." In *Changing Men and Masculinities in Latin America*, edited by Matthew C. Gutmann, 134–52. Durham: Duke University Press.

Gago, Verónica. 2017. *Neoliberalism from Below: Popular Pragmatics and Baroque Economics.* Durham: Duke University Press.

Gandolfo, Daniella. 2009. *The City at its Limits: Taboo, Transgression, and Urban Renewal in Lima.* Chicago: University of Chicago Press.

Gandolfo, Daniella. 2013. "Formless: A Day at Lima's Office of Formalization." *Cultural Anthropology* 28, no. 2: 278–98.

Gandolfo, Daniella. 2014. "Illegality: Deviation." Cultural Anthropology. https://culanth.org/fieldsights/580-illegality-deviation.

García, María Elena. 2013. "The Taste of Conquest: Colonialism, Cosmopolitics, and the Dark Side of Peru's Gastronomic Boom." *Journal of Latin American and Caribbean Anthropology* 18 (3): 505–24.

García-Quijano, Carlos. 2007. "Fishers' Knowledge of Marine Species Assemblages: Bridging between Scientific and Local Ecological Knowledge in Southeastern Puerto Rico." *American Anthropologist* 109, no. 3: 529–36.

Gestión. 2013. "Lloret de Mola: Gladys Triveño esta malinformando a Humala sobre la pesca de Anchoveta." March 21, 2013.

Gestión. 2014a. "Construcción del Puerto pesquero 'Bahía Blanca' en el Callao avanza al 41%." February 19, 2014.

Gestión. 2014b. "Pescadores artesanales trasladarán sus embarcaciones durante modernización de Muelle Norte." August 26, 2014.

Gestión. 2014c. "Chancay tendrá un complejo portuario de US $1,600 millones." August 31, 2014.

Gestión. 2017. "Giuffra: 'Alistamos un shock de inversiones en los desembarcaderos para la pesca artesanal.'" January 2, 2017.

Gill, Lesley. 2016. *A Century of Violence in a Red City: Popular Struggle, Counterinsurgency, and Human Rights in Colombia*. Durham: Duke University Press.

Goodale, Mark, and Nancy Grey Postero, eds. 2013. *Neoliberalism, Interrupted: Social Change and Contested Governance in Contemporary Latin America*. Palo Alto: Stanford University Press.

Goodson, Gar. 1988. *Fishes of the Pacific Coast: Alaska to Peru, including the Gulf of California and the Galapagos Islands*. Palo Alto: Stanford University Press.

Gootenberg, Paul. 1993. *Imagining Development: Economic Ideas in Peru's "Fictitious Prosperity" of Guano, 1840–1880*. Berkeley: University of California Press.

Gordillo, Gastón. 2004. *Landscapes of Devils: Tensions of Place and Memory in the Argentinean Chaco*. Durham: Duke University Press.

Grandia, Liza. 2012. *Enclosed: Conservation, Cattle, and Commerce among the Q'eqchi' Maya Lowlanders*. Seattle: University of Washington Press.

Greene, Shane. 2006. "Getting over the Andes: The Geo-Eco-Politics of Indigenous Movements in Peru's Twenty-First Century Inca Empire." *Journal of Latin American Studies* 38, no. 2: 327–54.

Griffith, David, Carlos García-Quijano, and Manuel Valdés Pizzini. 2013. "A Fresh Defense: A Cultural Biography of Quality in Puerto Rican Fishing." *American Anthropologist* 115, no. 1: 17–28.

Gupta, Akhil. 1995. "Blurred Boundaries: The Discourse of Corruption, the Culture of Politics, and the Imagined State." *American Ethnologist* 22, no. 2: 375–402.

Gutmann, Matthew C. 2007. *Fixing Men: Sex, Birth Control, and AIDS in Mexico*. Berkeley: University of California Press.

Gutmann, Matthew C., ed. 2003. *Changing Men and Masculinities in Latin America*. Durham: Duke University Press.

Hale, Charles. 2002. "Does Multiculturalism Menace? Governance, Cultural Rights, and the Politics of Identity in Guatemala." *Journal of Latin American Studies* 34, no. 3: 485–524.

Han, Clara. 2012. *Life in Debt: Times of Care and Violence in Neoliberal Chile*. Berkeley: University of California Press.

Haraway, Donna. 2016. *Staying with the Trouble: Making Kin in the Chthulucene*. Durham: Duke University Press.

Hardin, Garrett. 1968. "The Tragedy of the Commons." *Science* 162 (3859): 1243–48.

Harvey, David. 1974. "Population, Resources, and the Ideology of Science." *Economic Geography* 50: 256–77.

Harvey, David. 1982. *The Limits to Capital*. Oxford: Blackwell.

Harvey, David. 2003. *The New Imperialism*. Oxford: Oxford University Press.

Harvey, David. 2008. "The Right to the City." *New Left Review* 53: 23–40.

Harvey, Penny, and Hannah Knox. 2012. "The Enchantments of Infrastructure." *Mobilities* 7, no. 4: 521–36.

Hay, Douglas, Peter Linebaugh, John G. Rule, E. P. Thompson, and Cal Winslow, eds. 1975. *Albion's Fatal Tree: Crime and Society in Eighteenth Century England*. London: Allen Lane.

Helmreich, Stefan. 2009. *Alien Ocean: Anthropological Voyages in Microbial Seas*. Berkeley: University of California Press.

Hetherington, Kregg. 2011. *Guerrilla Auditors: The Politics of Transparency in Neoliberal Paraguay*. Durham: Duke University Press.

Heynen, Nik, James McCarthy, Scott Prudham, and Paul Robbins, eds. 2007. *Neoliberal Environments: False Promises and Unnatural Consequences*. New York: Routledge.

Higgins, James. 2005. *Lima: A Cultural History*. New York: Oxford University Press.

High, Casey. 2010. "Warriors, Hunters, and Bruce Lee: Gendered Agency and the Transformation of Amazonian Masculinity." *American Ethnologist* 37, no. 4: 753–70.

Holston, James. 2008. *Insurgent Citizenship: Disjunctions of Democracy and Modernity in Brazil*. Princeton: Princeton University Press.

Igoe, Jim. 2017. *The Nature of Spectacle: On Images, Money, and Conserving Capitalism*. Tucson: University of Arizona Press.

International Finance Corporation. 2013. "Callao Muelle Norte: Environmental and Social Review Summary." Accessed October 12, 2016. http://ifcextapps.ifc.org /ifcext/spiwebsite1.nsf/78e3b305216fcdba85257a8b0075079d/1da3bbfc9d8cd89385257 afd007183da?opendocument.

Johnson, Nathaniel C. 2014. "Atmospheric Science: A Big Boost in El Niño." *Nature Climate Change* 4: 90–1.

Joseph, Miranda. 2002. *Against the Romance of Community*. Minneapolis: University of Minnesota Press.

Kirksey, Eben. 2015. *Emergent Ecologies*. Durham: Duke University Press.

Krupa, Christopher. 2010. "State by Proxy: Privatized Government in the Andes." *Comparative Studies in Society and History* 52, no. 2: 319–50.

Krupa, Christopher, and David Nugent, eds. 2015. *State Theory and Andean Politics: New Approaches to the Study of Rule*. Philadelphia: University of Pennsylvania Press.

La República. 2004. "La otra 'Guerra' por los puertos del Pacífico y el rostro oculto de Dionisio Romero." October 3, 2004.

La República. 2009. "Protestan a bordo de naves en Ancón." April 5, 2009.

La República. 2011a. "Según Humala, Alan se burla al devolver dinero." February 14, 2011.

La República. 2011b. "Retiran a Pescadores del Callao." October 20, 2011.

La República. 2012. "Sí hubo irregularidades en concesión de los puertos." June 20, 2012.

La República. 2013. "Chancay: Pescadores artesanales bloquean Panamericana norte." March 3, 2013.

La República. 2014a. "Invertirán 2,800 millones de dólares en complejo portuario en el norte de Lima." August 30 2014.

La República. 2014b. "Humala inspeccionó labores en el Terminal Norte del Puerto del Callao." September 13, 2014.

Leal Martínez, Alejandra. 2016. "'You Cannot be Here': The Urban Poor and the Specter of the Indian in Neoliberal Mexico City." *The Journal of Latin American and Caribbean Anthropology* 21, no. 3: 539–99.

Lefebvre, Henri. 1991. *The Production of Space*. Cambridge, Mass.: Blackwell.

Lefebvre, Henri. 2003. *Urban Revolution*. Minneapolis: University of Minnesota Press.

Li, Tania Murray. 2014. *Land's End: Capitalist Relations on an Indigenous Frontier*. Durham: Duke University Press.

Linebaugh, Peter. 2008. *The Magna Carta Manifesto: Liberties and Commons for All*. Berkeley: University of California Press.

Linebaugh, Peter. 2010. "Enclosures from the Bottom Up." *Radical History Review* 108: 11–27.

Linebaugh, Peter. 2014. *Stop Thief! The Commons, Enclosures, and Resistance*. Oakland: PM Press.

Longo, Stefano B., Rebecca Clausen, and Brett Clark. 2015. *The Tragedy of the Commodity: Oceans, Fisheries, and Aquaculture*. New Brunswick, N.J.: Rutgers University Press.

Loring, David C. 1971. "The United States-Peruvian 'Fisheries' Dispute." *Stanford Law Review* 23, no. 3: 391–453.

Lowe, Philip, Jonathan Murdoch, Terry Marsden, Richard Munton, and Andrew Flynn. 1993. "Regulating the New Rural Spaces: The Uneven Development of Land." *Journal of Rural Studies* 9, no. 3: 205–22.

Luke, Steven. 1999. "Environmentality as Green Governmentality." In *Discourses of the Environment*, edited by Eric Darier, 121–51. Oxford: Blackwell.

Luxemburg, Rosa. 1951. *The Accumulation of Capital*. New Haven: Yale University Press.

Maldonado Félix, Héctor, and María Elizabeth Puertas Porras. 2011. "La pesca industrial peruana antes de la anchoveta (1923–1955)." *Investigaciones Sociales* 15, no. 27: 559–73.

Malm, Andreas. 2016. *Fossil Capital: The Rise of Steam Power and the Roots of Global Warming*. London: Verso.

Mangin, William, and John Turner. 1968. "The Barriada Movement." *Progressive Architecture* 49: 152–62.

Mansfield, Becky. 2004. "Neoliberalism in the Oceans: 'Rationalization,' Property Rights, and the Commons Question." *Geoforum* 35: 313–26.

Martínez-Reyes, José E. 2016. *Moral Ecology of a Forest: The Nature Industry and Maya Post-Conservation*. Tucson: University of Arizona Press.

Marx, Karl. 1990. *Capital: Volume 1: A Critique of Political Economy*. New York: Penguin Books.

Masseur Stoll, Edwin. 1993. "Comentarios a la nueva Ley General de Pesca." *Pesca* 60, no. 1–2: 4–19.

Mathews, Andrew. 2008. "State Making, Knowledge, and Ignorance: Translation and Concealment in Mexican Forestry Institutions." *American Anthropologist* 110, no. 4: 484–94.

Matos Mar, José. 1984. *Desborde Popular y Crisis del Estado*. Lima: Instituto de Estudios Peruanos.

Maurtua, Víctor M. 1906. *Juicio de Límites entre el Perú y Bolivia*. Barcelona: Imprenta de Henrich y Comp.

McCay, Bonnie J. 1987. "The Culture of the Commoners: Historical Observations on Old and New World Fisheries." In *The Question of the Commons: Culture and Ecology of Communal Resources*, edited by Bonnie J. McCay and James M. Acheson, 195–216. Tucson: University of Arizona Press.

McCormack, Fiona. 2017. *Private Oceans: The Enclosure and Marketisation of the Seas*. London: Pluto Press.

McClintock, Cynthia. 1983. "Velasco, Officers and Citizens: The Politics of Stealth." In *The Peruvian Experiment Reconsidered*, edited by Cynthia McClintock and Abraham F. Lowenthal, 275 –308. Princeton: Princeton University Press.

McClintock, Cynthia, and Abraham F. Lowenthal. 1983. "Preface." In *The Peruvian Experiment Reconsidered*, edited by Cynthia McClintock and Abraham F. Lowenthal, iii–xvi. Princeton: Princeton University Press.

McGoodwin, James R. 2006. "Integrating Fishers' Knowledge into Fisheries Science and Management: Possibilities, Prospects and Problems." In *Traditional Ecological Knowledge and Natural Resource Management*, edited by Charles R. Menzies and Caroline Butler, 174–92. Lincoln: University of Nebraska Press.

Meltzoff, Sarah Keene. 2013. *Listening to Sea Lions: Currents of Change from Galapagos to Patagonia*. Lanham: Altamira Press.

Menzies, Charles R. 2016. *People of the Saltwater: An Ethnography of Git lax m'oon*. Lincoln: University of Nebraska Press.

Millar, Kathleen M. 2018. *Reclaiming the Discarded: Life and Labor on Rio's Garbage Dump*. Durham: Duke University Press.

Miller, Peter, and Nikolas Rose. 2008. *Governing the Present*. Cambridge: Polity Press.

Ministerio de la Producción. 2012a. "I censo nacional de la pesca artesanal ámbito marítimo, primeros resultos." http://www.detrasdelacortina.com.pe/download/censo-pesquero-artesanal.pdf.

Ministerio de la Producción. 2012b. "Principales indicadores del pescdor artisanal, ámbito marítimo." http://www.oceandocs.org/handle/1834/8423.

Mirowski, Philip. 2013. *Never Let a Serious Crisis Go to Waste: How Neoliberalism Survived the Financial Meltdown*. London and New York: Verso.

Moore, Amelia. 2012. "The Aquatic Invaders: Marine Management Figuring Fishermen, Fisheries, and Lionfish in the Bahamas." *Cultural Anthropology* 27, no. 4: 667–88.

Moore, Jason. 2015. *Capitalism in the Web of Life: Ecology and the Accumulation of Capital*. New York: Verso.

Moore, Jason. 2016. "Anthropocene or Capitalocene? Nature, History, and the Crisis of Capitalism." In *Anthropocene or Capitalocene? Nature, History, and the Crisis of Capitalism*, edited by Jason Moore, 1–11. Oakland: PM Press.

Muehlmann, Shaylih. 2013. *Where the River Ends: Contested Indigeneity in the Mexican Colorado Delta*. Durham: Duke University Press.

Muñoz, Braulio. 2008. *Alejandro and the Fishermen of Tancay*. Tucson: University of Arizona Press.

Ñiquen C., Miguel, and Marilú Bouchon. 1995. "Información estadística de la pesquería pelágica en la costa Peruana." *Informe* no. 107. Callao: IMARPE.

Nixon, Rob. 2011. *Slow Violence and the Environmentalism of the Poor*. Cambridge: Harvard University Press.

North, Liisa. 1983. "Ideological Orientations of Peru's Military Rulers." In *The Peruvian Experiment Reconsidered*, edited by Cynthia McClintock and Abraham F. Lowenthal, 244–74. Princeton: Princeton University Press.

North, Liisa, and Tanya Korovkin. 1981. *The Peruvian Revolution and the Officers in Power, 1967–1976*. Montreal: Centre for Developing-Area Studies, McGill University.

Nugent, David. 2010. "States, Secrecy, Subversives: APRA and Political Fantasy in Mid-20th-Century Peru." *American Ethnologist* 37, no. 4: 681–702.

Orlove, Benjamin. 2002. *Lines in the Water: Nature and Culture at Lake Titicaca*. Berkeley: University of California Press.

Ortiz, Marienella. 2014. "Decreto supremo 005 elevó pesca negra y redujo consume directo." *El Comercio*, October 1, 2014.

Ostrom, Elinor. 2008. *Governing the Commons: The Evolution of Institutions for Collective Action*. Cambridge: Cambridge University Press.

Panfichi, Aldo. 1995. "La urbanización de Lima, 1535–1900." In *Mundos Interiores: Lima 1850–1950*, edited by Aldo Panfichi and Felipe Portocarrero, 15–42. Lima: Universidad del Pacífico.

Paxson, Heather. 2010. "Locating Value in Artisan Cheese: Reverse Engineering Terroir for New-World Landscapes." *American Anthropologist* 112, no. 3: 444–57.

Probyn, Elspeth. 2016. *Eating the Ocean*. Durham: Duke University Press.

Pálsson, Gísli, and E. Paul Durrenberger. 1990. "Systems of Production and Social Discourse: The Skipper Effect Revisited." *American Anthropologist* 92, no. 1: 130–41.

Paolisso, Michael. 2007. "Taste the Traditions: Crabs, Crab Cakes, and the Chesapeake Bay Blue Crab Fishery." *American Anthropologist* 109, no. 4: 654–65.

Paulik, Gerald J. 1981. "Anchovies, birds, and fishermen in the Peru Current." In *Resource Management and Environmental Uncertainty: Lessons from Coastal Upwelling Fisheries*, edited by Michael H. Glantz and J. Dana Thompson, 35–80. New York: John Wiley and Sons.

Paredes, Carlos, and María Elena Gutierrez. 2008. *La industria anchovetera peruana: costos y beneficios*. Lima: Instituto del Perú, Universidad de San Martín de Porres.

Peterson, Nicole D. 2014. "Breaking the Bounds of Rationality: Values, Relationships, and Decision-Making in Mexican Fishing Communities." *Conservation & Society* 12, no. 3: 245–56.

Peterson, Nicole D., and Cindy Isenhour. 2014. "Introduction: Moving Beyond the 'Rational Actor' in Environmental Governance and Conservation." *Conservation & Society* 12, no. 3: 229–32.

Poole, Deborah. 1997. *Vision, Race, and Modernity: A Visual Economy of the Andean Image World*. Princeton: Princeton University Press.

Povinelli, Elizabeth. 2011. *Economies of Abandonment: Social Belonging and Endurance in Late Liberalism*. Durham: Duke University Press.

Prince, Carlos. 1890. *Lima Antigua: Tipos de antaño*. Lima: Imprenta del Universo.

Quiroz, Alfonso W. 2013. *Historia de la corrupción en el Perú*. Lima: Insituto de estudios peruanos.

Rama, Angel. 1996. *The Lettered City*. Edited and translated by John Charles Casteen. Durham: Duke University Press.

Ramírez, Josué. 2009. *Against Machismo: Young Adult Voices in Mexico City*. New York: Berghan.

Ramírez, María Clemencia. 2011. *Between the Guerrillas and the State: The Cocalero Movement, Citizenship, and Identity in the Colombian Amazon*. Durham: Duke University Press.

Riofrío, Gustavo. 1991. *Producir la ciudad (popular) de los 90: entre el mercado y el estado*. Lima: DESCO.

Roemer, Michael. 1970. *Fishing for Growth: Export-led Development in Peru*. Cambridge: Harvard University Press.

Ros-Tonen, Mirjam A. F., and John H. van Boxel. 1999. "El Niño in Latin America: The Case of Peruvian Fishermen and North-East Brazilian Peasants." *European Review of Latin American and Caribbean Studies* 67: 5–20.

Rostworowski de Diez Canseco, María. 1981. *Recursos naturales renovables y pesca, siglos XVI y XVII*. Lima: Instituto de Estudios Peruanos.

Rostworowski de Diez Canseco, María. 1999. *History of the Inca Realm*. Cambridge: Cambridge University Press.

Ruiz de Somocurcio, Jorge. 2015. "Costa Verde, club Regatas y Pescadores." *El Comercio*. June 26, 2015.

Saénz, Isaac. 2005. "La urbe y el mar." *Derroteros de la Mar del Sur* 13: 123–43.

Scott, James C. 1985. *Weapons of the Week: Everyday Forms of Resistance*. New Haven: Yale University Press.

Scott, James C. 1998. *Seeing Like a State: How Certain Schemes to Improve the Human Condition Have Failed*. New Haven: Yale University Press.

Scott, James C. 2012. *Two Cheers for Anarchism*. Princeton: Princeton University Press.

Sider, Gerald M. 2003. *Between History and Tomorrow: Making and Breaking Everyday Life in Rural Newfoundland*. Orchard Park, NY: Broadview Press.

Smetherman, Bobbie B., and Robert M. Smetherman. 1973. "Peruvian Fisheries: Conservation and Development." *Economic Development and Cultural Change* 21, no. 2: 338–51.

Smith, Neil. 1984. *Uneven Development: Nature, Capital, and the Production of Space*. Oxford: Blackwell.

Sociedad Nacional de Pesquería (SNP). "DS 005, mutila 5 millas marinas." *Peru Pesquero* 2012, no. 6: 4.

Sodikoff, Genese Marie. 2012. *Forest and Labor in Madagascar: From Colonial Concession to Global Biosphere*. Bloomington: Indiana University Press.

Steinberg, Phillip E. 2001. *The Social Construction of the Ocean*. Cambridge: Cambridge University Press.

Steinberg, Philip, and Kimberley Peters. 2015. "Wet Ontologies, Fluid Spaces: Giving Depth to Volume through Oceanic Thinking." *Environment and Planning D: Society and Space* 33: 247–64.

Stoler, Laura Ann. 2013. "Introduction 'The Rot Remains': From Ruins to Ruination." In *Imperial Debris: On Ruins and Ruination* edited by Laura Ann Stoler, 1–35. Durham: Duke University Press.

Strathern, Marilyn. 2000. "Introduction: New Accountabilities." In *Audit Cultures: Anthropological Studies in Accountability, Ethics and the Academy*, edited by Marilyn Strathern, 1–18. New York: Routledge.

Swanson, Heather Anne. 2015. "Shadow ecologies of conservation: Co-production of salmon landscapes in Hokkaido, Japan, and southern Chile." *Geoforum* 61: 101–10.

Swanson, Kate. 2010. *Begging as a Path to Progress: Indigenous Women and Children and the Struggle for Ecuador's Urban Spaces*. Athens, Ga.: University of Georgia Press.

Tilic, I. 1963. "Material estadístico sobre la industria peruana de harina de pescado." *Informe* no. 14. Callao: IMARPE.

Thompson, E. P. 1963. *The Making of the English Working Class*. New York: Pantheon Books.

Thompson, E. P. 1991. *Customs in Common*. New York: New Press.

Thorp, Rosemary. 1983. "The evolution of Peru's economy." In *The Peruvian Experiment Reconsidered*, edited by Cynthia McClintock and Abraham F. Lowenthal, 39–64. Princeton: Princeton University Press.

Thurner, Mark. 1997. *From Two Republics to One Divided: Contradictions of Postcolonial Nationmaking in Andean Peru*. Durham: Duke University Press.

Tracy, Megan. 2013. "Pasteurizing China's Grasslands and Sealing in Terroir." *American Anthropologist* 115, no. 3: 437–51.

Tsing, Anna Lowenhaupt. 2015. *The Mushroom at the End of the World: On the Possibility of Life in Capitalist Ruins*. Princeton: Princeton University Press.

Turner, John. 1977. *Housing by the People: Towards Autonomy in Building Environments*. New York: Pantheon Books.

United Nations General Assembly. 1982. "Convention on the Law of the Sea." http://www.refworld.org/docid/3dd8fd1b4.html.

Urciuoli, Bonnie. 2011. "Semiotic properties of racializing discourses." *Journal of Linguistic Anthropology* 21, no. S1: E113–22.

Vasquez Aguirre, Isaac, Augusto Paz Torres, and Raúl Hidalgo Reyes. 1970. "Desembarque de pescados, mariscos y otros animals marions durante 1970." *Serie de informes especiales* no. IM–80. Lima: IMARPE.

Viatori, Maximilian. 2010. *One State, Many Nations: Indigenous Rights Struggles in Ecuador*. Santa Fe: School for Advanced Research Press.

Viatori, Maximilian. 2015. "Rift, Rupture and the Temporal Politics of Race in Ecuador: Whiteness and the Narration of Neoliberal Futures during and after the Cenepa War." *History and Anthropology* 26, no. 2: 187–205.

Viatori, Maximilian. 2016a. "Public Secrets, Muzzled Science: Agnotological Practice, State Performance, and Dying Salmon in British Columbia." *Political and Legal Anthropology Review* 39, no. S1: 89–103.

Viatori, Maximilian. 2016b. "Upheaval and the Maintenance of Indigenous Alterity: Borders, Crises and Racecraft in Ecuador, 1941–2008." *Ethnohistory* 63, no. 3: 497–518.

Viatori, Maximilian. 2016c. "Defending White-Mestizo Invisibility through the Production of Indigenous Alterity: (Un)Marking Race in Ecuador's Mainstream Press." *Anthropological Quarterly* 89, no. 2: 483–512.

Walker, Charles. 1999. *Smoldering Ashes: Cuzco and the Creation of Republican Peru.* Durham: Duke University Press.

Walker, Charles. 2008. *Shaky Colonialism: The 1746 Earthquake-Tsunami in Lima, Peru, and its Long Aftermath.* Durham: Duke University Press.

Walley, Christine J. 2004. *Rough Waters: Nature and Development in an East African Park.* Princeton: Princeton University Press.

West, Paige. 2012. *From Modern Production to Imagined Primitive: The Social World of Coffee from Papua New Guinea.* Durham: Duke University Press.

West, Paige. 2016. *Dispossession and the Environment: Rhetoric and Inequality in Papua, New Guinea.* New York: Columbia University Press.

West, Paige. 2017. "Dispossession." Theorizing the Contemporary. *Cultural Anthropology.* June 28, 2017. https://culanth.org/fieldsights/1150-dispossession.

Wintersteen, Kristin. 2014. "The Smell of Money: Fishmeal on the Periphery of the Global Food Economy." *Harvard Design Magazine* 39: 34–40.

Wolff, Thomas. 1980. *In Pursuit of Tuna: The Expansion of a Fishing Industry and Its International Ramifications—The End of an Era.* Tempe: Center for Latin American Studies, Arizona State University.

Index

Page numbers in *italics* represent illustrations.

166–167, 182; for tourist rides, 24, 81, 142, 178; zapatos, 97–98
boliches, 11, 53–59, 78, 89, 154, 161, 164–171
bonito (*Sarda chiliensis*), 10, 43–44, *44*, 53, 76, 92–93, 159–160, 166
Bourbon Reforms, 35, 70, 186
Brenda (Interviewee), 105–109
buzos, 120, 122

caballa (*Scomber japonicus*), 8
CAG (Guano Administration Company), 43, 75–76
Callao, Peru, 48, 68, 69–70, 74, 77, 89, 92–93, 102, 105
Callao Province, 28
capital: in the 1980s, 49; and artisanal fishers, 78, 141–142, 168, 173, 179; and dispossession, 15; and ecology, 110; and food kiosks, 179; global, 65, 90; human, 153; and inequality, 188; and nationalization, 47; and nature, 12, 15, 33, 192; and politics, 26–27, 32, 34, 43, 47–48, 103, 185; and privatization, 48, 50, 51; social, 22, 101, 158, 163; and surplus value, 26; and tourism, 65; and uneven development, 89–110, 186–192. *See also* accumulation; capitalism; economy; labor; profit
capitalism: and climate change, 189, 191; and dispossession, 15, 114; and nature, 12–13, 33, 191; and politics, 34; and separations, 19–20, 186–192; and uneven development, 89–110. *See also* accumulation; capital; economy; labor; profit
Carlos (Interviewee), 182
carnets, 122–125, 126. *See also* licensing
certifications, 107–108
César (Interviewee), 162, 165, 166, 172, 181–182
ceviche, 81–84, 136
chalanas, 5, 97
Chancay, Peru, *2*, 94, 102–103, 104
chanque (*Concholepas concholepas*), 120

children, 24, 98, 117, 136, 137, 156, 174, 175, 176, 181
Chile, 90, 101
Chimbote, Peru, 47, 48
cholera outbreak (1991), 32, 80–84
cholos/cholas, 72
Chorrillos, Peru: according to government, 103–104; and APCV, 84–85; day in the life of, 116–120; guilds, 70; history, 6, 68, 71–72, 77, 186; and IMARPE, 78, 89, 95; location, *2*, *3*; Municipality of Chorrillos, 128–135, 139, 145, 169–170; police department, 169–170; and regional dynamics, 35–36, 188; registry of fishers, 76; as research setting, 28–33. *See also* artisanal fishers; boats; fishers' association (of Chorrillos); wharf, Fishers' (Chorrillos)
Cilus gilberti (corvina drum), 96
Circuito de Playas, Chorrillos, *3*, 120
citizenship: and comportment, 18, 36, 107, 112, 135; cultural, 152–183; and hierarchies, 71, 171–174; and Indigenous peoples, 73; and neoliberalism, 17–18, 187; and responsibility, 67, 77, 86–87. *See also* rights
civil war, 65, 79
clam, razor (*Ensis macha*), 120
Claros, Ricardo, 101
class: and cholera outbreak (1991), 82–84; and climate change, 37, 185, 189; and Costa Verde development, 188; and cultural citizenship, 152–183; and ecology, 26, 185, 192; and entrepreneurialism, 25; and hygiene, 80–82, 134, 140, 179; inequalities, 15, 171–174, 188; and licensing, 122–123; and neoliberalism, 18, 113–114; and Produce, 111–114, 126–127; and responsibility, 111–150; solidarity, 135–149; and urban development, 32. *See also* capital; capitalism; discourse; elites; rights; society
Claudio (Interviewee), 159–161, 166, 184–185, 191

of regulations, 52, 85, 112, 129, 133, 135, 167–168, 171, 173; and industry and labor, 74–79, 185; and nationalization, 46–48; and national territorial waters, 14, 51, 185; and rights, 170; and vendors, 180–181; and visibility, 17, 36, 111, 113, 120–126, 151, 180, 187. *See also* governance; neoliberalism; politics

subsidies, 12, 63, 117, 168

Supe, Peru, 48

Supreme Decree 001-2015, 61

Supreme Decree 011-2013, 61

Supreme Decree no. 005-2012-PRODUCE. *See* "005" (Supreme Decree no. 005-2012-PRODUCE)

Supreme Decree no. 012-2001-PE, 53

Supreme Decree no. 017-92-PE (five-nautical-mile protection), 52, 53, 57

sustainability: and "005," 59, 60; in Ancón, 102, 104; and artisanal fishers, 122, 190; and capital, 12, 26; and the commons, 115; and the market, 106–109; and neoliberalism, 51; and regulations, 41–45; and the state, 63; and uneven development, 90; and the wharf, 139, 145

swordfish (*Xiphias gladius*), 96

Taira, Jaime Sobero, 49–50

taxation, 111–112, 122, 123, 147, 187

technology, 75–76, 78–79. *See also* modernity; progress

temperatures: and El Niño, 9, 47, 49, 56, 94–95, 162; and the Humboldt Current, 10, 43, 45, 105; oscillations of, 13–14. *See also* ocean natures

Terminales Portuarios Chancay (TPCh), 102

Thunnus albaceres (yellowfin tuna), 96

tourism: in Ancón, 99; boat rides, 24, 81, 142, 178; and cholera outbreak (1991), 81; and Costa Verde development, 84–86;

and food kiosks, 136–137, 139–140; and global capital, 65; and the Global South, 90; history of, 71–72; and livelihood diversification, 24; and the wharf, 6, 17, 36, 112, 141–142, 146–149, 172–173

TPCh (Terminales Portuarios Chancay), 102

Trachurus murphyi (jack mackerel), 89

Triveño Chan Jan, Gladys, 56

Tumbes, Peru, 105–106

tuna, yellowfin (*Thunnus albaceres*), 96

Ugarteche, Manuel Prado, 43

unions, 17, 36, 74–75, 77, 125–127, 147–150. *See also* associations; labor

urbanization, 30, 32, 47, 65–66, 68–71, 74, 78–80

urban renewal, 65, 66, 84, 87, 88, 186

Urquizo Maggia, Jose, 56, 121–122

U.S. Fish and Wildlife Service, 75–76

Velasco Alvarado, Juan, 46–48, 51, 77, 168

vendors, 24, 29, 36–37, 115, 117–120, 135–145, 154, 173–181, 183, 188. *See also* food kiosks; wharf, Fishers' (Chorrillos); women

Venezuela, 12–13

Villa Maria fish market, 144, 147, 159, 175

visibility: and the commons, 115–120; of dispossessions, 183; and fishing rights, 35, 71; and history, 26, 31, 53, 67, 185; to the state, 17, 36, 111, 113, 120–126, 151, 180, 187

wealth, 10, 14, 15, 34, 49, 152, 170, 186, 188. *See also* capital; capitalism; elites; poverty

wharf, fishers' (Chorrillos), 26; and autonomy, 149, 182; as commons, 20; and Costa Verde development, 86–87, 112, 129, 131; and culture, 64–65, 75, 87, 118–119, 131, 135, 161, 182–183; and ethnographic research, 30; fish market, 135–149,

wharf, fishers' (Chorrillos) (*continued*)
174–181; and food kiosks, 24, 135–145, 179;
and gender, 135–145; and government
jurisdictions, 134; history, 92–93; and
investors, 139; location, *3*, 120–121; and
Produce, 127, 134, 145, 147, 169; renovation of, 36, 138, 145–149; and responsibility, 86, 127–135, 180–183; review team,
128–135; the space, 17, 20, 118; and the
union, 125–127; and visibility, 120–125. *See
also* Chorrillos, Peru; fishers' association
(of Chorrillos); tourism; vendors

women: and associations, 29; and autonomy,
24, 37, 136, 150, 175; day in the life of,
117–120; Indigenous, 72–73; and labor, 19,
23–24; at the wharf, 135–145, 150, 174–
181. *See also* food kiosks; gender; vendors

Xiphias gladius (swordfish), 96

Yacht Club, *3*, 6–7, 17, 72, 86, 131, 145–149,
148, 169–170, 186

zapatos, 97–98